Countryside Leisure

ep EP PUBLISHING LIMITED
1977

Stonehenge, Wilts

EXPLORING EARLY BRITAIN

by MICHAEL SWANTON

The author and publishers would like to thank the following for supplying the photographs used in this book and for allowing them to be reproduced:

Aerofilms Ltd for the cover transparency of Maiden Castle; the Ashmolean Museum, University of Oxford, for photographs appearing on pages 37, 59, 114, 132; The Royal Commission on Ancient and Historical Monuments in Wales, p. 85 (Crown copyright reserved); Mr W. A. Baker, p. 66; B. T. Batsford Ltd, p. 48 (we regret that we are unable to trace the copyright holder); A & C Black Ltd, p. 68 left (originally appeared as plate XII (a), Margary, *Roman Roads in Britain*, John Baker Publishers Ltd, 1973, 3rd edn); Janet and Colin Bord, pp. 108 top, 109, 131; The Cambridge University Collection, pp. 19, 21, 35, 41, 91, 136; Mr Peter Chèze-Brown, p. 69; Department of the Environment, frontispiece and pp. 27, 44, 63 right, 81, 95, 98, 106, 112, 121 (all Crown copyright: reproduced with permission of the Controller of Her Majesty's Stationery Office); Department of the Environment (Edinburgh), pp. 88, 108 bottom, 129 (all Crown copyright: reproduced by permission of the DOE); Geological Survey and Museum, p. 16; Dr Paul Mellars, p. 18; National Maritime Museum, London, p. 64; Royal Commission on Historical Monuments (England), p. 10 (Crown copyright), p. 11 (Crown copyright Central Office of Information), p. 75 (copyright A. F. Kersting), p. 122 (Crown copyright), p. 126 (copyright J. Smith); Royal Commission on Historical Monuments (England), Air Photographs Unit, pp. 68 right, 78, 82 (all Crown copyright); Mrs Margaret Rylatt, p. 94; Scottish Tourist Board, p. 24; Dr Graham Webster, p. 56; West Country Tourist Board, p. 31; Mr Roger J. A. Wilson, p. 52 both pictures.

ISBN 0 7158 0472 3

Published by EP Publishing Ltd., Bradford Road, East Ardsley, Wakefield, West Yorkshire, 1977

Printed in Great Britain by
Butler & Tanner Ltd, Frome and London

CONTENTS

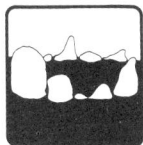

For Oliver, Alexander and Richard
Always look carefully, never stop asking 'Why?'

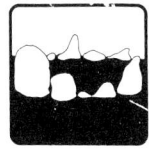

INTRODUCTION

Men have lived in Britain for half a million years. Very slowly at first, but then with increasing rapidity, the nature of early human society changed. The primitive subsistence eked out by the hunters and fishers of the late Ice Age gave way to the more settled pastoral and farming communities of Neolithic and Bronze Age times, to be replaced in turn by the sophisticated urban society of Roman Britain. The surface of the land, dug into and built upon for ten millennia or more, bears continuing witness to the means by which these early inhabitants of Britain gradually gained control of their frequently hostile environment. These remains are often the sole evidence we have for the economic and social life of our remote ancestors. We can trace the outlines of their dwelling-places—caves or mere flimsy shelters at first, but growing increasingly sophisticated. And we can see the more substantial defences they eventually found necessary for their protection. It is possible to discover evidence of the agricultural and industrial activities by which they lived, and to follow the routes by which scattered communities maintained trading and other links with one another. We can recognise temples and ceremonial sites which bespeak some non-material aspirations—however incompletely glimpsed by us. And everywhere lie the funerary monuments from which we can infer their anticipation of an afterlife. But succeeding generations have tended to build over

and obliterate the remains of their predecessors, despoiling their houses and temples as quarries for road construction or for their own buildings. At the present time the demand for new houses, factories and roads is far from sated; every year in Britain fifty thousand acres of land are built over, and consequently many thousands of archaeological sites destroyed. Even in remote countryside, ancient mounds and ditches are vulnerable, since they are found to impede the new machinery used in our increasingly intensive and mechanised agricultural methods.

If the remains from half a million years of occupation should sometimes seem so slight, it is important to remember that the population of Britain at the end of the Ice Age was probably no more than a few hundreds. The New Stone Age farmers numbered only twenty thousand or so, and even by the time of the Roman conquest the total population probably amounted to little more than four hundred thousand.

While the remains of early man often seem merely vestigial—a slight shadow picked out on uneven ground—some other early monuments are very impressive indeed; structures like the great stone circles and massive Roman fortifications have formed objects of continuing wonder for generations. The study of antiquities in the field—'field archaeology' as it is called, compared with excavation or the study of objects transferred to museums—has a long and

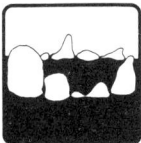

creditable history in Britain. For centuries it formed a traditional recreation of country gentry and country parsons who had a natural eye for the lie of the land and who took an active interest in the rural scene in all its varied aspects. During the nineteenth century, systematic field-archaeology was given an enormous boost through the co-ordination of interested amateurs into learned antiquarian and archaeological societies organised on a local or national basis. This did much to draw to public attention the importance of this part of our national heritage. And the twentieth century has witnessed a growing body of professional official archaeologists, employed by various branches of local and national government. During the 1950s and 60s, however, popular interest in archaeology received an unprecedented stimulus through the media of television and the colour-supplement press, while the spread of weekend motoring increasingly enables the interested layman to explore the countryside in search of remains of the past for himself. During 1975 Stonehenge attracted almost seven hundred thousand paying visitors—second only to The Tower of London in this respect. Even relatively unimportant sites receive a steady stream of visitors during the summer months. During the month of July 1975 scarcely a minute of the day passed without there being at least one visitor's car parked by the sign-posted path leading to the ruined megalithic tomb of Pentre Ifan in Pembrokeshire.

Of course major sites like Stonehenge, in the guardianship of the Department of the Environment, are admirably laid out with markers, plans and explanatory leaflets—although even some of these assume a considerable degree of prior knowledge. But it was clear that the vast majority of visitors to Pentre Ifan found this monument, although undoubtedly impressive, quite puzzling—which only a few words of explanation could have corrected. It is the object of this volume to help the casual visitors to understand something of the nature and purpose of some of the various ancient remains they will find during their exploration of the countryside during holidays and at weekends.

Even where not labelled and set off by close-cut green lawns, it is difficult to visualise these monuments in their original condition. The peaceful earthen mounds and grassy banks of prehistoric hillforts were once startling and violently new intrusions on the scene—gleaming white chalk walls, with freshly-cut new timber revetments, gates, stockades and walkways, surrounded by steep and dangerously deep-dug ditches. Even the fine country houses of Roman aristocrats, their roofs long tumbled, and the walls robbed by later builders, are for the most part reduced to mere foundations and lower courses.

During recent years several attempts have been made to reconstruct ancient buildings from their ground-plans, both in the interests of research—in order to discover the means by which early man may have overcome various practical problems—and incidentally to present a more graphic and easily understood picture to the general public. In order to study problems involved in the construction of earthworks, and to record the progress of their decay, the British Association for the Advancement of Science has built embankments on Overton Down, Wiltshire, SU 129706, which will be inspected at periodic intervals over the years as part of a long-term practical experiment. A variety of prehistoric huts have been reconstructed at different times in the open-air Avoncroft Museum of Buildings at Stoke Prior, near Bromsgrove, Worcestershire. At the Lunt Roman fort near Coventry, with the assistance of the Royal Engineers using traditional tools and methods, archaeologists have reconstructed the timber gateway of the fort and a length of rampart, together with one or two internal buildings (see p. 94). At Cirencester the Corinium Museum has been laid out to resemble the interior of a Roman house, while at Fishbourne, near Chichester, the original flower-beds of a Roman garden have been laid out with plants known to have been common in Roman times

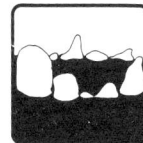

(see p. 29). At Butser Hill on the Hampshire–Sussex border, the British Association for the Advancement of Science has sponsored a large-scale research project into ancient methods of farming. Experiments in progress include cultivation with ox-ploughs, yield-testing prehistoric strains of cereal crops, and various kinds of animal husbandry. This experimental station is not normally open to public inspection, but visitors to the Butser Hill plots in the nearby Queen Elizabeth Country Park on the A3 south of Petersfield, SU 716185, can see prehistoric cereals under cultivation, ancient breeds of domestic animals and a variety of reconstructed farm buildings.

The original setting of these monuments is even harder to visualise than their original form. It is well known that the landscape of lowland Britain as we now know it—characteristically covered with small fields, bounded by hedgerows and banks, dotted with coppices—was largely a creation of the late eighteenth- and early nineteenth-century Enclosure Acts. Prior to that the English landscape presented a much more open aspect. We know that in remoter times still, much of the land surface was covered with swamps or forest. Relative changes in land and sea levels mean that at one time large areas of what is now dry land may have formed inland lakes or lagoons. At various times some areas have been inundated, while others were left high and dry as the shoreline has receded. Large parts of what was once dry land now lie beneath the North Sea. The scientific analysis of soil samples together with the plant and tree pollen they contain, obtained from deep borings, indicate considerable changes in climatic conditions during prehistoric times, together with consequent changes in overall vegetation cover.

Although the sites mentioned in this book are easily located and plainly visible, an observant visitor will notice many lesser remains in the vicinity of major monuments, as well as elsewhere. The mounds and ditches of earthworks which may seem all but obliterated under the midday sun will be thrown into high relief in the evening when the sun is at a low angle and the shadows lengthen. While most people naturally have greatest opportunity to look at ancient monuments during summer holidays, visits at other times of the year can be rewarding, revealing different features. During the winter months the vegetation which sometimes obscures the less-frequented monuments is reduced. Although beech woods tend to be clear of undergrowth all year round, most wooded sites are clearest during the winter, while bracken-covered sites are best visited in the spring, when the cover has been beaten down by the winter's storms. Heather is more troublesome to the visitor, although even this is occasionally burnt off. In any case, winter is a good season for field archaeology. Flooding fills depressions and emphasises the lines of the slightest banks. Frosts with differential melting-rates, or wind-blown snow lodging in otherwise indiscernible hollows, can pick out vestigial features as if they were part of a gigantic fingerprint.

Where a site has been ploughed completely flat, variations in the quality of colour or the soil may sometimes be recognised. The rubble core of a burial mound, or the flinty material along the line of a Roman road is readily distinguished from the soil round about. Ditches or post-holes which have filled up level with the surrounding surface are invariably marked by darker, softer and finer silt. Grass or crops such as corn grow especially well over the rich soil of silted-up ditches, and the darker healthier foliage often stands out in marked contrast to that round about. Conversely, crops growing in thin, poor or impacted soil over building foundations or the rubble core of old roads tend to be pale, stunted and sparse. This is especially noticeable at the height of the growing season from May to July. In high summer shallow-rooted grass often parches white over foundations and provides especially good evidence. From the air such crop-marks can reveal plans of ancient sites almost as exact as those recovered by excavation—a deserted Roman town, for instance, showing

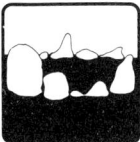

the entire layout of streets, houses, shops, temples, baths and so on. During the course of lengthy droughts like those of 1975–6, many hundreds of new sites can be discovered with the aid of aerial photography.

Some monuments, especially those in the care of the Department of the Environment or the National Trust, are well sign-posted. But ordinarily anyone intending to visit sites by car or on foot will have recourse to the appropriate Ordnance Survey map. These are cheap enough to buy, although public libraries can usually supply them. Probably the most useful for the motorist or walker is the 1 : 50,000 scale series—i.e. about $1\frac{1}{4}$ inches to the mile. This will be

Little Woodbury, Wilts: plan of excavated section (after Bersu)

Little Woodbury, Wilts: aerial photograph showing crop-mark site

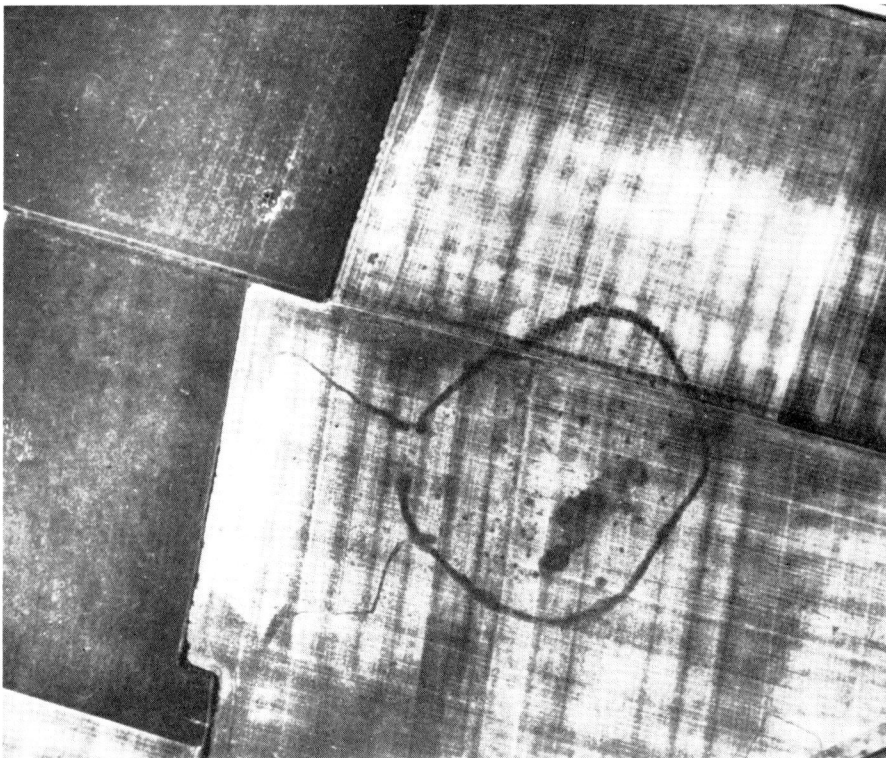

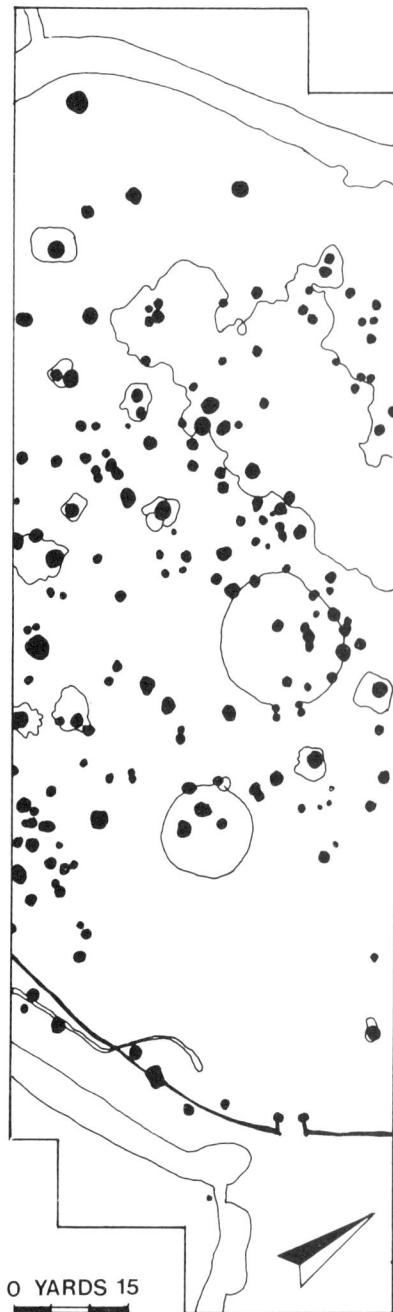

0 YARDS 15

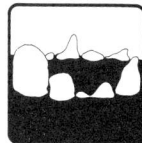

adequate for locating all of the major sites mentioned in the course of this book. Larger-scale sheets at $2\frac{1}{2}$ or 6 inches to the mile allow more precise detail to be shown, and have room to mark the location of a host of lesser monuments, and even the find-spots of minor archaeological remains now in museums or elsewhere. All these maps, and some others, like those issued by the Automobile Association, employ a

Little Woodbury, Wilts: reconstruction of Iron Age farmstead

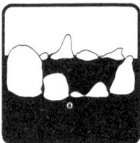

simple but precise system of standard grid-references, allowing locations to be defined with complete precision. The National Grid divides the country into a number of squares, each identified by double letters; and each of these large squares is divided into a number of smaller squares. A reference is given by citing the appropriate letters, and then co-ordinating first the numbers running horizontally along the top or bottom (usually to the third point), with those running vertically up either side. For instance, on the map on p. 134, Stonehenge lies at grid reference SU 123422. Six-figure grid-references are cited for each of the sites mentioned in this book.

Public rights of way are clearly marked on all 1¼-inch Ordnance Survey maps. Where it is necessary to cross open fields, however, the responsible field-archaeologist will always respect the land, keeping to footpaths or the edges of fields, being particularly careful of growing crops (remembering that long grass can represent a valuable hay-crop). Sometimes it is advisable to seek prior permission from the owners of the land, although invariably this is readily given. The few instances where this is specifically necessary for the sites referred to in this book are mentioned in the Appendix. For safety's sake some monuments, like those containing subterranean chambers, are normally kept locked, but the keys are usually lodged at a nearby house. Of course those who intend exploring the caves, mines or chambered tombs described below would be wise to wear old clothes and to take a torch. Pencil and paper are always useful. A minute or two spent in making a short note or rough sketch sharpens the observation, helps you remember what you have seen, and adds enormously to the enjoyment in retrospect. Short distances can be paced out—the length of an easy pace for the average man measures roughly one yard. Wherever practical, measurements of length cited in this book are given in yards, while heights are given in feet.

When walking, it is always worth while casting an eye over the surface of ploughed fields, rabbit-scrapes or otherwise disturbed soil. Especially after rain, casual finds of flint, fragments of pottery, coins or other evidence of former occupation may sometimes be found. These can be identified by comparison with others displayed in local museums. Do not hesitate to ask for one of the curators in charge; it is their job to assist enquiries, and they in turn may be very interested in your find. It is not necessarily the most impressive find—let alone the most valuable in money terms—that is of the greatest archaeological importance. It was the chance discovery of some very ordinary pieces of Roman tile which led to the unearthing of the Fishbourne Roman palace—a building unique in northern Europe, while the collection of apparently insignificant fragments of pottery by amateurs walking on the top of a hillfort at South Cadbury in Somerset led archaeologists to the identification of what is almost certainly the site of Arthur's Camelot. Even a casual stray find may be of importance in extending the archaeologists' distribution-map. In any case, it is important to know the precise find-spot. And you should make a note of this—at least in terms of a six-figure grid-reference. If you can mark it by pacing the distance from the nearest fixed feature like a gatepost, then so much the better. You should of course resist any temptation to dig for yourself; archaeological excavation requires considerable resources of both labour and experience. There are regular 'digs' taking place in most regions at all times, where offers of help, however inexperienced, will be welcome. Your library or museum will supply details (ask for the *C.B.A. Calendar of Excavations*).

Some monuments—especially those in the care of the Department of the Environment—include small site-museums containing illustrative material from excavations on the site. Finds of the greatest importance are naturally housed in one of the major national collections, such as the British Museum in London, the National Museum of Antiquities, Edinburgh, or the National Museum of Wales, Cardiff. But more

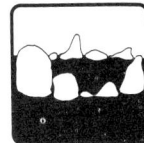

often than not, material from excavations will find its way to the local museum, exhibited with plans and photographs of other monuments in the area. Time spent by the field-archaeologist in visiting museums is invariably worth while, providing useful information beforehand, or afterwards helping to resolve puzzling features found in the field.

Clearly the better-informed we are, the more profitable our examination of monuments on the ground will be. Most public libraries will provide a good selection of books on local and regional archaeology. Two general surveys may be warmly recommended to the beginner: Eric Wood's *Field Guide to Archaeology* (Collins, 5th edn, 1977) and the Ordnance Survey publication *Field Archaeology in Great Britain* (Southampton, 5th edn, 1973); both contain good bibliographies. A number of regional guides, describing a comprehensive selection of visible remains in particular areas have been published over the years, but particularly valuable—up-to-date and well-written—are the Faber Archaeological Guides: *Scotland* by Euan Mackie, 1975; *Wales* by Christopher Houlder, 1974; and *Southern England* by James Dyer, 1973. The Department of the Environment publishes an admirable series of illustrated regional guides dealing with the particular monuments in their care: *Scotland*, *Wales*, *Southern England*, *East Anglia and the Midlands* and *Northern England*. These, like the Department's authoritative pamphlet guides to certain major monuments, may be bought from the site custodians. The Ordnance Survey issues a number of specialised maps, each marking between one and two thousand sites (not all visible): *Ancient Britain: North* (1964) and *South* (1977), *Southern Britain in the Iron Age* (1964), *Roman Britain: North* and *South* (1977), and detailed maps of *Hadrian's Wall* (1972) and *The Antonine Wall* (1969). Examples of books dealing with special subjects include: C. H. D. Cullingford, ed., *British Caving* (Routledge, 1962); H. C. Bowen, *Ancient Fields* (EP Publishing, 1963); I. D. Margary, *Roman Roads in Britain* (John Baker, 1967); A. H. A. Hogg, *Hillforts of Britain* (Hart-Davis, MacGibbon, 1975); Evan Hadingham, *Circles and Standing Stones* (Heinemann, 1975); R. J. C. Atkinson, *Stonehenge* (Penguin, 1960); L. V. Grinsell, *The Ancient Burial Mounds of England* (Methuen, 1953).

More detailed information on particular sites can be found in accounts published in the year-books of local archaeological societies—mostly organised on a county basis. These may be consulted at reference libraries and museums. Many have been in existence for a hundred years or more, and consequently represent a considerable storehouse of information on local antiquities of all kinds. Some have cumulative indexes so that it is easy enough to find your way about them. But where these do not exist, the county library or society headquarters can occasionally provide access to an unpublished index of some kind. The librarian or secretary will be willing to answer enquiries by post—in which case it is important that your queries should be as specific as possible.

County and smaller local societies organise programmes of lectures, excursions and excavations. Membership is open to anyone for a small subscription, and is strongly recommended for those of any age who might wish to visit monuments in the congenial company of like-minded people. Reduced subscriptions are generally available for those who wish to attend meetings but do not need to subscribe to the year-book, which they can read in the local library.

The earliest inhabitants of Britain lived in frozen conditions close to the edge of the ice-cap during the last phase of the Great Ice Age, or subsequently in a somewhat warmer climate when the ice-cap retreated farther north. They eked out a subsistence-living by hunting the herds of wild animals that roamed the tundra, fishing where this was available, and gathering edible plants, roots, leaves, berries and nuts.

The tools and weapons which they made by shaping flakes and cores of flint or whittling pieces of bone, are found extensively in the gravels of southern Britain. But the temporary shelters they constructed for themselves seem to have been of only the flimsiest kind: a few branches roofing over a shallow hollow scooped out of the ground. These may have occurred singly, or in a small group clustered round a spring. Such slight constructions can often only be inferred by archaeologists from traces of hearths or a scatter of tools and other occupation-debris. None leaves any visible remains on the present-day surface. But one excavated example is preserved under cover at Abinger Manor, Surrey, TQ 112459. A shallow, roughly oval pit, 3 feet deep at maximum and about 5 yards long by 3 yards wide, was dug into the natural Greensand rock. At the farthest end of the interior a natural ledge or bench had been left to provide a suitable place for seating or sleeping. Just clear of the

pit to the west, two post-holes suggest the existence of a rough frame against which thin branches or saplings might have been leant to form a roof. Probably this was then thatched with bracken or grass, or covered with skins. A concentration of burnt earth and stones indicates that a cooking hearth lay close to the entrance, under cover but so placed as to allow the smoke to escape outside. The marks of other open-air hearths have been located on the outside to the north and south of the hut. In and around the hut were found several thousand 'microliths' (small pieces of flint flake originally used to tip arrows, or set in a framework of wood or bone to form cutting tools), which shows that this hut was built and occupied during Mesolithic or Middle Stone Age times, about 8000 BC.

Other early peoples took advantage of natural fissures and hollows in the rock, setting up home in the mouths of caves or beneath the shelter of overhanging rocks—the entrances of which might be further protected by a screen of branches. Caves are relatively rare in Britain, found largely in the belt of limestone which runs diagonally across the country from Devon to Yorkshire—and in parts of Wales. The caves we see now are inevitably somewhat different in appearance from when they were lived in by early man. Falls of rock and the slow accumulation of debris means that the surface occupied by Stone Age

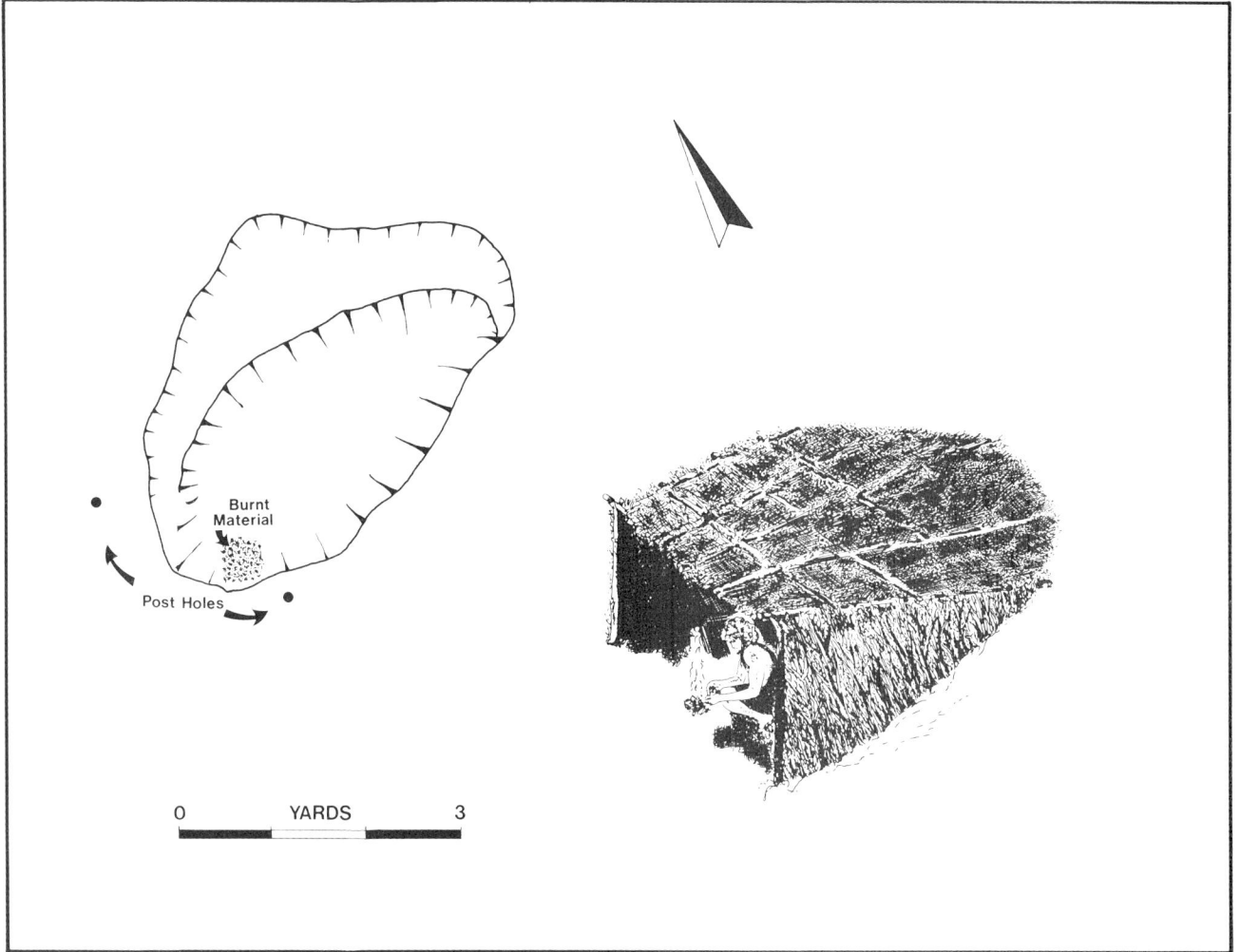

Mesolithic hut at Abinger, Surrey: plan and artist's reconstruction

man may lie at a considerable depth below the present floor-level of the caves (although sometimes excavation has cleared right down to the natural rock). And of course the surrounding scene may have changed radically, altering the position of the cave relative to rivers, lakes or sea-shore. Often these caves were occupied by wild animals before being used by man. Excavators may find the remains of tropical or subtropical species such as hippopotamus, straight-tusked elephant, lion and the rare sabre-toothed tiger; the upper more recent levels contain the remains of animals which lived in the colder ice-cap conditions: woolly rhinoceros, mammoth, cave-bear, bison, wolf, reindeer and so forth. Not all these animals necessarily *lived* in these caves; frequently they seem to have been the dens of packs of hyaenas, and piles of gnawed bones represent the carcasses of their prey dragged inside to be eaten.

One of the best known of such caves, familiar to many holiday-makers, is Kent's Cavern, lying in the side of a valley half a mile east of Torquay harbour, Devon, SX 934642. This consists of two main lofty chambers with a series of lesser galleries leading off in all directions. Two separate entrances, about 6 feet high and some 15 yards apart, lead into the two main caverns, which are linked internally. The remains of a wide variety of animals have been found here, including bones of the sabre-toothed tiger. The remains of early man discovered in the cave include various kinds of flint tools, barbed bone and reindeer-antler harpoon-points, a bone sewing needle, and pieces of a shaped ivory rod. Similar rods or batons have been found in other cave-dwellings, and they may have served some ritual or ceremonial function. The varieties of stone tools found show that the period during which Kent's Cavern was occupied was particularly lengthy, running from about 100000 to 8000 BC. The southern chambers were occupied during the earlier part of the period, and the more northerly rather later.

Other well-known caves inhabited by early man are

Oldbury, Kent: rock-shelters on eastern flank of hill

found in the limestone gorges of the Mendips. Particularly impressive is Wookey Hole, Somerset, ST 532480, consisting of a series of caves through which runs the River Axe—but only the opening chamber of which was occupied. Of a number of separate caverns in Cheddar Gorge, Somerset, the most important is Gough's Cave, ST 466538—still impressive, although its original appearance is obscured by concrete floors laid for the convenience of visitors. The range of stone tools found indicates that the outer chamber was occupied during the last phase of the Ice Age, from about 25000 to 10000 BC. Some 8 feet deep was found the grave of an adult male. He had been buried together with a simply-decorated baton of reindeer antler, and a necklace of perforated periwinkle shells. Stone Age man seems to have attached some special significance to this kind of sea-shell since they are found commonly in cave-dwellings of this period, and often far inland. The grave had been scattered over with horse teeth. A second baton found in this cave was apparently made from a human arm-bone. Further burials of this date were found in Aveline's Hole in Burrington Combe on the northern edge of the Mendips in Avon, ST 476587, one of which was accompanied by a periwinkle necklace and scattered over with deer teeth. However, the most important burial of this date came from Goat's Cave, Paviland, West Glamorgan, SS 437859. This is a deep cleft some 25 yards long, 30 feet up in a cliff on the south coast of the Gower peninsula, 15 miles west of Swansea. The original sea-level was rather lower, and instead of dropping straight on to the shore-line as now, the cave would have looked out over a narrow plain towards the sea. Flint tools show the site to have been occupied from about 25000 to 10000 BC. About 16500 BC (dated scientifically by analysis of the radio-active carbon content), a young man 25 years old was buried with a large boulder at his head and feet. He carried with him an ivory armlet, wolf-tooth pendants, and a number of small ivory rods. A handful or two of periwinkle shells may possibly represent a necklace, or food intended for the afterlife. Nearby, and presumably part of the ceremonial burial, lay the skull of an elephant. The whole grave had been sprinkled with red ochre, occasionally found in other burials of this date, and supposed to be symbolic of blood—perhaps representing the womb of Mother Earth.

A mile farther to the east, with a more accessible entrance on the top of the cliff, is Long Hole, SS 452851. Also on the Gower peninsula at Parc le Breos about a mile inland from Penmaen, is the cave of Cat's Hole, SS 538900, high in the side of the wooded Parc Cwm valley, 50 feet above the bed of the stream. Other caves occupied by early man in South Wales include Hoyle's Mouth, near Tenby, SN 111003, and Priory Farm Cave, near Pembroke, SM 979017. In North Wales, Cae Gwyn and Ffynnon Beuno are two separate but adjacent caves lying in the side of a gorge opening into the Vale of Clwyd, SJ 058724.

An important series of caves and rock-shelters

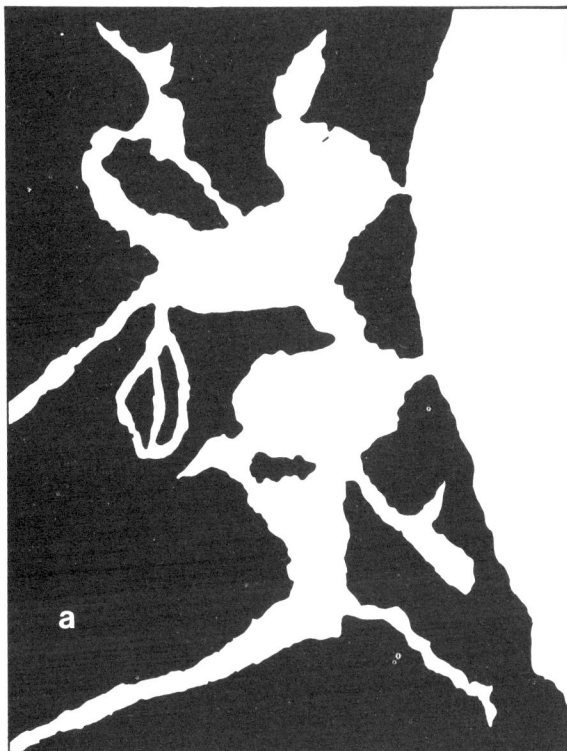

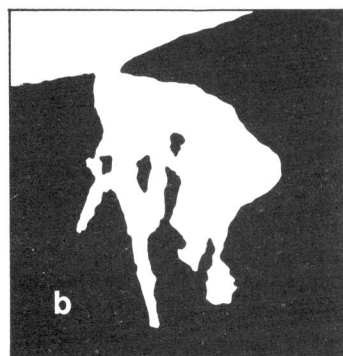

Ground-plans of cave dwellings: (a) Kent's Cavern, Devon; (b) Robin Hood's Cave, Derbys

0   YARDS   20

occurs either side of a limestone ravine on the Derby–Nottinghamshire border at Cresswell Crags, centre SK 535742: on the south side Church Hole, and on the north side Pin Hole, Robin Hood's Cave and Mother Grundy's Parlour. Most had been hyaena dens at some stage, but numerous flint and bone tools show them to have had a lengthy history of human occupation from about 50000 to 2000 BC and later. These caves provide our only evidence for cave-art from Britain—in the form of pieces of bone bearing engraved drawings of a reindeer, a horse's head and a human figure. Of course those who inhabited these Cresswell caves were on the very periphery of European Stone Age society, and it is perhaps scarcely surprising that, compared with material from the Continent, artistic finds are scarce and of poor quality. And there is no evidence for cave-paintings of the kind found in southern France and northern Spain.

Two other important cave-dwellings—both at one time also hyaena dens—are to be found at Victoria Cave, high up on the moors 1500 feet above sea level, near Settle, Yorkshire, SD 838650, and King Arthur's Cave, in the side of a hill 300 feet above the River Wye, near Ross, in Herefordshire, SO 545155.

In the south-east, two overhanging rock-shelters—the softer sandstone hollowed out beneath the harder greensand—provided shelters for Stone Age men at High Rocks, Sussex, TQ 561382 and Oldbury Hill, Kent, TQ 585562.

Other rock-shelters in the vicinity of Oban on the west coast of Scotland—notably the MacArthur and Druim Vargie caves, NM 855308, 855320, open on to a former beach, now 25 feet above sea level due to a change in relative land and sea levels. (Britain has tilted slightly since the Ice Age, the north-west rising and the south-east subsiding a little.) These were occupied by post-glacial Mesolithic 'strand-loopers', hunters and fishers, whose middens are still visible as mounds along the line of the beach. These refuse dumps consist largely of the remains of shellfish and crab claws, but show that they also caught

seals, and trapped deer, wild pigs and smaller game. Good examples of middens can also be found along the shores of the island of Oronsay (Caisteal nan Gillean, Cnoch Sligach, Croch Sligach and Croch Riach,

Caisteal nan Gillean, Oronsay, shell-midden: (left) section of deposit; (right) close-up of structure—almost entirely composed of limpet shells

NR 350870 centre), and on the east coast along the southern shore of the Firth of Forth at Inveravon, NS 952798. No doubt groups of hunters camped along the beaches of southern Britain also, but the rising sea level consequent upon the melting of the ice cap—which flooded the North Sea and eventually about 8000 BC severed the land-bridge which connected southern Britain with the Continent—has scoured any middens out of existence.

Names like Robin Hood's Cave remind us that the occupation of caves was not confined to Stone Age man. Many caves throughout the country show evidence of having afforded refuge to medieval hermits, outlaws and vagrants of all periods to the present day.

The period during which early man eked out a pre-

carious living, preying on herds of wild animals and gathering shellfish and edible roots, lasted for some 500000 years. Then from about 4000 BC with the Neolithic Age, the introduction of simple methods of farming enabled man gradually to gain some degree of control over his environment. By cultivating rather than gathering certain plants—cereals in particular—and by domesticating and breeding certain kinds of animals, a more reliable and abundant source of food was obtained. Gradually the subsistence economy gave way to one in which a more or less predictable surplus could be produced. Released from the interminable food-quest of earlier times, man was enabled to develop a more complex society, and eventually urban communities, supporting a wide variety of specialised trades, including a priestly caste. The introduction of metals, first bronze and then iron, about 1800 and 500 BC respectively, gave man even more secure control of his environment.

A more settled economy permitted the development of increasingly substantial dwellings. From Neolithic times onwards men constructed a variety of simple timber houses, most commonly circular but occasionally rectangular in plan, apparently with pitched roofs thatched with grass or reeds. Some gained greater headroom by continuing to scoop out the floor in the manner of the early Abinger hut. They occur alone, or clustered in small groups within palisaded enclosures, like a modern African *kraal*. Sometimes these palisades were reinforced or replaced by banks of earth and stone, which survive more readily than the buildings within. Only where stones were incorporated in the structure as rough footings do visible remains survive on the surface at the present time. Generally throughout lowland Britain a continuous history of subsequent farming, especially the use of the plough, has obliterated all surface traces of housing, although extensive remains frequently appear as crop-marks in aerial photographs.

Similarly the well-known 'lake villages' of early times have mostly disappeared without trace. These

Holbeach Drove Common, Lincs: aerial photograph showing crop-marks of early field plans

were settlements of huts built on artificial platforms made of earth and stones and layers of brushwood set on former lakesides or the edges of broad rivers like the Thames. Most famous is that excavated in the Somerset Levels near Glastonbury, where between sixty and seventy circular huts were found over an irregular area of about $3\frac{1}{2}$ acres—now merely a series of low mounds in a marshy valley, ST 493407. Wet conditions allowed the preservation of basketwork, wooden boxes and other domestic utensils, which can be seen in museums at Glastonbury and Taunton. Other such lakeside settlements are known to have existed in Holderness in East Yorkshire, in the Vale of Pickering, in Norfolk, Suffolk and south-west Scotland.

The most numerous visible remains of dwellings from this date are the 'hut-circles' familiar in upland regions of Britain. But even in upland areas more suitable for pasture than arable farming and therefore little cultivated in subsequent ages, the concentrations of stones representing early settlement sites formed con-

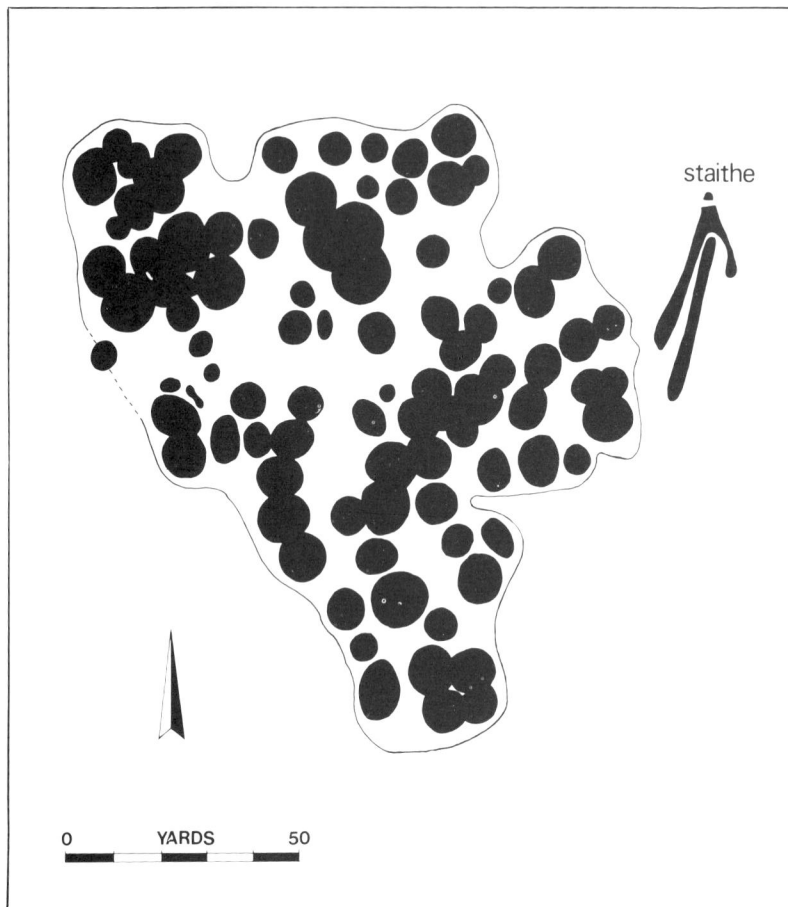

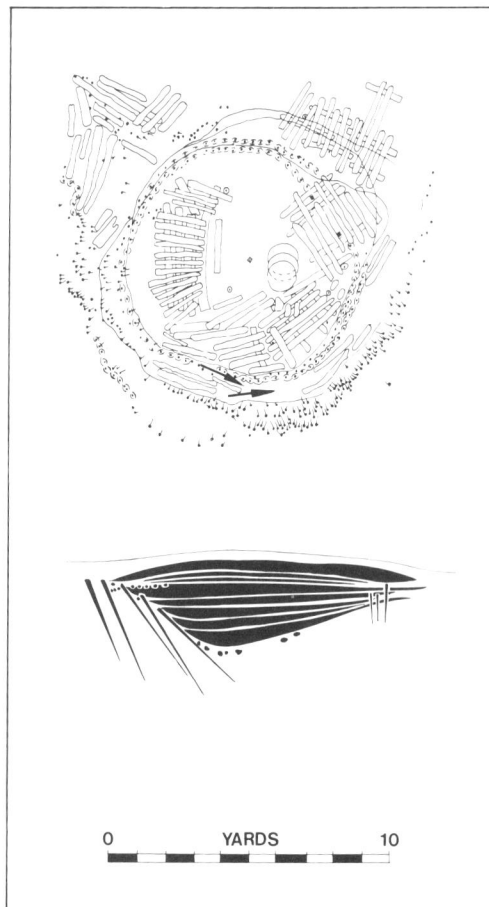

Iron Age lake village at Glastonbury, Somerset: (left) general plan; (right) plan and section of a hut showing sequence of floor-levels (after Bulleid)

venient quarries for those in search of material for dry-stone walling or other purposes. Much evidence has been lost in this way in relatively recent times. We know that even a major Dartmoor settlement site like Grimspound is less easily recognisable for what it is today than it was at the turn of the century when it formed the dramatic setting for scenes in Conan Doyle's *The Hound of the Baskervilles*. Nevertheless, the granite moorlands of the south-west are still prolific in visible remains of this kind. 'Hut-circles' represent what is left of the footings or lower courses of houses—some of which may have been built entirely of stone, beehive fashion, but most of which had timber superstructures. They employ the simplest kind of dry-stone walling, the gaps presumably plugged with moss or grass. They are single-roomed huts invariably circular in plan, varying between 2 and 8 yards in diameter. They occur either singly as isolated homesteads, or in various sized groupings, sometimes up to sixty or seventy together representing quite large villages. Often they are enclosed with an embankment, and occasionally associated garden plots and fields can be identified (see below, p. 34). Seventy or more hut-circles lie scattered on Standon Down, 1100 feet above sea level on the west of Dartmoor, SX 554824, and must have accommodated a considerable community in Bronze Age times, from about 1400 to 800 BC, when rather drier climatic conditions permitted occupation and cultivation at levels which would be impractical or impossible at the present time.

Of the very many settlement sites on Dartmoor, perhaps the most accessible is Grimspound, lying in a small valley about five miles south-west of Moretonhampstead, SX 701809. A massive dry-stone granite wall, about 3 yards across and originally some 6 or 7 feet high, encloses an oval 'pound' of about four acres. There is a single paved entrance on the eastern side. Water is supplied by a small stream running through the enclosure passing beneath the boundary wall. The pound now contains about two

The Rings, Devon: a Bronze Age enclosed settlement, SX 680645

dozen hut-circles, some scattered freely over the interior, others bonded into the enclosure wall. Typically the circles are some 5 yards across, the walls 4 to 6 feet thick, and seldom now more than 4 feet high, made of turf or loose stones contained by vertical slabs. A central stone provided a firm base for a post supporting a conical roof of branches which rested on the outer walls, and was probably thatched or covered with turf. A low entrance, about $2\frac{1}{2}$ by $3\frac{1}{2}$ feet, is usually formed of two upright stones supporting a lintel. There are sometimes signs of a rough porch or extension—and no doubt additional screens of branches or wattle might further protect the entrance. The floor was of beaten earth, sometimes with small areas of stone paving. These huts are most commonly sited on sloping ground so that drainage was no problem. The interior was usually provided with a low stone bench on one side for sleeping or seating, while on the other side a sunken hearth in the floor is marked by fire-crazed stones, fragments of which can still be picked up. Half a dozen other less substantial huts without hearths probably served various domestic functions such as storage or workshops. Three or four cattle-pens are built against the enclosure wall.

In the far north in Orkney and Shetland there survive the remains of much more substantially-built nuclear villages. In 1850 gale-force winds stripped the accumulation of drifted sand along the shore of the Bay of Skaill at Skara Brae on the west coast of Orkney, HY 231188, to reveal a cluster of seven squarish stone-built huts. Each hut is about 5 or 6 yards across. Well constructed from blocks of flat stone, the walls still stand up to 8 feet high in some places. The separate house units are connected by a series of paved alleyways, drained by underfloor channels and roofed over with slabs to keep out the rain. And the whole group of houses faced inwards to afford some degree of protection against the severe weather in these parts. Timber being unobtainable in Orkney, the roofs may have been constructed of stone, beehive- or igloo-fashion, presumably leaving a hole to let out the smoke, or perhaps more likely were made of turves supported by whale-bone ribs— often washed ashore in these parts. Low doorways about 3 or 4 feet high opened out on to the covered alleyways. Each house had a central hearth. All the interior fittings were made of stone slabs. There were box-beds with recessed cupboards in the wall above; and in each case against the rear wall stood a two-shelf dresser on three legs. Preserved in stone, these give a good idea of what must have been possible using timber elsewhere, and how snug the accommodation could be. Tanks set into the floor were presumably used to hold water or shellfish.

Although originally standing above ground, the village was surrounded by its middens, which had accumulated against the exterior walls to such an extent that it must have seemed almost subterranean. Excavation revealed no evidence for agriculture—perhaps understandable in these northern climes. But an enormous number of cattle and sheep bones, together with shells in the middens, indicate that the inhabitants depended largely on stock-raising and shellfish. Textile-manufacturing implements are absent from the range of tools found, suggesting that the Skara Brae people dressed in animal skins. They wore beads made of bone, teeth and walrus ivory. Small stone or whale-bone cups containing red, yellow and blue pigments suggest that they may have favoured body-painting. The village was occupied from about 1600 to 1400 BC.

The remains of a similar village are visible on the shore at Jarlshof in the southernmost point of Shetland, HU 398096. Later, at about the time of Christ, a new type of house was introduced here—the so-called 'wheelhouse'. A similar building technique was employed, but the plan was totally innovative. It consisted of a circular outer wall with an open space in the centre, and stone partitions radiating like spokes in a wheel dividing the interior into a number of wedge-shaped living compartments, each looking

Skara Brae, Orkney: plan of Neolithic village (after Childe)

Skara Brae, Orkney: interior of hut showing furnishings built from stone slabs

into the open area in the middle. In another type these spokes stop short of the wall, leaving an outer corridor.

Similar kinds of villages are known to have existed in the south-west of England. Still substantially intact is that at Chysauster, Cornwall, SW 473350. Some eight units of housing are ranged along either side of a 'street', each with a small stone-walled garden-plot at the rear (see p. 42 below). The walls, built of an earth and rubble core with dry-stone facing, still stand 5 or 6 feet high in places. Each unit is roughly oval in plan, and consists of a number of separate rooms opening off a central courtyard. They are well-paved, and drained by covered gullies. Evidence for central hearths indicate which were living rooms, and no doubt others served as workshops or animal-pens. The outlines of other houses lie off the main street, one having beneath it the remains of a fogou, which probably served as a cold-store for food (see below, p. 44). The Chysauster villagers probably gained their living by 'streaming' tin nearby.

The greater part of the British population continued to live in buildings of the Grimspound or Chysauster types well into the first centuries AD. But the occupation of Britain by Roman imperial forces from AD 55 resulted in the introduction of wholly new domestic standards. Soon after the pacification of the lowlands, at least the principal families were encouraged, as they had been in Gaul, to adopt Mediterranean-style dwellings. Wealthy landowners could commission large well-planned rectilinear houses built to the highest technical specification, providing advanced standards of comfort and hygiene.

In the country they chose well-favoured sites for their villas, characteristically lying on a sheltered slope facing south or east, with a good supply of running water nearby. They were single-storied, half-timbered buildings, standing on stone foundations. The lower walls were constructed from courses of fine, well-mortared masonry, plastered and often finely decorated on the interior with mural paintings. The timber super-

Darent, Kent: stoke-hole and tile floor-supports of hypocaust system of a Roman villa, photographed during excavation, 1894, TQ 563707

structure supported a tiled roof of modern type. Fragments of tile can usually be picked up in the vicinity of Roman buildings in large quantities and is almost invariably the first sign of a newly-discovered villa site. Patterned and sometimes elaborately figured mosaic floors were common. The main rooms were usually heated by a hypocaust-system—a furnace providing hot air which circulated beneath floors raised on small brick pillars.

Generally such buildings are provided with suites of baths. These were based on the Turkish bath principle, with a series of three or more rooms, varying in the degree to which they were heated, and containing hot and cold plunges. Such facilities clearly became a desirable status symbol for the prosperous native farmer, and detached bath-houses are sometimes found in isolation, the only stone and mortared construction among the otherwise timber buildings of a Romano-British homestead.

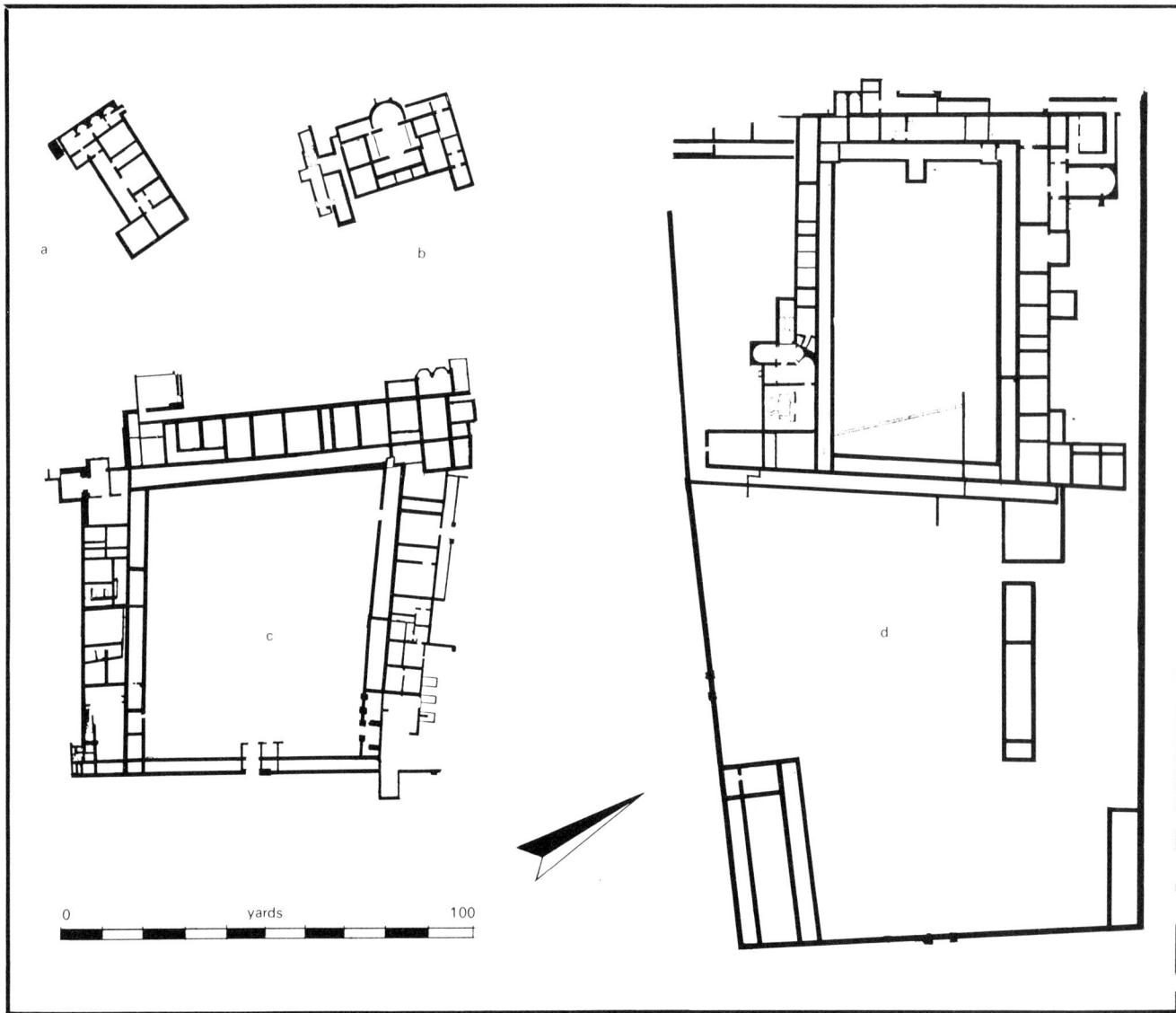

Comparative plans of Roman villas: (a) Newport, Isle of Wight; (b) Lullingstone, Kent; (c) North Leigh, Oxfordshire; (d) Bignor, Sussex

Roman villas varied greatly in size and complexity of plan. The simplest kind of building, seen for example at Newport on the Isle of Wight, SZ 502886, consisted simply of a range of rooms leading off a corridor or veranda which runs along the front of the house. Frequently a short wing was added at either end of the main range. At Newport it was the western wing which contained the elaborate bath system. It was entered by way of a vestibule at the west end of the veranda; there one might disrobe and take advantage of the cold plunge; thereafter a series of three apsidal-ended chambers became increasingly hotter as they approached the furnace at the north end. The water was supplied from an outside cistern at the southern end of the wing.

The remains of a similar villa lies on the edge of the cliff above Folkestone, Kent, TR 241370, with a superb view out across the Channel. The evidence of stamped tiles suggests that this fine house was built for a high-ranking officer of the Roman Channel Fleet based at Dover.

The largest and richest Roman villas were built round four sides of a courtyard, like that at North Leigh, Oxfordshire, SP 397154. Situated on sloping ground above the River Evenlode, the main house covers an area of some hundred square yards, ranged round a courtyard about 70 yards long by 50 wide. It was entered by a large gate on the lower south-eastern side with a porter's lodge beside it. A tessellated corridor ran all the way round, broken by steps as it gradually ascended the slope. No less than three suites of baths have been identified; and a kitchen wing lay close to an elaborate dining-room with heated floor and walls—both walls and ceiling painted with an olive branch design. Traces of many auxiliary buildings, presumably connected with the management of the estate, have been located on the south towards the river.

The remains of other fine courtyard villas can be seen at Rockbourne, Hampshire, SU 120170, or Great Witcombe, Gloucestershire, SO 899142. More elab-orate still, with double courtyards, are those at Chedworth, Gloucestershire, SP 053135, within easy reach of the cosmopolitan spa at Bath (see below, p. 31), or at Bignor, Sussex, SU 988147, which boasts particularly fine mosaics with classical subjects.

Lullingstone, Kent: part of the mosaic on the dining-room floor, depicting the abduction of Europa by the god Jupiter in the guise of a bull; the inscription at the top refers to the likely jealousy of Jupiter's wife Juno

A wide variety of villa plans existed, however. For example, at Brading in the Isle of Wight, SZ 599853, the courtyard was open to the east where the land slopes down to the sea, and the main house lay at the farther western end, flanked by detached farm buildings including an aisled hall or barn connected to the main house only by a wall. At Lullingstone in Kent, TQ 529651, a remarkable villa was built on an artificial terrace cut into the hillside above gardens running down to the River Darent. It displays a complex but compact plan in which pride of place was given to a superb apsidal reception or dining-room. This is accompanied by so few other chambers, that it may represent the country pleasure-house of a man

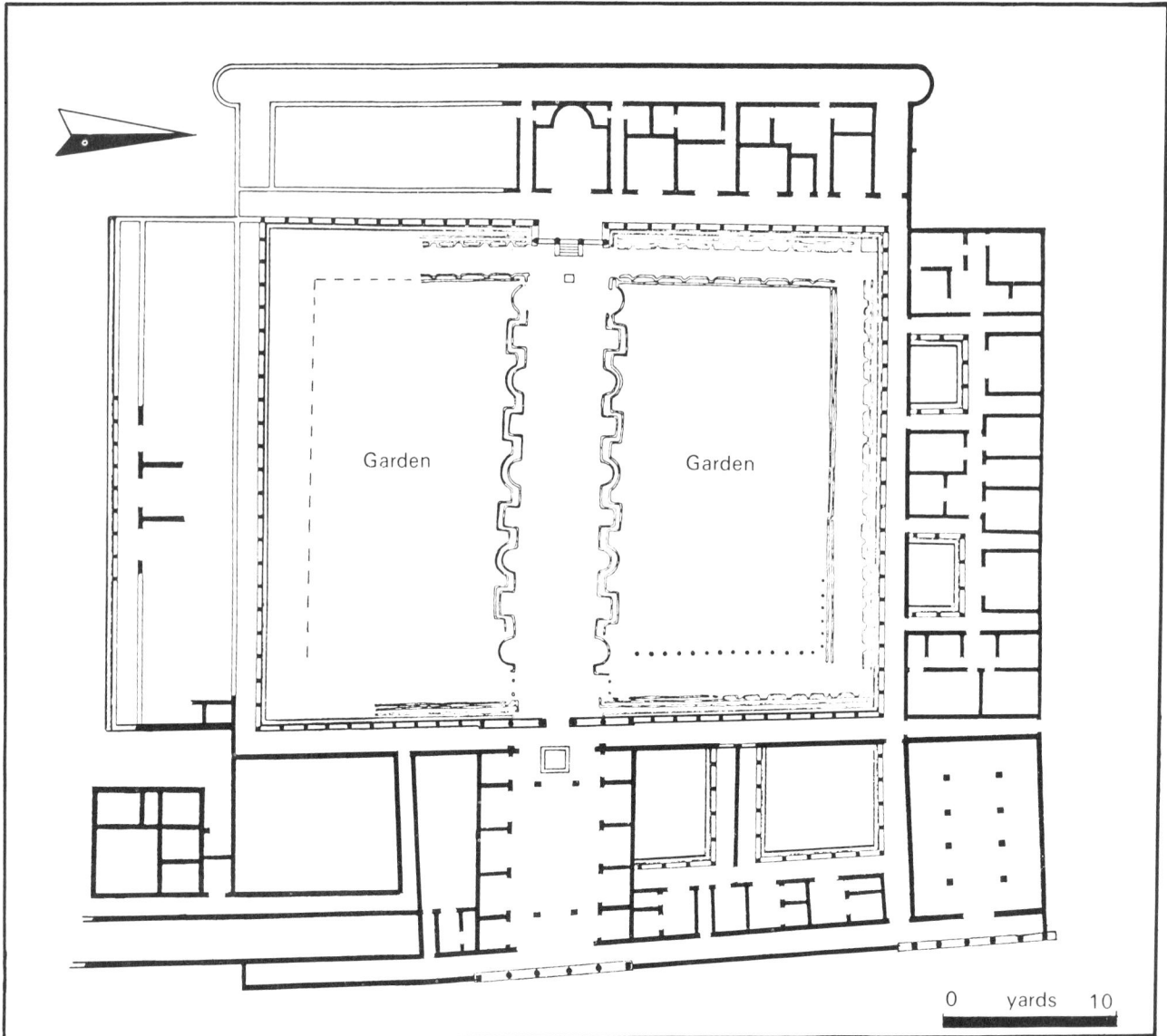

Fishbourne, Sussex: plan of Roman palace (after Cunliffe)

who had business interests in London, just 15 miles away. Marble portrait-busts, presumably of members of his family, occupied wall-niches. Some time in the fourth century the family was converted to Christianity, and designs painted on the wall plaster, including robed figures in an attitude of prayer, indicate that certain rooms were converted to use as a Christian chapel.

However, the most exceptional private house of all, both in its size and ground-plan, is to be seen at Fishbourne in Sussex, SU 841047. Lying close to the sea at the head of a creek just a mile west of the Roman town of Chichester, this is the only known example of a villa built wholly in the classical Italianate manner anywhere north of the Alps. For parallels we must look to places like Pompeii. Founded shortly after the Roman conquest, there is good reason to suppose that this fine palace (the term 'villa' is scarcely adequate), was built for the local British collaborator, the princeling Cogidubnus, described on a plaque found at Chichester as 'King and Imperial Legate' (see below, p. 116). As yet the site is only half excavated but it is already clear that in its final form the palace complex covered some five and a half acres. The main building was ranged round four sides of a large formal garden planted with trees and shrubs and containing fountains and statues. The house was entered through a colonnade and a large open entrance hall, about 35 yards long by 15 wide, from which a straight broad path passed through the garden to a flight of steps leading to an upper level on which lay a formal apsidal audience-chamber. Virtually all the rooms were sumptuously decorated with mosaics (earlier a restrained geometric black-and-white, later coloured pictures), moulded stucco decorations and marble wall-veneers. The main living-quarters of the owner lay facing the sea in the southern wing. Further small colonnaded courtyards or gardens are incorporated within the side ranges, and another more natural garden lay beyond the house on the seaward side.

The sites of some six hundred villas are known, dis-tributed generally throughout the lowland zone and usually coinciding with rich arable land. However, the major innovation of the Roman period was the creation of sophisticated urban life in Mediterranean style, based on well-planned and substantial cities linked by a network of major roads. Some cities, like Lincoln or Colchester, were deliberately founded as self-governing colonies of retired Roman legionaries—and were thus technically inhabited by Roman citizens. Others, like Canterbury, Chichester or St Albans, were tribal capitals, serving as the commercial and administrative centre for their region. Others still, like Bath, never acquired an extensive administrative or commercial function, but could boast a rich cosmopolitan spa life. And there were a host of minor settlements which grew up to serve a variety of economic functions. Some, like Wall in Staffordshire, SK 098066, or Great Casterton on the border of Leicestershire and Cambridgeshire, TF 002091, represent small staging-posts along major routes, providing overnight accommodation and stables where official messengers could change horses. Others like London or Wroxeter in Shropshire, SJ 565087, were originally military forts, and occasionally remained garrison towns, the forts continuing to occupy an important place in the town plan.

Roman towns varied greatly in size. Caistor St Edmund, Norfolk, TG 230035, covered a mere thirty-five acres, while Roman London was ten times that size, spreading over some three hundred and thirty acres in all. As with London, many Roman towns continued to flourish in later times and thus lie buried deep beneath their modern successors, to be glimpsed only in fragments—the remains of a bath-house or a stretch of walling. But others, like Caistor, Wroxeter or Caerwent (ST 469905), were abandoned to the plough, and now stand in more or less open countryside. The best known, because fully excavated (although now back-filled), is at Silchester in Hampshire, SU 640625, the tribal capital of the Atrebates. Now only a farmhouse and a medieval church stand

TOWCESTER

BATH

Amphitheatre

LONDON

Modern farm buildings
and medieval church

SALISBURY

0   YARDS   300

WINCHESTER

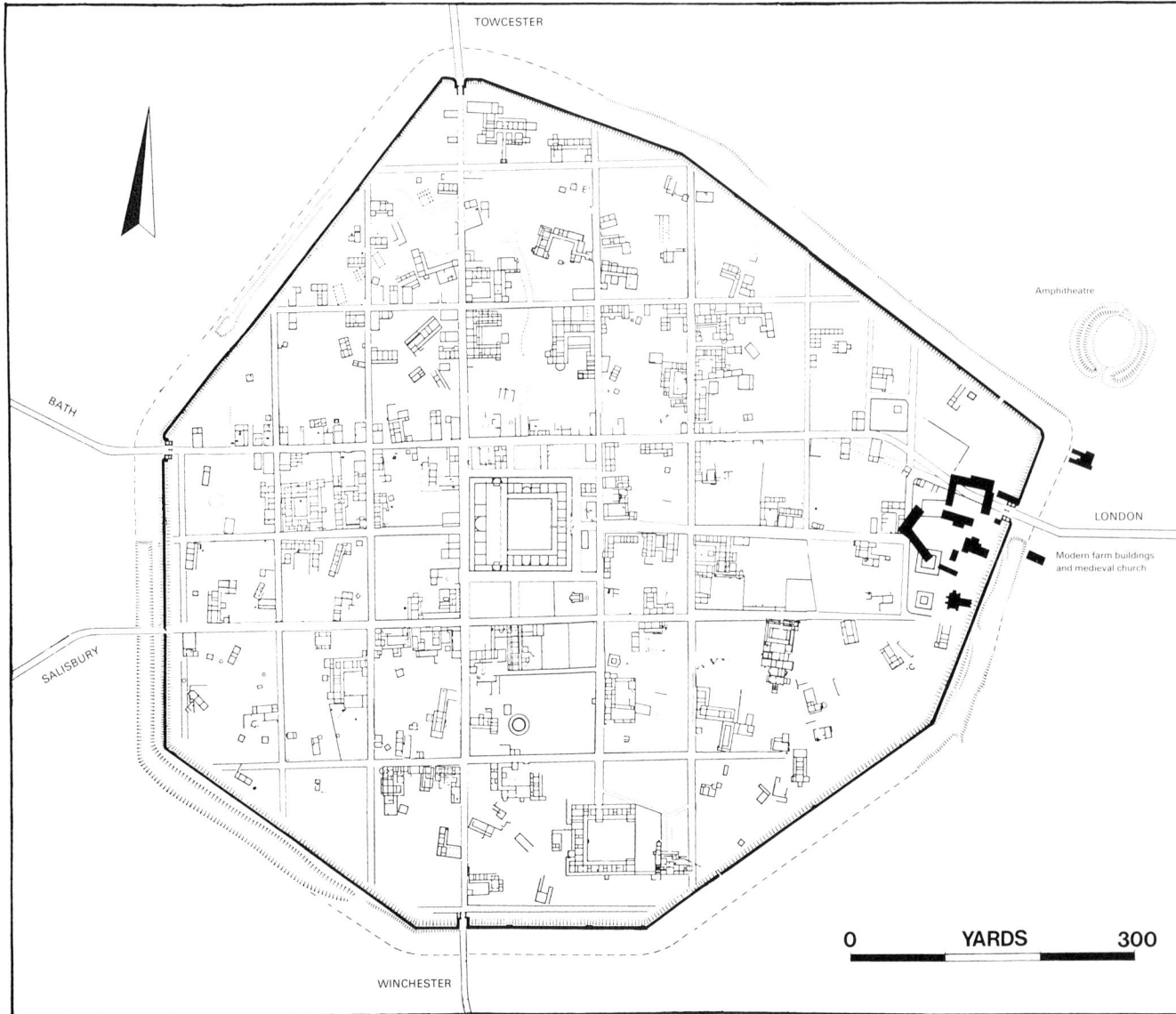

Silchester, Hants: plan of Roman town (after Boon)

inside the east gate. Although largely robbed of its facing stone, the perimeter wall is still impressive, standing 15 feet high. Like all Roman towns, the interior was laid out with a grid-pattern of streets centred on the forum. This was an open space or large courtyard about 50 yards square, enclosed by a colonnade, and which served as both market-place and civic centre. Adjacent was usually a large hall, the basilica, where the town magistrates met. The colonnade on one side of the Wroxeter forum is still visible. Large public baths formed an important feature of a Roman town. These were based on the same principle as those in private villas, but were larger and offered more elaborate facilities like exercise halls, such as befitted municipal pride. Jewry Wall at Leicester represents the remains of one such exercise hall, and there is another at Wroxeter, while an appropriately smaller establishment can be seen at Wall.

The thermal baths which rely on natural hot springs at Bath were, of course, unusual. In addition to conventional baths of the Turkish and Sauna varieties, there was a great swimming bath, 24 yards long by 10 yards wide and 5 feet deep, still lined with Roman lead, and still fed by the hot spring sacred to the native goddess Sulis, whom the Romans identified with Minerva, and whose temple formed part of the bath complex (see below, p. 116). Normally, however, a town's water supply had to be brought from a distance, either by a raised aqueduct, as at Lincoln, or in an open channel following the contours of the land, as at Dorchester (see below, p. 73).

Other important buildings in the town included temples and a hostelry, but most of the interior was taken up with housing. Much was of the simplest kind, consisting of a long, narrow building, the front abutting on to the street often used as a shop, the living quarters at the rear. Others, more spacious, were built four-square around courtyards, urban versions of the larger country villas. And like them, the finest were decorated with statuary, mosaics and wall paintings.

Bath, Avon: the great Roman bath showing its position relative to the medieval abbey; the superstructure is of a later date

Individual town-houses are visible at: St Albans, Hertfordshire, and Caerwent, and in Kent at Canterbury and at Dover, where finely painted plaster walls still stand to head height.

Outside the built-up area of the town there was room for an amphitheatre where public entertainments could be staged: gladiatorial combats, beast-shows, public executions and the like. These structures usually took the form of an oval space surrounded by tiers of wooden seats raised on an earth bank faced with timber or stone; an entrance lay at either end. Examples are visible at: Cirencester, Carmarthen, Dorchester or Chichester. They usually appear now merely as earthen banks. But similar amphitheatres were attached to military forts to serve as weapon-

training courts, and an outstandingly fine example is preserved at Caerleon on Usk (see below, p. 91). No site in Britain has yet been identified as a *circus* of the kind used for chariot-racing.

Urban theatres used for conventional dramatic performances existed in some places. A good example has been revealed by excavation at St Albans. It was basically a D-shaped building, open to the sky, the auditorium consisting of a semi-circular bank which carried tiers of wooden seating facing the acting area: an open space with steps leading to a back-drop of colonnade and a small inner stage. The citizens of St Albans must have been accustomed to dramatic performances of all kinds; the foundations of two monumental triumphal arches straddle the line of Watling Street where it passed through the city, one facing London, the other Chester.

At some stage in their development all important towns were provided with defences. To begin with, these usually just took the form of an earthen bank and exterior ditch. But before the end of the Roman occupation, this bank was usually strengthened by a massive stone wall, with projecting bastions which provided emplacements for heavy artillery—machine catapults and the like. Impressive gateways led out on to the major roads. The most complete and undisguised perimeter wall is to be found at Caerwent, abandoned since Roman times. But often these fine walls, refurbished in medieval times, survive to the present day, and large stretches can still be seen at Exeter, York, London and elsewhere. A Roman gateway, the Newport Arch at Lincoln, is still in use after almost two thousand years. And further substantial fragments remain at St Albans, Caistor St Edmund, Colchester, and at Aldborough in Yorkshire, SE 405665.

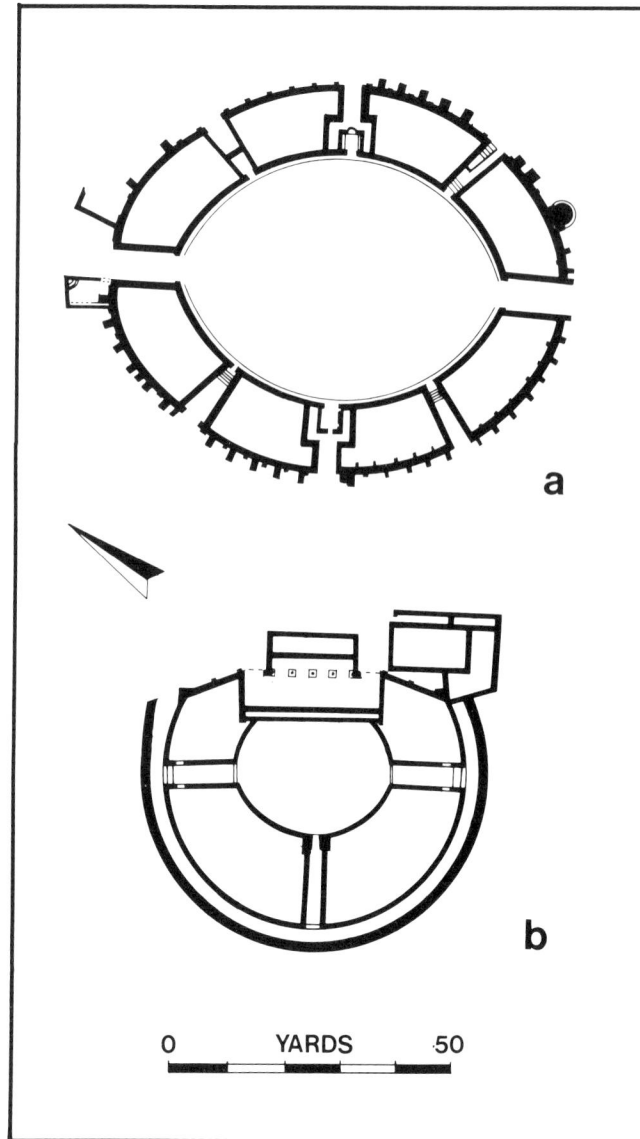

Plans of Roman theatres: (a) military ludus at Caerleon, Gwent; (b) town theatre at St Albans, Herts

AGRICULTURE

During the first half million years of his existence, man eked out a precarious living by hunting wild animals, fishing, gathering berries and leaves, and grubbing up such edible roots as he could find. Except for the occasional glut, when his group had the luck to kill a large animal, almost his entire existence was absorbed in the continual quest for food. The sole key to human advancement lay in food production rather than mere food collection. But farming is a comparatively recent innovation which did not reach Britain before some time in the 3rd millennium BC. The green revolution came about first in the lowlands, and then gradually infiltrated the upland regions of the north and west. No longer dependent on the unpredictable movements of wild animals, Neolithic man learned to domesticate and maintain controlled herds; and instead of gathering wild plants, he learned to sow the seed in identifiable plots and to reap a predetermined and concentrated harvest.

The examination of ancient pollen remains, preserved at lower levels in the soil, shows that there was considerable clearance of forest between about 4000 and 3000 BC. It was probably at this time that the large open stretches of downland and heath were formed. Using fire to clear the undergrowth, and polished stone axes to fell the larger trees, Neolithic farmers moved from one clearing to another as and when the land was worked out. And as areas ceased to be used for cultivation, there was an increase in scrub trees like birch, alder and hazel, as compared with the oak and elm of the forest. Together with the advent of large quantities of cereal pollen, we find the pollen of weeds like ribwort, associated with arable land. The wet clay of Neolithic potters sometimes picked up cereal grains, and from the impressions left on the finished pots we know that these early British farmers grew at least three kinds of cereals: Emmer and Einkhorn wheats and barley. Oats and rye seem to have been introduced later in the Iron Age.

The earliest methods of cultivation, using hoe or mattock, or the simplest kind of pointed-stick plough, can have left little or no permanent mark on the surface of the land. But careful excavation at South Street near Avebury, Wiltshire (see below, p. 105), has revealed the scratches of light ploughing preserved on the original land surface. The criss-cross pattern showed that the land was ploughed in two directions so as to break up the soil thoroughly. The surface had been sealed soon afterwards when a Neolithic burial-mound was built over the site, thus dating these cultivation marks securely to about 3000 BC. Similar but later plough marks have been found elsewhere, most notably under the banks of early fields on Fyfield Down, just east of Avebury. In the Iron Age a heavier kind of plough was introduced; using a metal arrow-shaped ploughshare, this could move the soil to one

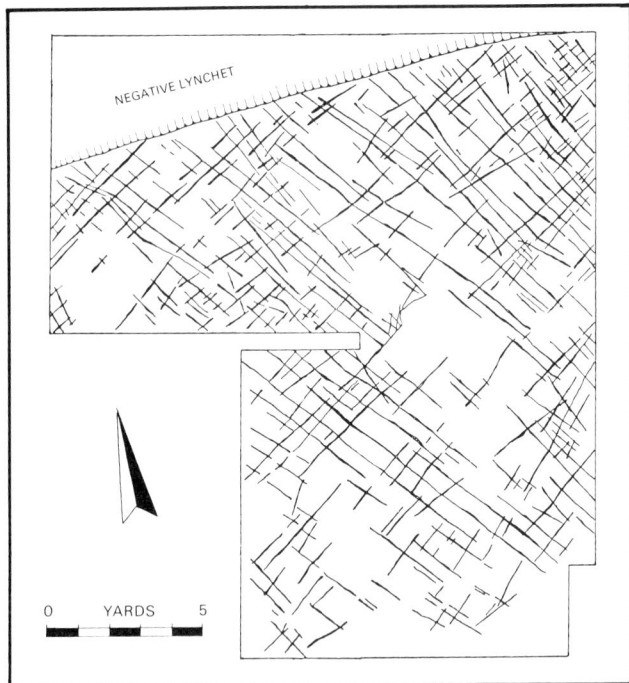

Neolithic plough-marks preserved beneath long barrow at South Street, Wilts

side, and allow more thorough working. In Roman times an improved model with an attached mouldboard actually turned the sod over.

In stony upland regions the outlines of small irregularly-shaped plots are marked by banks of stones cleared and dumped along the edges, both to allow easier working and to form recognisable boundaries to the area of cultivation. Such plots are commonly associated with the Neolithic and Bronze Age villages scattered across the granite moorlands of the southwest. Typical is the straggle of fields that lie for half a mile either side of an ancient trackway running along the slope below Rough Tor almost 1000 feet above sea level on Bodmin Moor, Cornwall, SX 144803.

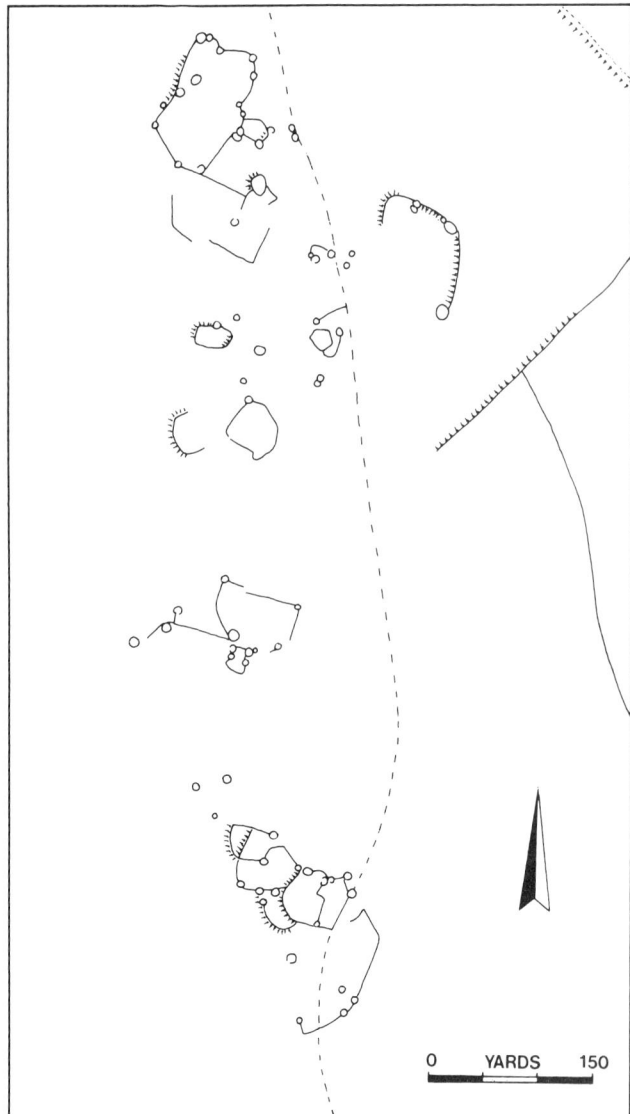

Bronze Age settlement below Rough Tor, Cornwall

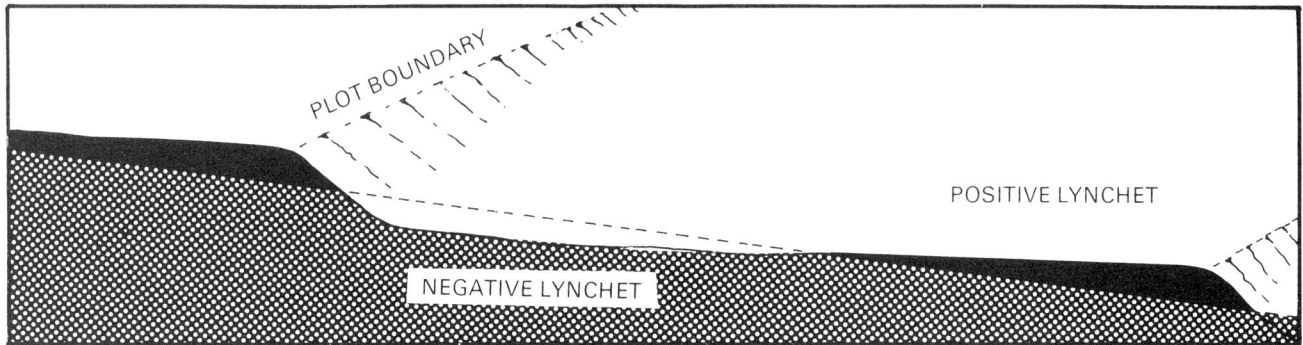

Diagram illustrating the development of lynchets

That such enclosures were worked fields rather than animal paddocks is shown by the development of cultivation terraces or 'lynchets'. Cultivation on sloping ground, however gentle, causes the disturbed soil gradually to creep downhill, leaving a marked hollow at the upper edge and a corresponding build-up of soil at the lower edge of the field. Once grass is allowed to grow over it again, the contours are fixed, unless disturbed by further cultivation. Very commonly, early fields are set diagonally on the slope, and then lynchets occur on all sides. This feature is even more marked where one field succeeds another down the hillside, when a series of cultivation terraces are often plainly visible. Sometimes lynchets are little more than 6 inches high, but on steep slopes they sometimes form deep scars measuring 20 feet or more in height. The fact that such steep hillsides were cultivated suggests that at some periods there was considerable demand for land.

In course of time the early irregular plots associated with hamlets of the Rough Tor type were replaced by extensive systems laid out in a more or less regular manner, including continuous straight boundary lines, suggesting that large-scale clearances were embarked upon by organised agricultural communi-

Lynchets at Mere, Wilts, ST 825335.

THE WARREN

DURDLE DOOR

0   ½   MILE   1

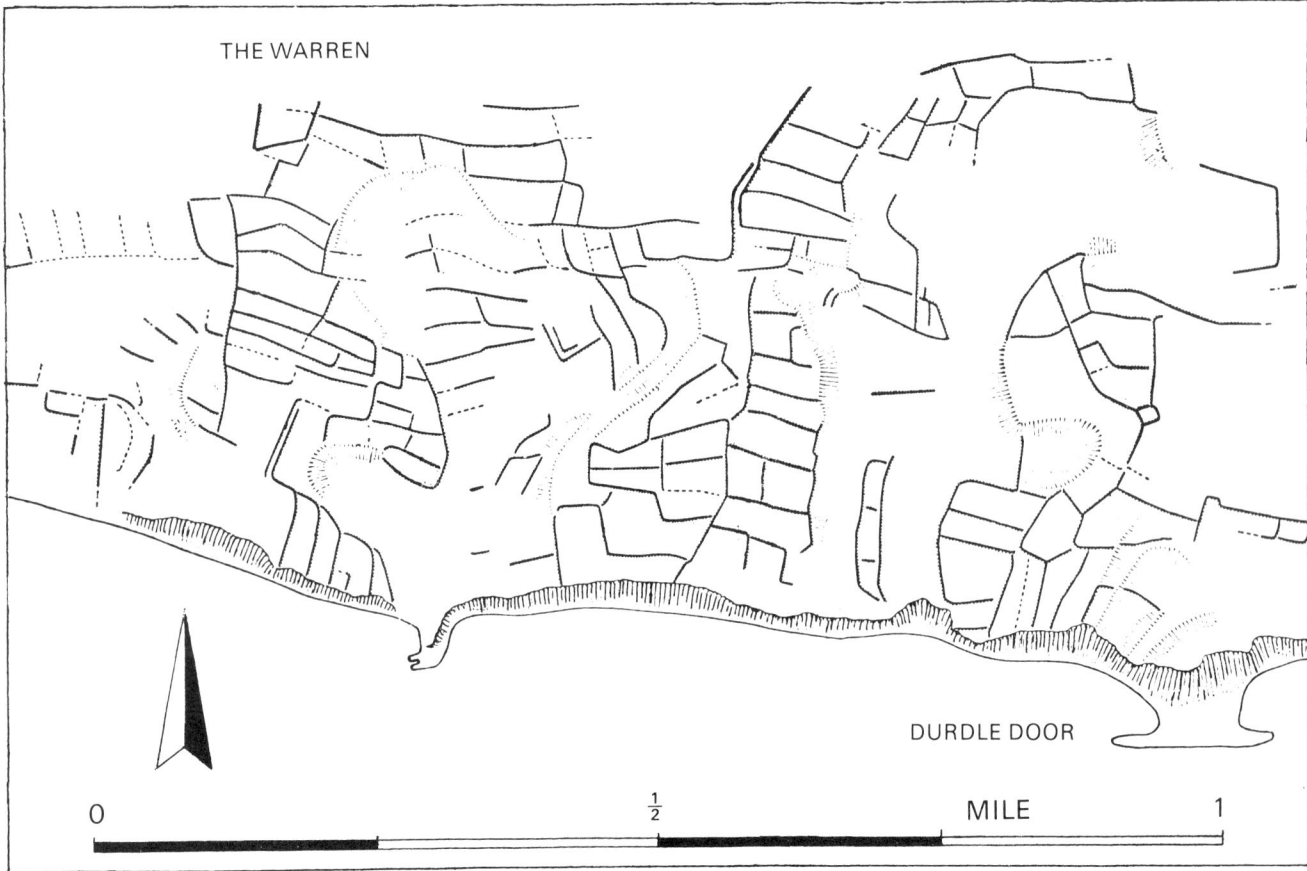

Plan of prehistoric fields on cliff edge west of Lulworth Cove, Dorset

ties. One might assume that this would have been characteristic of the Roman occupation and the period immediately prior to it. Extensive blocks of more or less rectilinear fields are widespread over much of the chalk downland of southern England from Dorset to Sussex, although they are often more readily identifiable from the air than on the ground. These 'Celtic' fields survive to the present day because they occupy only marginal arable land, given over to pasture when heavier Saxon ploughs made the more rewarding clay soil of the river valleys easier to work. Of course the demand for food production during two World Wars led to renewed ploughing of downland, and the consequent loss of much evidence. Elsewhere on lower ground continuous and intensive cultivation throughout the centuries has

Fyfield Down, Wilts: aerial view of square Celtic fields

obliterated all surface traces of early fields, although from the air field-systems can sometimes be picked up on the lighter gravel soils of river terraces. The great majority of early flint and bronze sickle-blades have been found in the Thames Valley and East Anglia, indicating that these were major corn-producing districts in early times.

On Fyfield Down west of Marlborough, Wiltshire,

SU 142710, several acres of fields exist enclosed by grass-covered banks now up to 10 feet high. Roughly squarish in plan, individual plots vary between a quarter and one and a half acres in extent. Sunken trackways between gave access to farm buildings, and led out to open pastures beyond. The original lay-out of a field was probably marked merely by a plough furrow. But excavation through the Fyfield lynchets

shows that early field boundaries sometimes took the form of a wooden fence, or a low wall formed by a row of stones dragged from the surface. One of many large stones on Fyfield Down bears grooves made by polishing stone axes, SU 128715.

In some cases the shapes of fields changed many times over the centuries during which they were in use. Ascribing any particular field-system to a given period is largely a matter of guesswork, unless the settlement to which it relates can be identified—which is rare—or unless an otherwise datable feature like a burial mound is constructed in a position under or over the field-system so as to provide a relative dating.

If animals were turned in to graze stubble, then the soil might be manured. But probably one field was cropped until the land was exhausted and the returns inadequate, when it would be abandoned in favour of a fresh site nearby until it had recovered by lying fallow for a lengthy period. Of course, restorative methods of land-husbandry such as manuring were unnecessary as long as land remained plentiful. However, the increasing population of Roman times—possibly well over ten millions—added to the persistent demands of military quartermasters, necessitated more systematic agricultural methods. Large-scale land-drainage was embarked upon to turn the East Midlands fenland into a rich corn-producing district under state management; and advanced agricultural techniques such as crop-rotation were introduced.

One elementary kind of land-management took the form of improving a sandy or clayey soil by 'marling' with chalk or lime. This was quarried for the purpose from distinctive shafts known now as 'Dene-holes', so-called because popularly believed to have been places of refuge from Danish or Viking raiders in Saxon times. The Roman geographer Pliny, writing about Britain in AD 70, describes the method and refers to shafts up to 100 feet deep, but most known examples are much smaller, typically only 20 or so feet deep. A narrow shaft, often little more than a yard

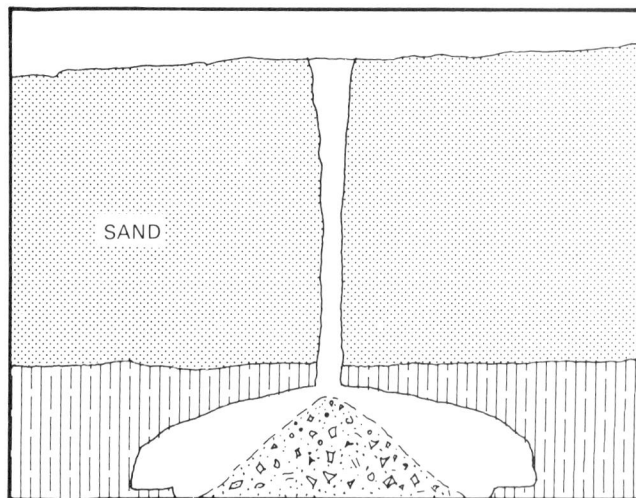

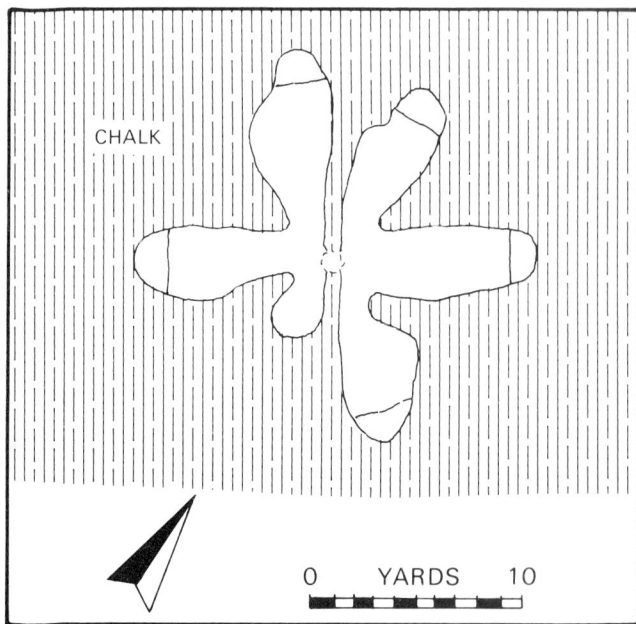

SAND

DEBRIS

CHALK

0 YARDS 10

Plan and section of dene-hole at Joyden's Wood, Kent

across, is dug through the covering of sand or clay to the chalk below, where a series of lateral galleries branch out in a trefoil or cinquefoil pattern. Surviving dene-holes are confined to the south-east of England. They are now often plugged as a safety factor, but examples still open (and therefore dangerous!), can be found in Joyden's Wood, Kent, TQ 507714, and in Hampshire near Four Marks and Basing Park, SU 682339, 697278. This method of extracting chalk for marling has been in use until comparatively recent times. The well-known caves at Chiselhurst in the London Borough of Bromley, TQ 431696, were extensively worked in the eighteenth and nineteenth centuries, although they almost certainly had an early origin. The horizontal galleries driven into the hillside here cover an area of almost twenty acres.

For some time throughout Britain, and perhaps always in the less hospitable climate of the far north, cultivation played a less significant role in the economy than stock-breeding. Excavation of the middens of communities like that at Skara Brae shows that cattle were by far the most important element: a large ox with a broad skull and long horns. Presumably these beasts were used as draught animals where required, hauling carts and pulling ploughs. Next in importance was the pig, and then goat-horned sheep. By the Iron Age a smaller type of cattle with shorter horns had been introduced, while sheep had replaced pigs in order of importance: a slender large-horned animal not unlike the present-day Soay sheep which can be seen at the Butser Hill experimental station (see p. 9).

From Neolithic times animals were probably herded from the backs of ponies, and certainly with the aid of dogs—something like a largish fox terrier, the skeletons of which have been found in excavations. Originally herds of cattle and sheep could probably be grazed in the open pasture-lands which lay beyond the small enclosed arable fields clustered round the settlement. But with the passage of time, both to counter the pressure on land space from neighbouring communities, and to discourage possible rustling, it proved expedient to lay out extensive 'ranches' with continuous boundaries running over many miles. From the air over parts of the chalk downland of southern England, it is possible to trace running lengths of banks and ditches which divide the land into large blocks, each covering up to ten square miles.

A classic example of such prehistoric ranch boundaries has been plotted enclosing large tracts of land on the Wiltshire—Hampshire border south-west of Andover. The course of the River Bourne seems to have been used as one baseline for the layout. Then roughly at right-angles, ditches were laid out running up the slopes. There they linked with others which were laid out using prominent hills like Sidbury or Quarley Hill as sighting points. The fact that these ditches were subsequently built over by the ramparts of Iron Age hillforts, proves that the ranches the ditches relate to had their origins at least as early as the Bronze Age. The area incorporates large tracts of smaller 'Celtic' fields. Where they drop into the valley-bottom the line of these ditches is often lost due to present-day soil conditions; but where they have been located on the chalk, excavation shows them to have been usually V-shaped, up to 3 or more yards across and about 4 feet deep.

Similar cross-country earthworks still visible from the ground are probably ascribable to the Iron Age. The Grim's Ditch series lying just north of the Berkshire Ridgeway, SU 423845–542833 and 546785–570792, represent a boundary system enclosing some twenty-two square miles in all. Although averaging now only some 6 feet between the bottom of the silted-up ditch and the top of the degraded embankment, excavation shows that these were once formidable barriers, a large V-shaped ditch, 6 feet deep and about 7 yards across, backed by a mound of proportionate size made from the upcast. The name Grim's Ditch suggests that the pagan Saxons attributed these large earthworks to the chief of their

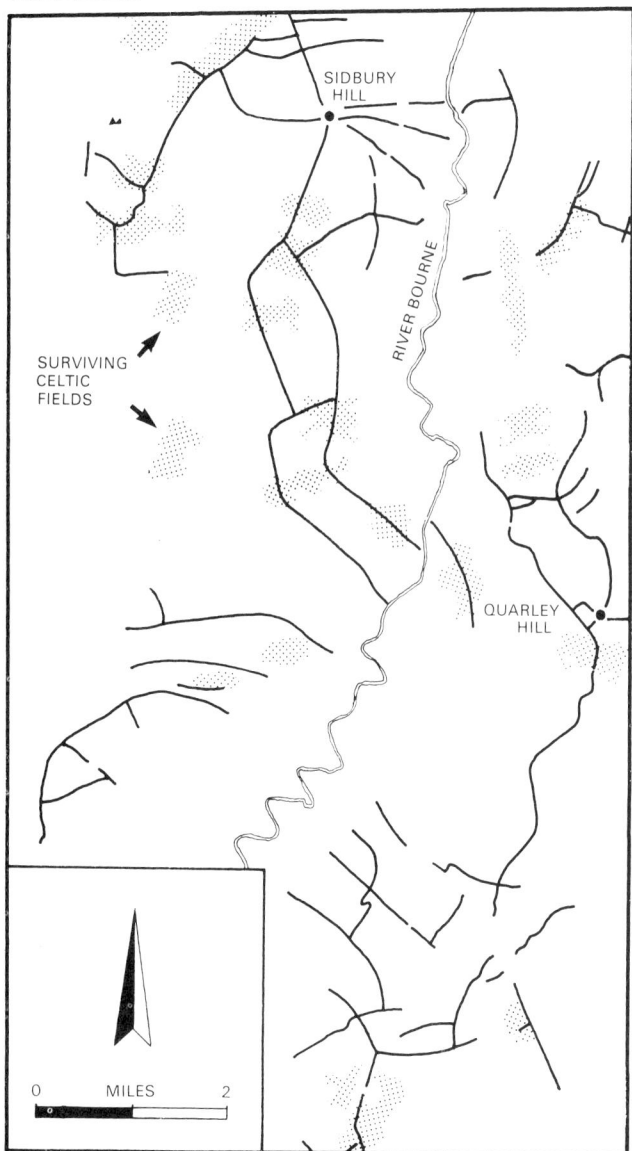

Bronze Age ranch-boundaries on the Wilts/Hants border, showing surviving areas of prehistoric fields

gods, Woden, one of whose nicknames was Grim. There is another so-called Grim's Ditch running through the central Chilterns in Buckinghamshire— best seen at Great Hampden between SP 835022 and Hampden church, or on Pitstone Hill, SP 952148 where it lies beside patches of 'Celtic fields' and close to the hollows left by ancient flint mines. Another large boundary system can be traced on the golf-course at Minchinhampton Common, south of Stroud, Gloucestershire, SO 857004–865013.

The Neolithic stock-breeders of southern England constructed a distinctive type of 'causewayed enclosures', which seem to have been used for periodic round-ups. Before the development of self-contained ranches, scattered pastoral communities needed periodic gatherings to arrange stock-trading and marking; and no doubt the associated festivities attracted tribesmen from a wide region. These enclosures consist of between one and four concentric ditches in discontinuous lengths, breached by numerous causeways of reserved ground allowing access to the interior. Low internal banks, broken by gaps corresponding to the ditch causeways, may have supported light palisades.

These causewayed camps vary considerably in size. The largest examples, like the classic site on Windmill Hill near Avebury in Wiltshire, SU 087714, cover more than twenty acres in all, while the smallest known example on Combe Hill, near Eastbourne, Sussex, TQ 574021, encloses little more than three acres. Other good visible examples include that at Whitehawk on Brighton Racecourse, TQ 330048, or on the Wiltshire downland at Knap Hill near Pewsey, SU 121636, or Whitesheet Hill near Mere, ST 802352. Enclosures of this kind are best preserved on the chalk downlands between Dorset and Sussex, but aerial photography has revealed similar structures on the gravel river terraces of the Thames at Abingdon in Berkshire, Staines in Greater London, and elsewhere.

Although in no way defensive in themselves, the sites of these camps were sometimes subsequently

Windmill Hill, Wilts: partly excavated ditches of Neolithic causewayed camp

occupied by Iron Age forts. This is usually revealed only by excavation, as at Maiden Castle, Dorset (see p. 81), but a good example still visible within the later defensive ramparts is found in The Trundle above Goodwood Racecourse on the South Downs, SU 877110. Excavation of causewayed camps has revealed no trace of internal buildings, and they certainly do not represent permanent settlement sites. They are best interpreted as places of occasional assembly which served some ceremonial function significant to the pastoral economy. The large quantities of cattle bones, including poleaxed skulls, buried in the ditches, suggest that these meetings were the occasion for extensive slaughtering of the herds. Before the availability of silage as winter fodder, enabling large numbers of animals to be kept through the winter months—a comparatively recent innova-

tion—animals surplus to those required for breeding were slaughtered in November (the month the Saxons called 'blood-month').

The production of a large-scale surplus of food necessitated adequate means of storage. Grain was stored in timber-lined pits dug into the ground, or in small four-square granary buildings raised off the ground by corner posts. Roman military granaries formed distinctive buildings within each fort: large stone buildings with raised floors built as if for a hypocaust-system, but with side-ventilations allowing fresh air to circulate freely (see below p. 94).

In the farthest south-west and in the far north, distinctive kinds of subterranean storage-chambers were developed, called variously fogous in Cornwall and souterrains or 'earth-houses' in Scotland. These are generally associated with pre-Roman Iron Age

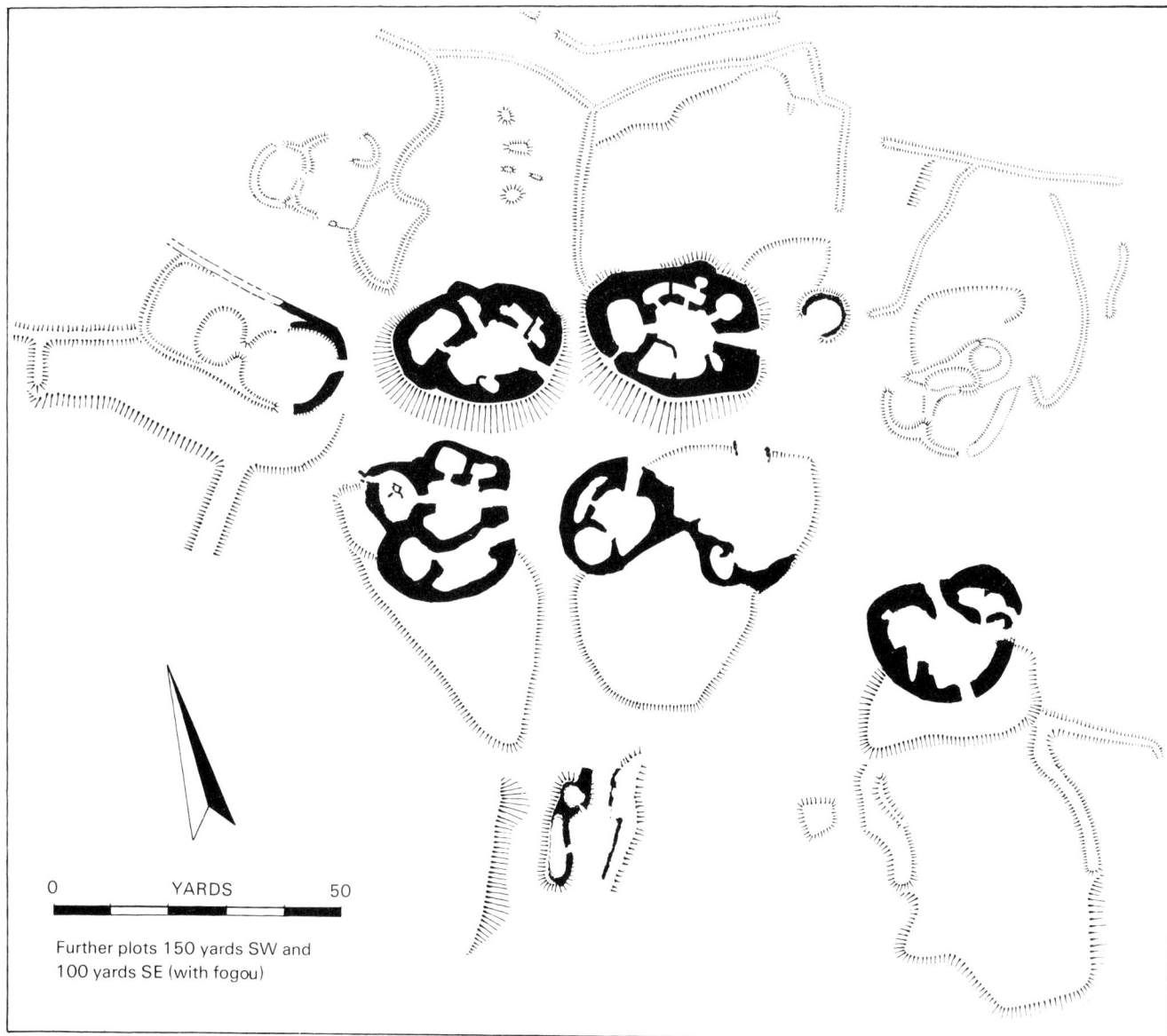

Chysauster, Cornwall: plan of Iron Age village showing garden plots (after Hencken)

0   YARDS   50

Further plots 150 yards SW and
100 yards SE (with fogou)

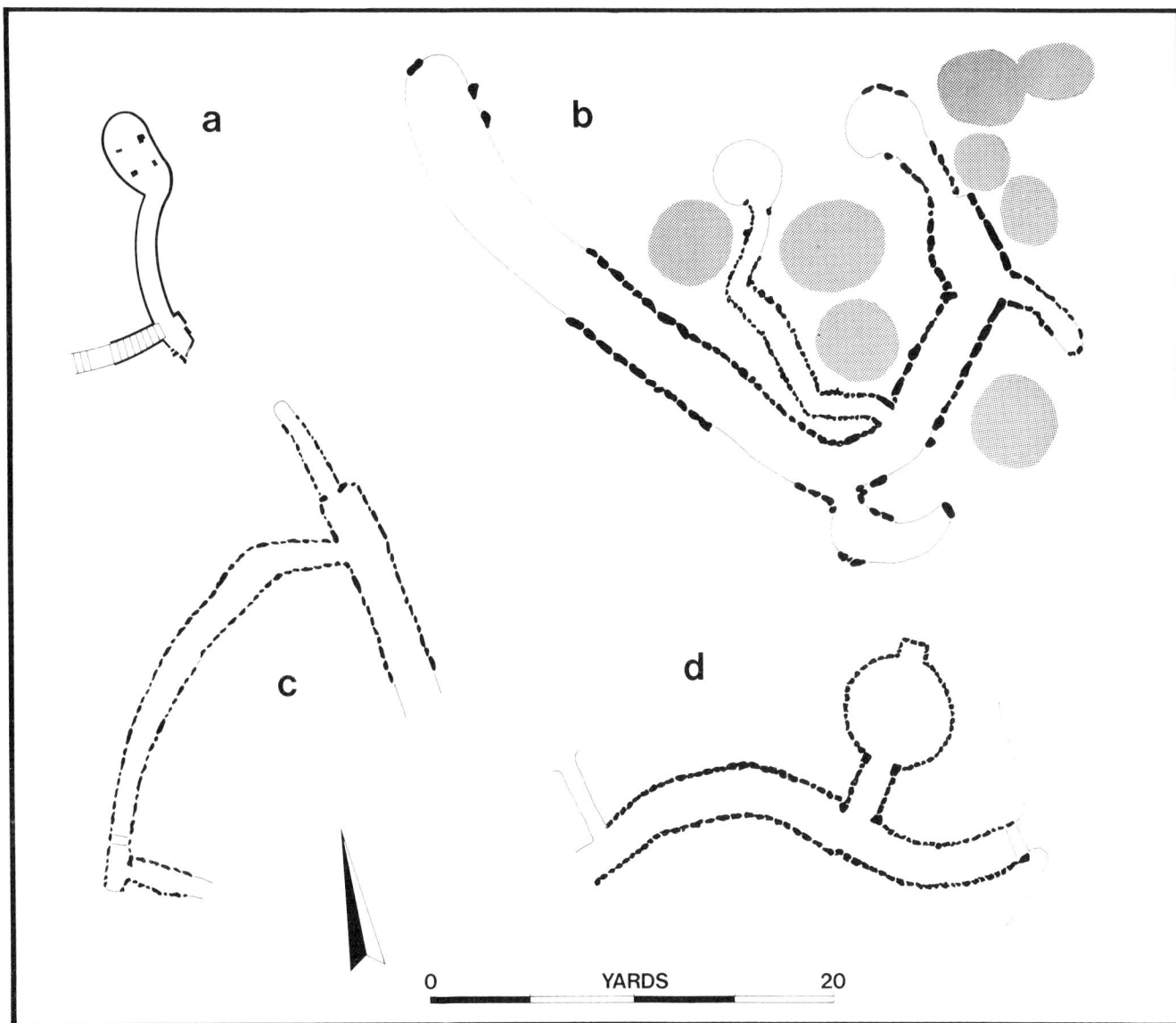

Comparative plans of souterrains and fogous: (a) Grain, Orkney; (b) Carlungie, Angus, showing relationship to huts; (c) Halligye, Cornwall; (d) Carn Euny, Cornwall

Carn Euny, Cornwall: interior of fogou

villages, normally lying immediately below one of the houses, as at Jarlshof or Chysauster (see p. 25). They consist of horizontal passageways running just a little way beneath the surface of the ground, lined and roofed with slabs of stone. A variety of plans occur. Often they have side-chambers or branch-passages.

Probably they were formed by digging out a trench, inserting the roof and then covering it with soil.

Most are now unroofed. But a Cornish fogou in a relatively well-preserved state can be seen in the Iron Age village of Carn Euny, SW 403288: a passageway 22 yards long, paved and drained and still retaining

its roofing stones in the central section. Close to the main entrance which opens from a dwelling in the village, lies a circular chamber; the other end is ruined, but there certainly existed at least one subsidiary entrance in a side-passage. At the farthermost end two niches, one either side of the passage, seem to be slots for holding a door. Another fine example, Y-shaped in plan and about 10 yards long, can be found beneath a bank behind Pendeen House high on the cliffs in St Just parish, SW 384355. Another at Halligye, SW 712238, passed beneath the ramparts of a fortified homestead, and possibly served as an additional exit, opening into the outer ditch.

The original purpose of these curious structures has been strongly debated. The exceedingly low roofs and permanent darkness make it improbable that they formed any kind of regular subterranean dwelling for man or beast. And although no doubt they could serve as hiding-places in an emergency, they are scarcely defensible points in the normal sense. Their interpretation as cold-larders for perishable foodstuffs seems the only reasonable one.

In Scotland particularly fine, and accessible, examples of souterrains occur along the east coast of Angus, at Ardestie, NO 502344 (an elaborate example some 45 yards long and requiring no drain since dug into coarse gravel, with one main and at least three subsidiary entrances) and Carlungie, NO 511359, or in Aberdeenshire, at Culsh, NJ 505055.

In Orkney, as at Rennibister, HY 397127, or Grain, HY 442117, souterrains are often only half subterranean, with a mound-like appearance from the exterior. Their chambers, entered now through a trapdoor, characteristically have roofs supported by pillars.

INDUSTRY

Once the production of a good surplus could be guaranteed, the economy had sufficient leeway to develop a wide variety of supplementary industries. Gradually there came into being the complex economy of modern society, in which man was no longer totally dependent upon the handicraft of himself and his family alone, but could call upon the services of various specialist tradesmen: miners, metalworkers, potters, weavers—craftsmen of all kinds, practising skilled arts in recognised centres.

The most immediately useful industry was the provision of those cheap and efficient tools with which man was slowly coming in control of his environment. The hunting and gathering communities of the Old Stone Age probably picked up the stone they needed for their implements casually from the surface, from river beds or wherever it came to hand. However, the farmers of the Neolithic Age found that the best flint came from thin seams bedded low down in the chalk of downland England. Probably this was first discovered by prising out nodules from where the chalk was cut through by river valleys. But later this assured source of first-rate flint was deliberately mined in a highly organised manner. Broad shafts up to 10 yards in diameter and 40 or more feet deep were sunk through the overlying burden of sand and clay and into the flint-bearing chalk beneath. The upper seams of inferior flint nodules were ignored in favour of the lower levels where the desirable 'floorstone' flint was to be found. There low galleries were dug radiating in all directions, sometimes up to 15 yards long and often with little more than 2 feet headroom. The seams were worked as efficiently as possible, leaving only very thin walls between the galleries, and frequently honeycombing, so as to join one shaft with another.

The miners' tools have been found in large numbers in abandoned shafts: wedges and pickaxes made from red deer antlers and shovels made from the shoulder-blades of oxen. Some still bear the fingerprints of those who last used them, pressed into the chalk dust caked on to the handles with sweat. For light the miners used chalk or pottery lamps burning animal fat. The soot-marks left by these lamps, as well as marks made by antler picks, still remain on the walls of the mine galleries. There are also systematic scratches which may be interpreted as the miners' tally-marks of production quotas. On the sides of the shafts can sometimes be found grooves made by the ropes in hauling baskets of flint up to the surface.

Probably no more than two or three shafts were open at any one time, the waste material from new shafts being dumped into an exhausted and abandoned mine. Gradually over the centuries several hundreds of shafts might be opened at one place.

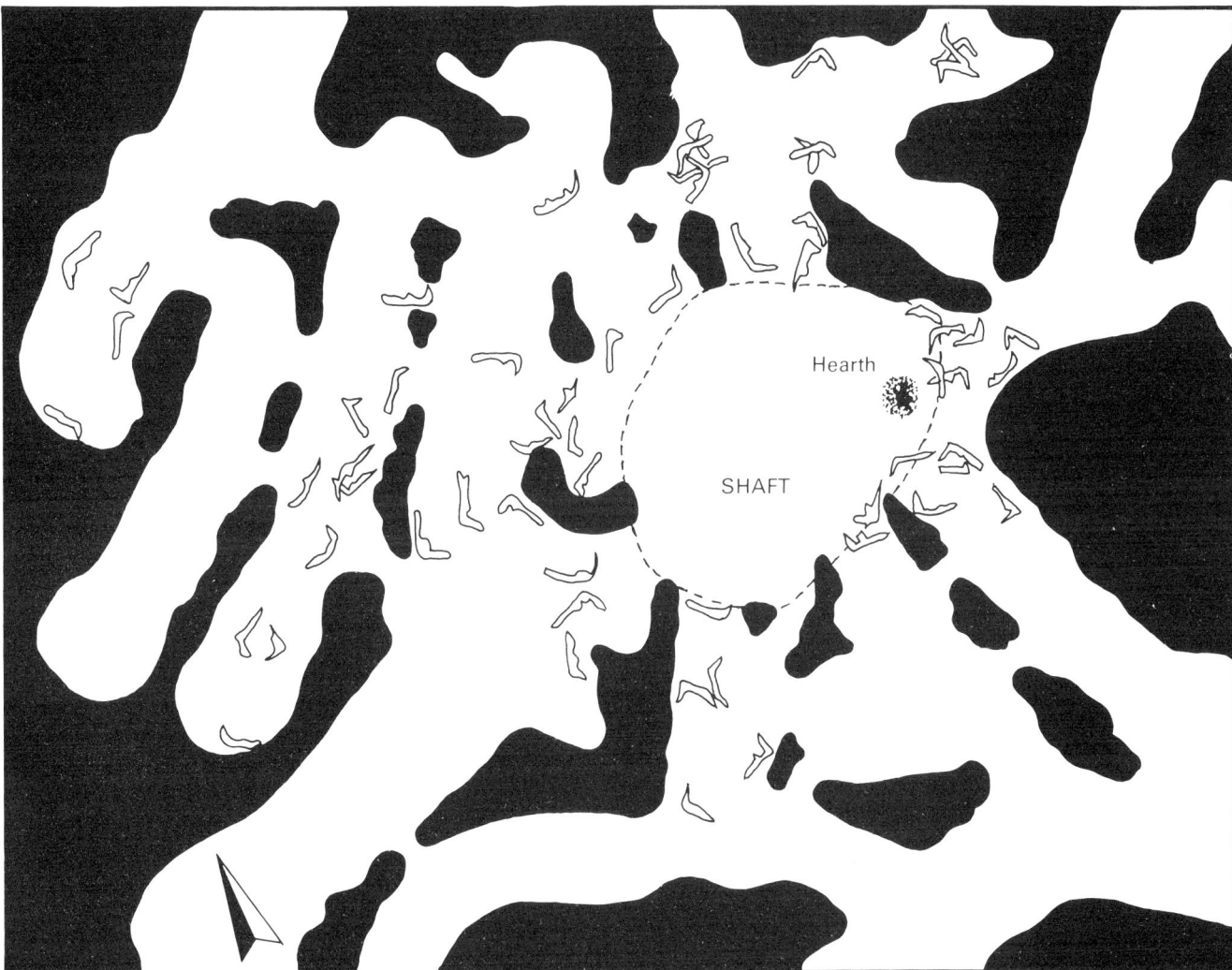

Grimes Graves, Norfolk: plan of a flint-mine, showing find-spots of antler pickaxes (after Armstrong)

0   YARDS   5

Now they are usually only visible as a series of pock-marks in the grassy surface—the hollows of collapsed shafts and mounds of waste material dumped on the surface round about.

The South Downs are particularly prolific in the remains of flint-mines. Large areas are recognisable behind Worthing in Sussex, at: Harrow Hill, TQ 081100, Blackpatch, TQ 094089, Church Hill, TQ 112083, or near to the Iron Age hillfort at Cissbury, TQ 137079, or farther east close to the Long Man hill-figure (see below, p. 116), at Windover Hill,

Grimes Graves, Norfolk: interior of Neolithic flint-mine

TQ 542034. Others are recognisable on downland elsewhere, in Wiltshire for instance at Easton Down, SU 236358, or close to the hillfort of Liddington Castle, SU 214799; and although not much good flint is found in the Chilterns, a small cluster of shafts is visible lying close to the line of a later ranch boundary-ditch on Pitstone Hill, Buckinghamshire, SP 950142. But the most famous flint-mines in England are those known as Grimes Graves, near Brandon on the Norfolk–Suffolk border, TL 817898. The rather odd name is once again attributable to the pagan Saxons, who thought of these hollows and scars as 'Woden's diggings'. They represent an industrial centre of some importance covering a considerable

area, with four hundred or more shafts sunk over an area about forty acres in extent. It was excavations of some of these, and of others at Harrow Hill, which has given us greatest insight into the activities and beliefs of Neolithic miners (see below, p. 102). One of the Grimes Graves shafts is kept open for public inspection. (The production of small flints for flintlock pistols and muskets traded to the natives in the old colonies, survived at Brandon into modern times, and small quantities are still produced there for the anti-quarian reproduction market.)

The raw flint nodules were usually trimmed by sur-face workers, and their dumps of waste chippings can often be found distributed round the mine-shafts. The characteristic product was a wedge-shaped tool which had multiple uses: hafted with the cutting-edge parallel to the handle to form an axe, or at right-angles to form either adze or hoe. Flint was a heavy commodity, and 'roughing-out' at an industrial centre close to the point of production had the double ad-vantage of testing the material for possible flaws and reducing the weight for ease of transport. They were probably traded to distant markets in this roughed-out form; the final shaping and grinding could be carried out almost anywhere. Perhaps some centres specialised in making up from raw materials produced elsewhere in the vicinity. At East Horsley on the North Downs in Surrey, TQ 097516, areas of flint debris mark the site of a factory. Pits dug nearby suggest that some raw material may have been obtained from surface workings. But adequate supplies would probably have had to be introduced from farther afield.

Flint occurs only in chalk and so its production was confined to the south and east of England. But many stones other than flint could be used for tools. Suit-able material was quarried from outcrops of rock in several parts of the highland zone to the north and west. And similar axe factories can be identified from the surrounding litter of waste flakes and broken rough-outs. Industrial waste from a factory using vol-

canic rock can still be found high up the mountainside at Corndon Hill in Shropshire, SO 304951. The rock used for most stone axes of this kind can be precisely identified by geologists, and attributed to their place of origin with some certainty, thus supplying proof of extensive cross-country trade links at this early date. Axes made from rock quarried at Corndon were distributed westwards to markets in the Midlands. In west Wales three shallow quarry pits surrounded by rings of debris are visible on Mynydd Rhiw in the Lleyn Peninsula, Gwynedd, SH 234299. We know that other axes were made from the distinctive white-spotted blue-grey rock outcropping at Carn Menyn in the Prescelli Hills of north Pembrokeshire, SN 1432, although no certain signs of quarrying have as yet been discovered. But industrial debris can still be picked up on the steep scree-strewn slopes of the Pike of Stickle, 1500 feet and more up on the north side of Great Langdale, Cumbria, NY 272072. The grey-green Borrowdale rock axes made here were traded to all parts of Britain and were apparently highly prized even on the southern downlands where they seem to have competed strongly for the home-market of the flint producers.

Good hard stone of this kind was needed for a variety of purposes. Quern- or mill-stones for grinding corn were valuable items which could be traded over large distances. Sandstone for this purpose was quarried from Pen Pits near Mere, where the workings cover an area of seven hundred acres of greensand escarpment at a point on the borders of Somerset, Dorset and Wiltshire, ST 767318. Stone quarries are normally not easy to date, but part of Pen Pits was overlain by the earthwork of an early Norman castle, thus confirming their relatively early origin. Unfinished mill-stones can still be seen in a quarry along Wharncliffe Rocks to the north-west of Sheffield, SK 296977–303971.

Large blocks of dolerite weighing about four tons each were quarried in the Prescelli Hills of Pembrokeshire and then transported as far as Salisbury Plain to be erected as part of the early ceremonial monuments at Stonehenge (see p. 110). Presumably some of the great monoliths erected at this time, either singly or in elaborate complex structures, could be found naturally, like the huge sarsens that litter the Marlborough Downs, but others may have been quarried (see p. 109).

The coming of the Romans resulted in large-scale systematic industrial quarrying of high-quality building stone to meet the extensive needs of military and civilian operations. Continuous subsequent quarrying on the same sites has almost invariably obliterated all traces of former workings however. Good free-stone could be obtained from sources like The Isle of Purbeck or the Cotswolds, but more often than not an adequate supply of building stone was available nearby. A deep quarry lies just beyond the south-west corner of the town wall at Aldborough, Yorkshire (see p. 32), while the source of building material used for the Roman villa at North Leigh in Oxfordshire, can be found in the woods 200 yards to the south of the building (see p. 27). In Edgar's Field on the south of the River Dee at Chester can be seen a bank of rock which is all that remains of a once large quarry, but which still bears the marks of pickaxes and a sadly dilapidated shrine to Minerva, patron goddess of Roman engineers (see below, p. 118).

From about 1800 BC weapons and tools made of stone were gradually replaced by those made of the hard metal alloy, bronze. Although perhaps at first imported, its two constituents, copper and tin, were readily available in Britain. Good copper ores lay in north Wales, under Parys Mountain in Anglesey, and Halkyn Mountain, Clwyd, or in south-west Scotland, while tin could be washed from alluvial beds, i.e. 'streamed', in Cornwall or on Dartmoor. But no visible evidence survives of its early working. Collections of bronze-founders' materials and equipment which occasionally come to light in all parts of the country suggest that at least part of the trade was carried on by itinerant smiths.

Then some time about 500 BC bronze was displaced by the stronger, more easily worked, more plentiful and therefore cheaper metal, iron. Unlike copper and tin, iron ore in one form or another is found in every part of Britain, and its working has left extensive traces. There is good evidence for iron-smelting in the form of hearths and slag in many pre-Roman settlements. And few communities can have been without their own blacksmith.

The major areas of iron exploitation in Roman times, and probably before, seem to have been the Weald of Kent and Sussex, and the Forest of Dean. Here good supplies of rich ore were to be found in conjunction with plentiful timber to provide the charcoal necessary for smelting. Probably many of the numerous slag-heaps to be seen in the Wealden region of East Sussex had their origin at this time. Large banks or spreads of cinder and other furnace debris, sometimes covering several acres, can be found at: Beauport Park, TQ 786140, Footlands, TQ 772198, Bardown, TQ 663293, Oldlands, TQ 476268 and Great Cansiron, TQ 448382, and elsewhere. A particularly instructive example is that at Walesbeech, TQ 395345, which has been cut in half by the water of the Weir Wood reservoir lake, and can be seen in section. Large quantities of slag were used to surface the Roman roads which ran through the area (see below, p. 69). There is good evidence that the Wealden iron industry was at least partly managed by military authorities on behalf of the Channel Fleet. Probably, indentured civilian or slave labour was used. Elsewhere the industry may have been wholly a matter of civilian enterprise.

In the Forest of Dean, excavation has shown that the Roman town of Ariconium, now Weston-under-Penyard near Ross-on-Wye, Herefordshire, was largely dependent on the iron-smelting industry, although nothing is now visible of what must have been a smokey, noisy, bustling hive of activity. But farther south at Lydney in Gloucestershire, within the ramparts of a disused Iron Age hillfort situated above the River Severn, the remains of a Roman iron-mine, albeit only a small exploratory one, can still be entered by way of a modern trapdoor (SO 615026). A narrow passage, or 'adit', was cut along the line of a joint in the limestone: first as an open cutting 6 yards long and about $1\frac{1}{2}$ yards wide, then a narrow tunnel only 18 inches to 2 feet wide running for a further 10 yards or so and sloping downhill at about 20 degrees from the horizontal before opening out onto the hillside below. One side of the cutting (the natural fault-line), is smooth, but the other face still bears marks of the miners' heavy iron pick-hammers. Part of the roof was hollowed out, allowing additional headroom. A considerable depth of debris lay uncleared on the floor. This mine presumably failed to produce adequate ore, since it was never opened up. Other trial shafts lie beneath the remains of a later Roman temple and bath-house built within the ramparts, and many hollows visible in the northern half of the interior probably represent other blocked shafts (see below, p. 120). Further workings may be found in the woods round about.

In addition to iron, the Roman geographer Strabo, writing some time about the birth of Christ, mentions lead and silver among a long list of British exports. And during the Roman occupation the exploitation of these obviously valuable metals became a highly organised and profitable enterprise, under official, and probably military, control. Technically, all mineral rights in the province were vested in the state. Pigs of lead and cakes of refined silver are sometimes found bearing imperial stamps showing their origin. Outcrop coal was mined for industrial purposes. Shale from Kimmeridge on the Dorset coast was turned on the lathe to produce personal ornaments and small furniture. And jet collected from the shore near Whitby on the Yorkshire coast was used for jewellery.

Of all Britain's natural resources, gold was for long among the most highly prized. The gold for ornaments sometimes found in Bronze Age burials was probably

LATER EARTHWORK

DEBRIS

HILLSIDE

0   YARDS   10

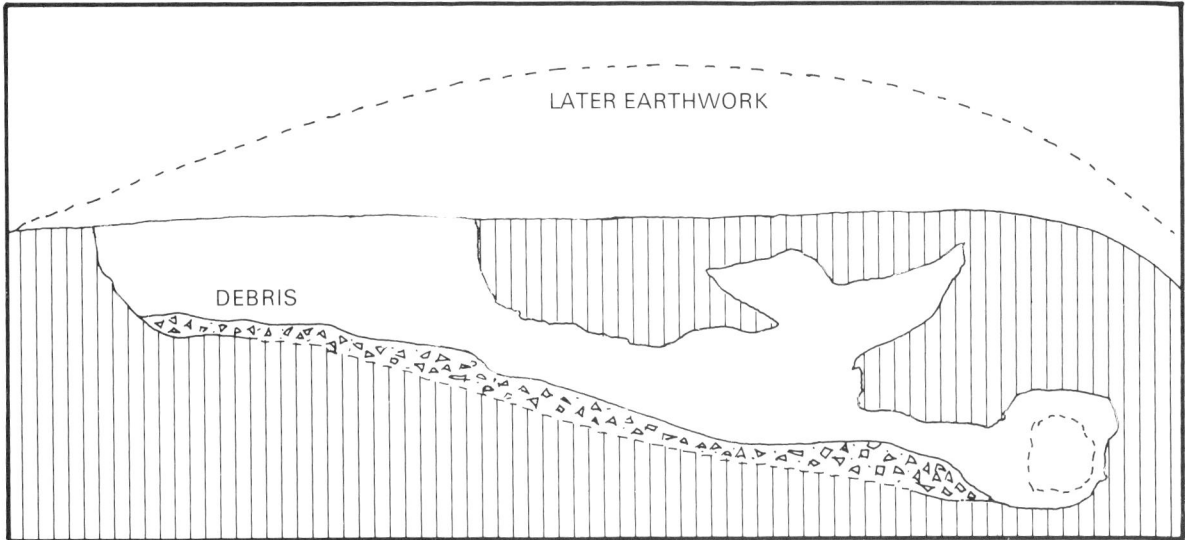

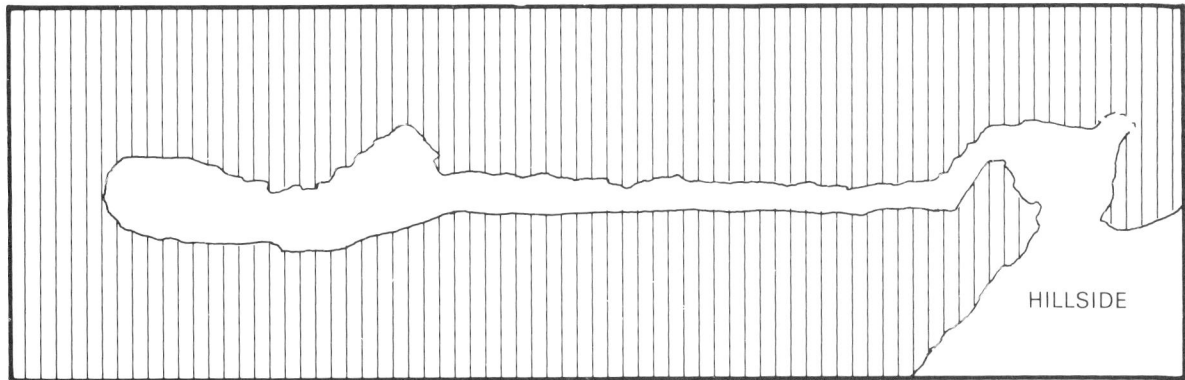

Lydney, Gloucs: plan and section of Roman iron-mine (after Wheeler)

51

Dolaucothi, Dyfed: entrances to Roman gold-mine tunnels

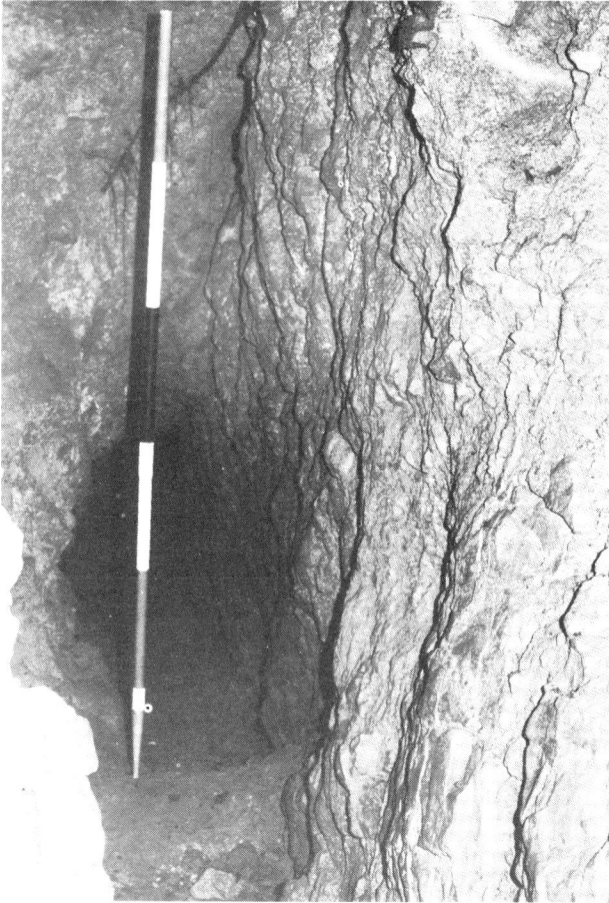

Lydney, Gloucs: interior of Roman iron-mine

seem to have been worked both open-cast and from underground mine-shafts. Among the jumble of later workings, it is still possible to recognise some of the original adits, and underground galleries have been traced in some instances to a distance of 18 or 20 yards below ground.

Large quantities of water were required for the various industrial processes involved. It was used for breaking down and sluicing out material from open-cast workings, for driving the machines used to crush the ore, and then for washing it. The necessary supply was brought to the site by means of aqueducts or channels cut into the hillside. One aqueduct can be traced along the side of the Cothi valley for a distance of seven miles, and another up the valley of the River Annell for about four miles, although some stretches of this are now obliterated. These channels supplied a series of large clay-lined collection-tanks or reservoirs, from whence it could be sluiced into the lower open-cast workings, or over a series of stepped washing-tables running down the hillside. The entire water system was probably capable of providing three million gallons a day to the workings. The pit-head bath-house found is more likely to have been for the

imported from Ireland. But quantities of low-grade gold-bearing rock exist in Wales, and were certainly worked in Roman times. The remains of one such works can be traced on the side of a mountain spur at Dolaucothi, between Lampeter and Llandovery, Dyfed, SN 665403. Gold-bearing veins of quartz

OGOFAU LODGE

0   YARDS   100

SHAFT

WASHING
TABLES

——— LEAT   ▪ RESERVOIR   ○ ADIT

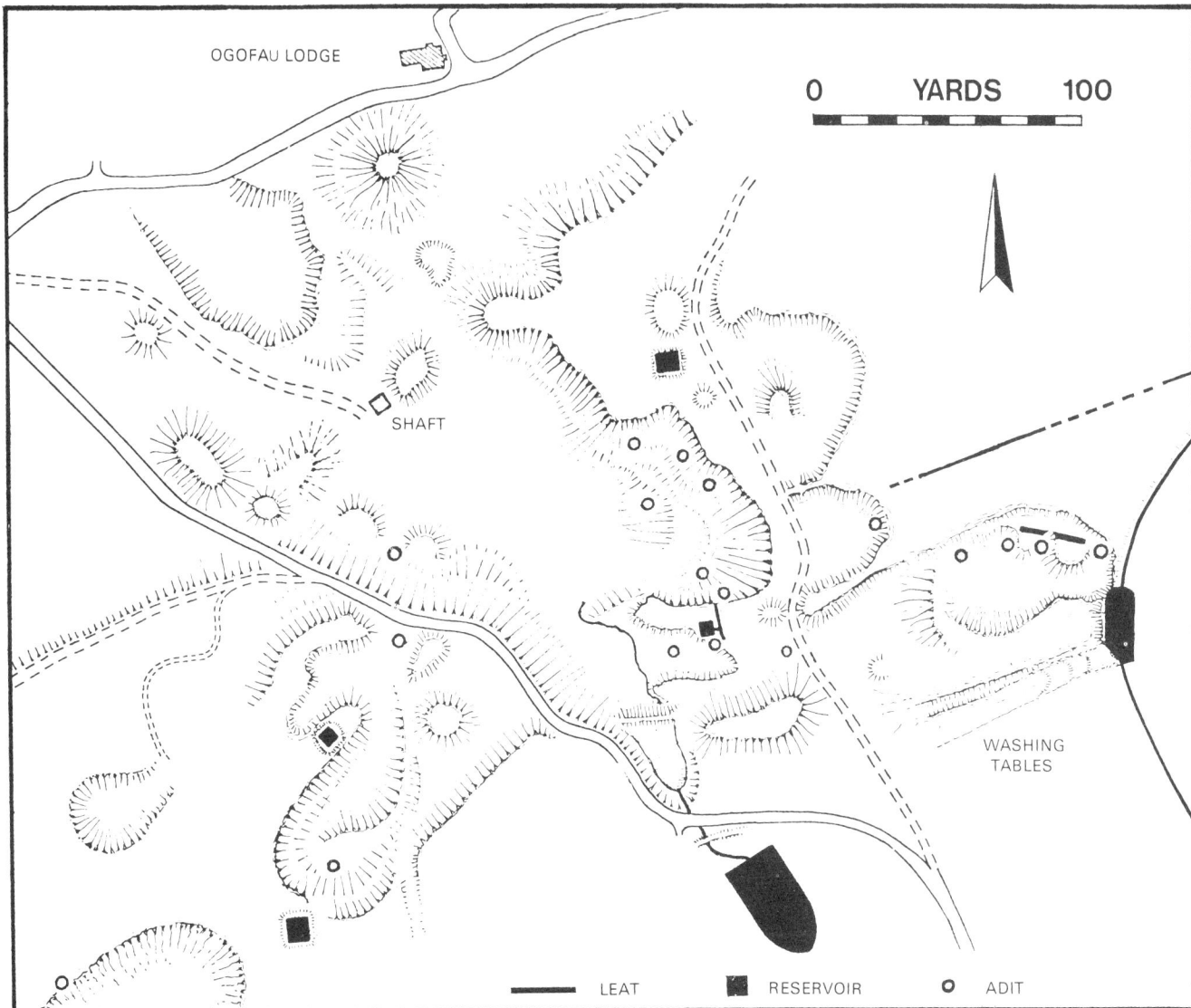

Dolaucothi, Dyfed: plan of main working in Roman gold-mine (after Jones)

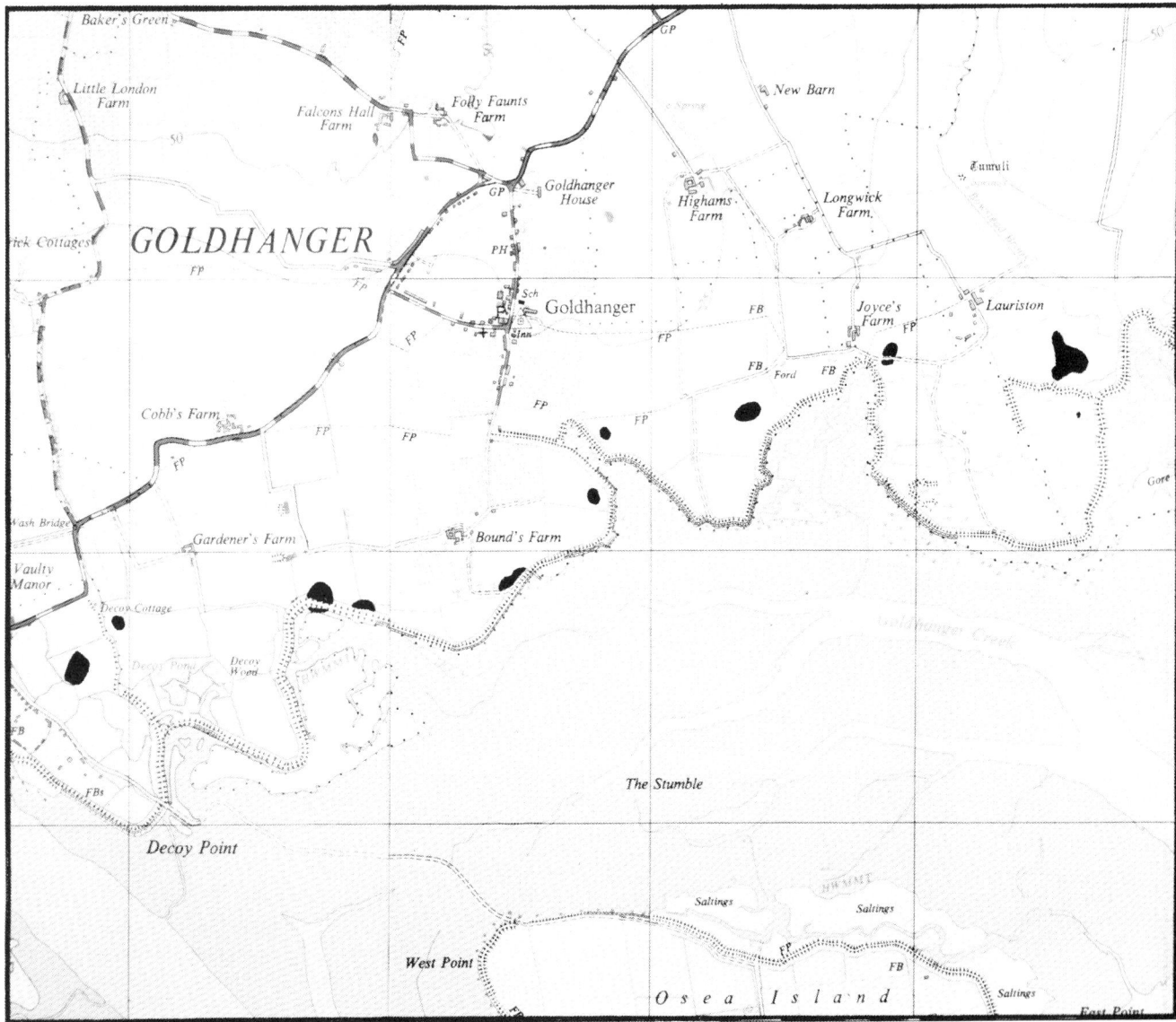

Plan of 'Red hills' salt-workings on the northern margin of the Blackwater estuary, Essex (based on Ordnance Survey 2½-inch map)

convenience of overseers than that of the work-force in general.

Among other industries, the production of salt was particularly important during early times. It was a necessary commodity for the preservation of food after the autumnal slaughter of livestock, and for curing hides and other purposes. The substantial inland sources which existed in the west Midlands around Northwich and Middlewich in Cheshire, and Droitwich in Worcestershire, were extensively exploited in Roman times, and perhaps before. The Roman name for Droitwich was Salinae, that is simply 'The Salt-Works'. More commonly, however, supplies were obtained from marine saltings, or enclosed areas of salt marsh, such as are found round the east coast from south Lincolnshire to north Kent. Sea water was boiled down and the resulting material moulded into blocks. The process was described by the Roman scientific author Pliny, who died in AD 78 as a result of wanting to examine too closely the eruption of Vesuvius which overwhelmed Pompeii. Large openwork stacks were built up from rough clay troughs containing brine, separated by clay spacing-bars and interlaced with brushwood which was then set alight. As the brine evaporated, more could be poured on top of the heated pile. The resultant mounds of waste material are found scattered in hundreds along the estuaries and tidal rivers of Essex and elsewhere. Characteristically reddened by fire, these are known locally as 'Red hills', low flattish mounds, little more than 4 or 5 feet above the level of the marshes, but varying in area from 20 or 30 square yards to four or five acres. Excavation shows them to consist of burnt red earth and wood-ash mingled with fragments of clay troughs, spacer-blocks and general briquetage, often glazed from spilt salt.

Among a variety of lesser industries, those of pottery- and tile-making have left recognisable marks on the landscape. Until shortly before the Roman invasion, pottery seems to have been largely a domestic concern, each small community, perhaps each household, providing for its own needs. But Roman building methods required the mass-production of bricks and tiles for roofing, bonding stone walls, lining furnaces and many other purposes. High-class tableware could be imported from the Continent; one Roman ship bearing a cargo of pottery apparently bound for the London market foundered on the Pudding Pan rock seven miles off the north Kent coast, and some of the barnacle-encrusted salvaged pots can be seen in Whitstable museum. But a vast quantity of pottery was made in Britain for the home market. Pots of all kinds would be necessary for a wide variety of purposes at a time when glass vessels were still a luxury, and plastic or cardboard containers were as yet unknown.

Raw clay is heavy. So normally it could be expected that the clay would be dug and made up on the spot. And potteries and tileries were generally situated where adequate supplies of a suitable clay could be found. The remains of digging can be recognised in the depression and dumps of waste at various places along the band of Wealden clay, for example, at Ewhurst, Surrey, TQ 083406, or in the Goose Green region of Alice Holt Forest on the Hampshire–Surrey border, SU 812412, where hundreds of mounds can be found covering several acres. The presence of kilns, however, is characteristically marked by quantities of broken sherds scattered from 'wasters', i.e. pots damaged in the firing process.

The Roman kiln was normally circular in plan. A hole was dug into the ground, usually 2 to 3 feet deep and 5 or more feet across. This contained the furnace, which was fed by a tunnel-like stoke-hole about 10 feet long and 18 inches to 2 feet across. Above this furnace, and supported by a stone pedestal, was inserted a clay floor on which the finished pots were placed in tiers. When fully stacked such a kiln might take up to a thousand pots at a time. Around the pile of pots was constructed an open cylinder of clay and straw; this ensured a considerable through-draught, resulting in very high firing-temperatures. At Water

occurred in convenient relationship to the market, large-scale industrial potteries were established, producing a wide variety of distinctive wares. Major Roman potteries of this kind were located in the New Forest region of Hampshire, and in the Nene Valley in Cambridgeshire. Along the River Nene around Sibson and Water Newton outside the now deserted Roman town of Durobrivae, TL 120970, more than seventy kilns have now been excavated, although this probably represents only a fraction of the whole. With say, two or three hundred kilns in full production, each capable of firing a thousand pots at a time, this part of the Fenland must have resembled latter-day Stoke-on-Trent! The profit-margins were considerable, and the fine houses and bath-suites of the factory owners and managers have been found. The Nene factories produced many kinds of pot: coarse cooking- and food-vessels of all kinds, and mortaria, i.e. dishes having the interior surface studded with grit for grinding food. But the local speciality was 'colour-coated' ware, made by dipping the naturally buff-coloured pots into slip containing iron salts, giving the surface a red or brown coat when fired.

Water Newton, Cambs: Roman pottery-kiln as excavated

Newton in Cambridgeshire, the potter had abandoned one kiln after the firing had gone wrong; he had not bothered to remove the bottom layer of cracked and spoilt pots, which thus remained virtually intact for the next 1700 years until discovered by the excavator.

Pottery-kilns were found in all parts of the province, some of them presumably supplying a purely local demand. The military seem to have provided at least part of their requirements from their own kilns. For instance the legion stationed at Chester was supplied from kilns eight miles down the river at Holt in Clwyd. But in certain places where suitable raw materials

Water transport was an important factor in the Nene Valley industry. There is no clay actually present at Water Newton, but the raw material could be brought along the Nene to the site from Jurassic beds two or three miles to the west. And the fragile finished product could be despatched to the markets more safely by barge than by the springless carts of the day. Using the rivers and dyke system of the north-east (see p. 70 below), Nene Valley pottery was distributed widely throughout midland and northern England.

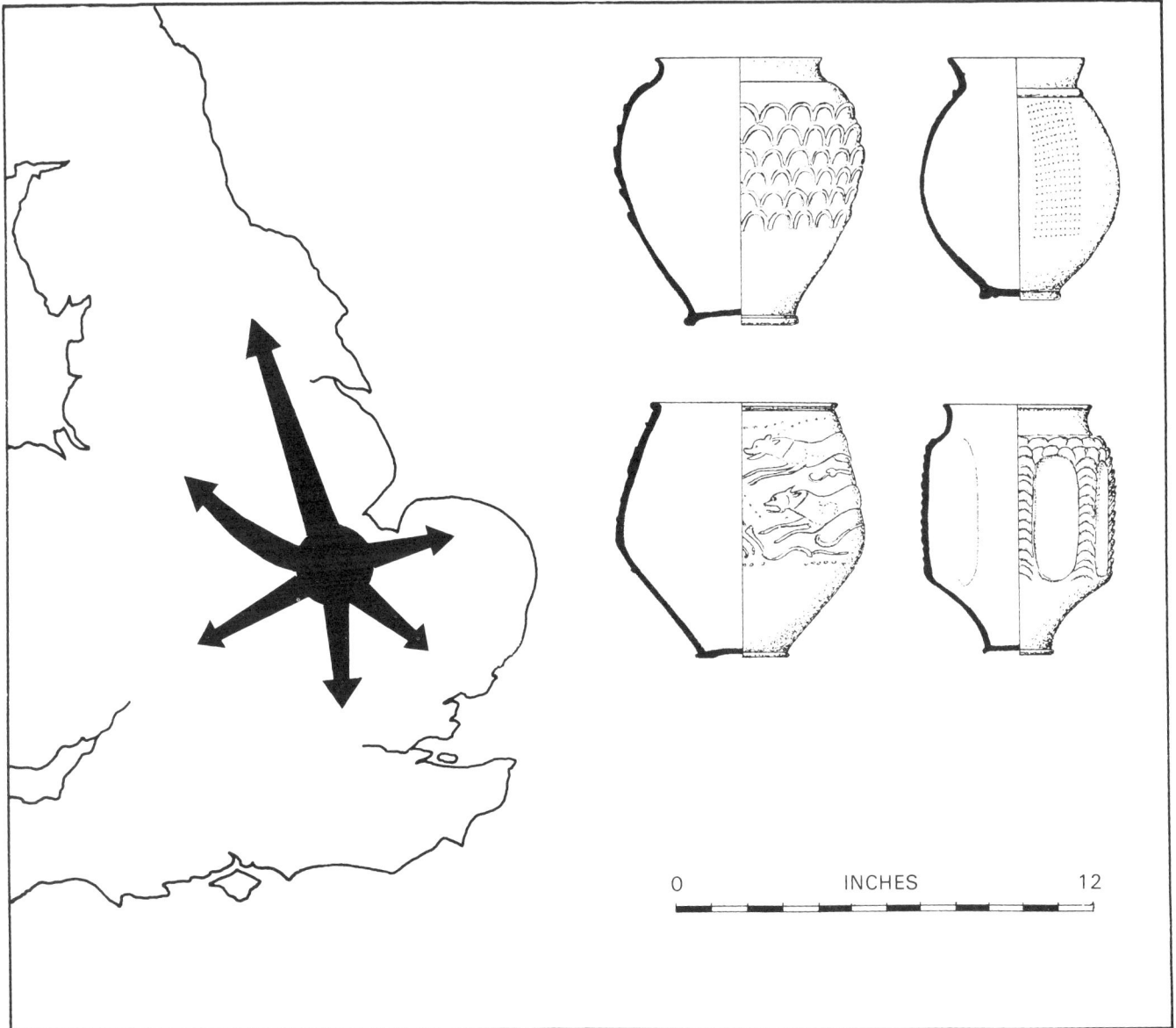

Some types of decorated pots made in the Nene Valley kilns and a sketch-map of their distribution

COMMUNICATIONS

In the sparse and fragmented society of the Old Stone Age, when the necessities of life were produced individually and locally, man had little or no need for systematic travel of any kind, other than to follow the migrations of the herds of animals on which he preyed. But the settled economy of Neolithic times brought with it the need for regular droveways along which pastoral communities could drive their stock to periodic assemblies (see above, p. 40), and to allow those producing flint and stone axes and querns, access to their cross-country markets. Of course river traffic and coastwise shipping must have played a considerable role in some trade-routes.

It is possible to reconstruct the 240-mile journey by which the Stonehenge bluestones were brought from Pembrokeshire to Salisbury Plain. The four-ton monoliths were probably taken on sledges or rollers for the first stage of the journey, running downhill the twenty miles from the quarry in Mynydd Prescelli to the estuary at Milford Haven. There they were loaded on to boats, or more likely rafts, to be taken along the South Wales coast and up the Bristol Channel to Avonmouth; from there, by a series of waterways—the Rivers Avon, Frome, Wylie and then the Wiltshire Avon—they arrived at a point relatively close to Stonehenge, from where they could once more be dragged overland along a ceremonial avenue to the site where they were to be erected (see p. 110).

The journey taken by the Stonehenge bluestones was a very particular one. For the most part, the course taken by overland journeys was dictated by the geology and lie of the land. Prehistoric tracks exploited natural routes running along the hill-scarps and ridges which cross the country, proceeding directly, but skirting the heads of valleys and avoiding obstacles such as swamps and river-crossings wherever possible. The general direction taken by such trackways is known from the distribution of prehistoric remains—both structures and portable objects—along their line; but with one or two exceptions these were natural 'routes' rather than constructed roads. Save for those laid out during the Roman occupation, roads in the modern sense of artificially paved or metalled ways were unknown before the eighteenth century. Short lengths of cobbled path are sometimes found leading to the entrances of Iron Age hillforts, and brushwood causeways were laid across swampy areas from very early times (see below, p. 62), but no system of constructed roads is known to have existed in prehistoric times. Nevertheless, well-maintained routes must have existed to take the not inconsiderable heavy waggon traffic of pre-Roman days.

The major cross-country route, bisecting England north-east/south-west is the so-called Jurassic Way. This follows the long ridge of Jurassic limestone

Icknield Way: the duplication of tracks crossing Therfield Heath, Herts

which runs across the country from the Cotswolds near Bath, through Northamptonshire and Lincolnshire to the Humber and beyond. It is an assumed route for the most part and we can seldom be sure of the precise line it took, save where the band of limestone narrows down to a mere ridge, as along the western rim of the Lincoln Edge. For this last stretch before the Jurassic Way reaches the Humber, a parallel route (the 'High Street'), runs north and south along the western escarpment of the Lincolnshire Wolds farther east. While the route north of the Humber is uncertain, the fact that it ends at the river's edge implies the existence of a ferry of some kind (see below, p. 63).

Other major trackways followed similar routes along lines of chalk in south and east England. Perhaps significantly, they converge on Salisbury Plain, crossing within a mile or two of Stonehenge. The Ridgeway advances along the Berkshire Downs, past Uffington Castle hillfort and the symbolic white horse (see below, p. 114), to ford the Thames somewhere near Goring. Thereafter known as the Icknield Way, it proceeds along the Chiltern escarpment and into Norfolk, passing close to the important flint-mining centre of Grimes Graves. Other routes crossed the country more directly east–west. One known popularly, but misleadingly, as the Pilgrims' Way, runs through Hampshire and along the escarpment of the North Downs through Surrey and Kent until reaching the Channel coast near Folkestone, thus implying embarkation for the Continent. A parallel route, but less well defined, ran along the South Downs, through the flint-mines clustered in Sussex, to a point somewhere near Beachy Head.

Whether it now takes the form of a metalled road, bridle-path or mere grassy track, the actual line followed today by the Pilgrims' Way for example, cannot be confidently accepted as the line used by prehistoric man. It is inconceivable that these ancient trackways should have been confined between narrow limits. Of necessity, unmetalled tracks tended to shift over a

Prehistoric trackways in England

broad band of ground. Before the invention of a good road surface, deep rutting of the earthen track by heavy traffic and consequent puddling in bad weather, would result in alternative parallel paths being taken time and time again, widening the route to an indefinite extent either side. Especially where the route descended a hill, the surface was easily worn away by heavy carts or pack-animals and by rivulets of water which in winter months would sluice away the loose material to form a sunken or hollow way. Sometimes several such 'hollow ways' are found adjacent to one another. A particularly steep descent might be managed by way of a zigzag route—often running along the terraces formed by lynchets.

In certain places alternative routes seem to have been duplicated on a more systematic pattern. Along the Pilgrims' Way between Guildford and Dorking, for example, the regular ridgeway runs along the upper line of the scarp from the Hog's Back along Albury Down, Hackhurst Down and Ranmore Common to Box Hill. Running close to the edge of the escarpment, it offers magnificent views across wide

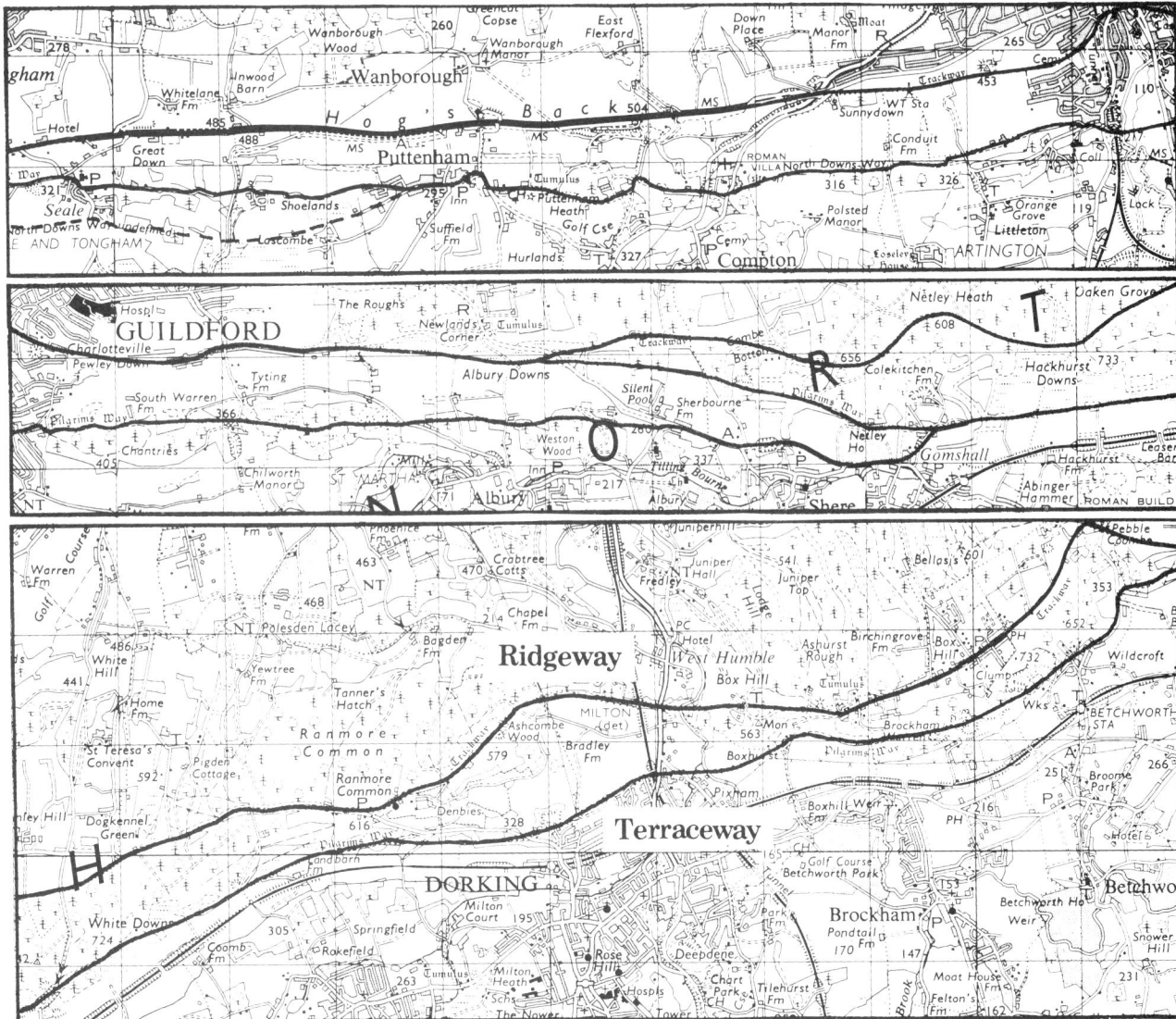

The 'Pilgrims' Way' and alternative routes between Guildford and Dorking, Surrey (based on Ordnance Survey 1-inch map)

distances of the Weald. This is an admirable route to follow during the summer months, since it is the most direct, least obstructed by valleys and river-crossings and because, being open, it is relatively cool. But during the winter, cold winds made this open aspect far less attractive, while rains rendered the sticky clay, which caps the chalk here, quite impassable. Then a relatively sheltered lower route was to be preferred, even though this might be less direct, requiring steeper descents and stiffer climbs negotiating intervening valleys. The terrace-way running along the bottom of the escarpment had the added advantage of passing through a continuous line of settlements along the spring-line, where accommodation and refreshment might be found, or business transacted. At places the terrace-way was supplemented by a further route running along the ridge of greensand which runs parallel about half a mile to the south. This was rather more devious, but at all times, prehistoric routes were conditioned by entirely local considerations of geology and topography.

In addition to major 'trunk' routes, there must have existed innumerable local lines of communication, no less important to the several communities they connected. And drove-roads would have allowed cattle to pass from farmstead to pasture. Occasionally these are marked by parallel lines of continuous field boundaries, or are recognised as short stretches of hollow way, like that to be seen running for a mile by the flint mines and later Iron Age cattle-enclosure on Harrow Hill, Sussex.

Where it was necessary to negotiate flooded or swampy areas, causeways of timber and brushwood could be laid. Remarkable survivals, overgrown by peat and splendidly preserved by the damp conditions, have been revealed by excavation in the Somerset Levels around Shapwick and Meare, in the Cambridgeshire Fens at Fordy, and at Brigg in Lincolnshire where large areas of swamp lay to the south of the Humber in early times. These swampland causeways incorporated large numbers of straight poles which

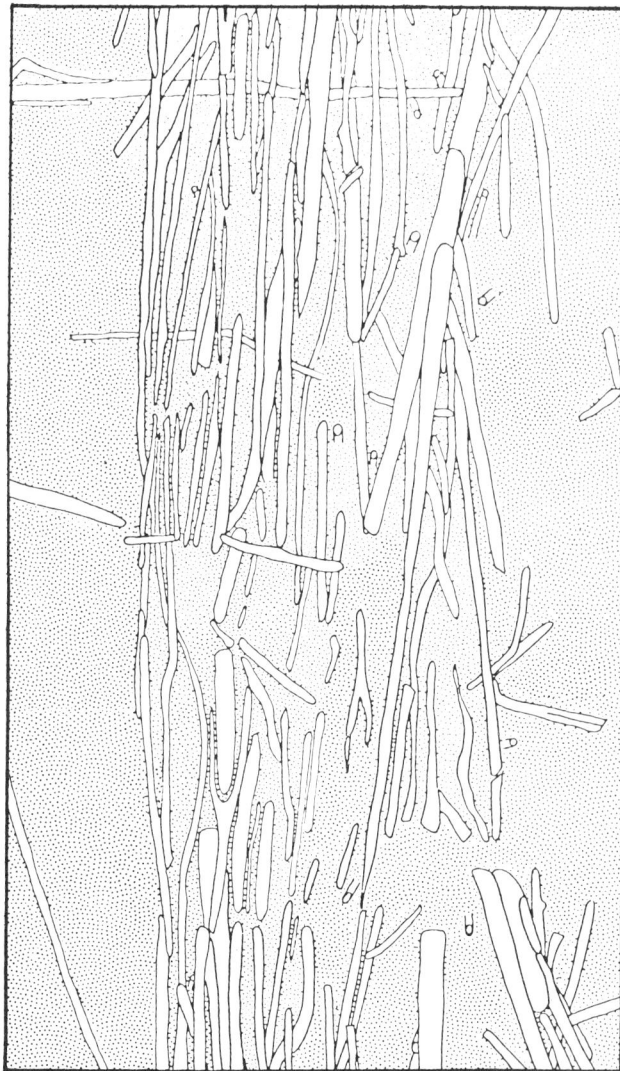

0   YARDS   2

Neolithic/Bronze Age trackway at Chilton, Somerset: plan of excavated section (after Somerset Levels Project)

62

A sunken way close to the flint-mines on Harrow Hill, Sussex

Tarr Steps, Somerset: clapper-bridge across the River Barle, Exmoor

must have been specially grown for the purpose. Some were relaid several times, but the earliest seem to belong to Neolithic times. For the most part they seem not to have been through-routes, but to have served purely local needs, for instance joining islands of dry land in the Somerset Levels with the 'mainland'.

Most rivers in Britain could be forded easily enough. No certain example of a prehistoric bridge is known, but it is clear that the kind of 'clapper-bridge' made from large slabs of stone found in some moorland places, had relatively early origins. One example well known to tourists, straddling the River Dart at Postbridge on Dartmoor, SX 648789, now consists of three slabs of stone each about 5 yards in length, supported by low piers made of rough stone blocks. In earlier times further spans may have existed either side. At Tarr Steps on Exmoor, SS 868322, the River Barle is spanned by one of the finest clapper-bridges in the country, some 60 yards long, and composed of about twenty slabs of stone roughly 3 yards long by 1½ wide supported on piers made from piles of loose stone.

The fact that some trackways end abruptly at the edge of large unfordable rivers like the Humber, implies the existence of ferries or water transport of some kind. We are fortunate now in having good archaeological evidence for the various types of vessels used for the Humber crossing. As they approached the river, the tracks along the Lincoln Edge and the Lincolnshire Wolds ran either side of a broad lagoon or lake leading into the estuary, now marked by the course of the River Ancholme. The swampy edges of this lagoon were traversed by a timber-and-brushwood causeway of the kind found in the Somerset Levels. A stretch was excavated at Brigg, SE 992075, and pollen analysis and radio-active carbon dating suggests that it was laid, or possibly relaid, during the late Bronze Age, some time about 600 BC. A hundred yards to the north, and presumably lying moored against a wooden staithe of some kind, was found a large raft. It was built from five thick oak planks made from split logs, 40 feet long, laid side by side and linked by ten transverse ribs of hazel passing through a series of integral cleats cut out of the oak.

The Bronze Age raft at Brigg, Lincs, during excavation, 1974

The planks were 'stitched' together with lengths of willow or yew fibre, and the whole caulked with clay and moss. The vessel is roughly rectangular, with a maximum beam of 9 feet, and slightly wedged-shaped either end to make steering easier. Whether there were any sides or superstructure can only be guessed. Presumably this type of raft or barge would be used to transport wagons and other heavier traffic. Dating by radio-active carbon methods shows that this vessel was in use some time during the late Bronze Age, between 700–500 BC.

At the end of the last century the construction of a gasometer about 400 yards south-east of the excavated section of trackway, revealed a large dugout canoe. Hollowed out of an oak log, this measured $48\frac{1}{2}$ feet long by 5 feet wide. The stern was made separately and the joint caulked with moss. Some holes in the gunwhale suggest the lashings for an outrigging of some kind to make the craft more stable. Presumably, like the raft, this boat would have been paddled or poled. And like the raft, the dugout canoe seems to belong to the later Bronze Age, being tentatively dated using radio-active carbon methods to about 800 BC.

On the opposite bank of the Humber at North Ferriby, SE 991252, the remains of no less than three massive boats have been found. These seem to have been built up from seven or more thick oak planks, about 45 feet long and 18 inches wide, probably making a boat about $8\frac{1}{2}$ feet in the beam. These are the oldest plank-built boats yet known in northern Europe, datable to some time in the 2nd millennium BC. But their method of construction was not markedly different from that of the Brigg raft: the planks fitted edge to edge with a rudimentary tongue-and-groove joint, caulked and stitched together with fibre and held by transverse ribs passing through cleats cut out of the oak planks.

On the southern shore of the Humber at South Ferriby was found the only known prehistoric example in Britain of the coracle. As described by classical authors like Solinus, writing in the third century AD, this was a light boat made of skins stretched over a wicker-work frame and capable of carrying just one or two men. Presumably it would have been used for only light ferrying work. The South Ferriby coracle has not survived, but the remains of one North Ferriby boat are being conserved at Hull Museum and of the Brigg raft at the National Maritime Museum, Greenwich, where eventually they will be displayed.

The Roman occupation brought with it the need for a close network of well-planned roads of modern type. These were first planned by military engineers to facilitate the efficient policing of the province by the occupying forces. Subsequently they would be maintained by the civil authorities to serve the administrative, commercial and industrial ends of a complex corporate state. Broad arterial roads reaching into every part of the province allowed government officials to employ a system of posting carriages. These were drawn by relays of horses changed at post-houses sited at strategic intervals. Ordinarily it was possible to cover 50 miles a day—much more in case of emergency. Accommodation was provided by hostels, placed about 25 miles apart. The settlements at Wall and Great Casterton had their origins in staging-posts of this kind (see above, p. 29).

Major routes were equipped with official milestones. These were usually cylindrical pillars about 18 inches in diameter and between 4 and 6 feet high, inscribed with the name of the reigning emperor and a mileage figure from a standard starting-point, which may or may not be specified. Occasional examples are found which have been recut for a new inscription—perhaps when the road was repaired—and these then are squarish in section. Most of the six dozen or so surviving examples have been taken into museums, although others may still remain to be discovered. Two old milestones were used in the building of the villa at Rockbourne, where they can still be seen (see p. 27). In Cumbria examples still in their original position can be found north-east of Hawking

Watling Street (now the A5) between Stretton and Weston-under-Lizard, Staffs

Hall, Middleton, SD 624859; and in a lay-by on the A66 half a mile south-east of Temple Sowerby, NY 620265. It is sometimes said that 'London Stone' in Cannon Street, on the former site of the governor's palace, was the point of origin for measuring all distances in Roman Britain, in the same way that a plaque in Trafalgar Square is now used officially.

To some extent of course the Roman engineer was influenced by the same geological factors that determined the routes of prehistoric trackways. Sometimes, as in the case of the Icknield Way, Roman roadmakers merely straightened out and used the prehistoric routes. But wherever possible they laid out their roads in a series of straight lengths, changing direction on hilltops or slight eminences from which a new stretch could be directly sighted. The characteristic straightness of Roman roads running for many miles across open country will be familiar to the motorist. But occasionally the terrain did not permit this, and

Roman road system in northern England

detours were necessary to avoid marshy ground or to skirt the head of a valley, for instance. In the relatively gentle lowlands, deviations from the straight ideal were rarely necessary. One instance occurs where the Cirencester to Winchester road makes a marked semicircular diversion round the rim of a deep dry valley at Hippenscombe on the Hampshire–Wiltshire border, SU 297581–322552. The Roman embankment constructed to take the road, 9 yards wide and up to 4 feet high, known as Chute Causeway, is still used by the modern road at this point. Even Watling Street, the great military arterial road linking London with Chester, twists slightly so as to avoid having to cross the meandering River Nene twice or more in a mile at Weedon Bec in Northamptonshire, SP 626612–635595.

The sudden brink of a steep scarp might be reduced by a cutting. But where it was unavoidable that the route met a steep hill head-on, the gradient was often negotiated by a series of zigzags. Of course, the slower traffic of the day would allow steeper gradients than modern traffic. But roads originally intended to carry companies of marching men or pack-animals who find the shortest route the most practical, however steep, were quite impractical for the heavier carts of civilian traders. In mountainous country physical obstructions would rarely permit straight sightings, and the road engineers were obliged to keep close to the contours, hugging the hillside. Sometimes the route is positively sinuous, as for example where the Eskdale road in Cumbria approaches Hard Knott fort, NY 218016. The highland zone was always subject to military considerations during the Roman occupation, and major highways like Dere Street across Northumberland and Roxburghshire or High Street and Maiden Way in Cumbria, run from peak to peak across exposed high plateaux—partly because engineering problems were eased, but also because routes through valleys and wooded gorges were easily ambushed by the still hostile native tribes. Even so, they were obliged to make use of natural gaps

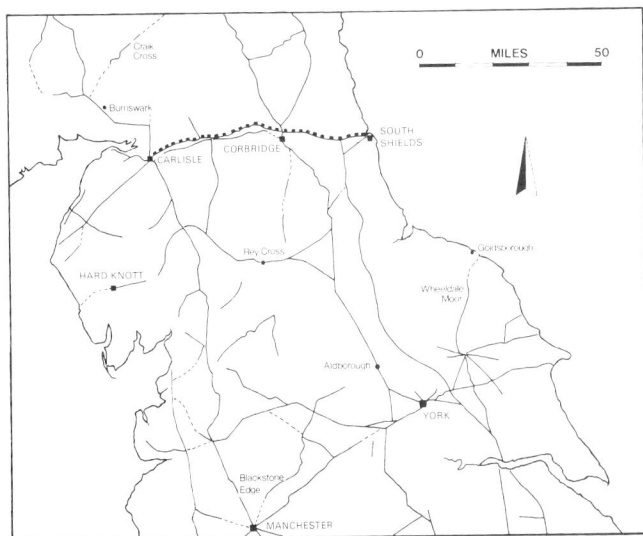

like the Wrynose Pass over Furness Fell or the Lune Gorge at Tebay; NY 273026 and NY 609012.

The importance of sound bottoming for an engineered road is obvious. In some terrain a firm base was offered by flat stretches of natural rock. At Craik Cross a remarkable stretch of road runs for some six miles over the high moor above Teviotdale on the Roxburgh–Dumfriesshire border, NT 267007–333075; it lies occasionally in 10-yard cuttings through the peat to the shale surface, which, allowing for a drainage ditch either side, gives a road surface of about seven yards across. On the Lancashire–Yorkshire border the natural rock surface was used for stretches at Blackstone Edge, SD 973170–988184. This was supplemented where necessary by rectangular stone blocks set in a bed of sand and rubble,

Roman road-surface descending Blackstone Edge, Lancs

to form a paved surface some 5 yards wide, with a central rib of larger blocks running lengthwise and transverse ribs at intervals. Where it descends the edge itself, the central rib has been hollowed out into a continuous trough, worn by the brake-poles of carts

slithering down the 1 in 5 gradient. Eventually this seems to have proved too troublesome for some traffic, since the line of an alternative route can be seen as a paler green line zigzagging down the hill close by.

Where good bottoming was not present, and to ensure good drainage, the road was commonly raised on an embankment, ordinarily 4 or 5 feet above the surrounding countryside. Sometimes these are found to have sunk into soft subsoil over the centuries. But

Ackling Dyke Roman road passing a group of Bronze Age barrows on Oakley Down, Dorset: the embankment cutting across the ditch of one of them, SU 007154

good lengths of road-embankment can often be seen. Particularly impressive lengths occur on Ermine Street running south from Lincoln to Stamford, or on Ackling Dyke running between Dorchester and Salisbury. The surface of most Roman roads was given a pronounced camber to throw off water, and sometimes they were flanked by V-shaped drainage ditches running either side. Paved surfaces of the Blackstone Edge kind were exceptional. Ordinarily the surface consisted of rammed gravel or similar small material

over a foundation of boulders. Where local material, rather than river gravel, was used for surfacing, the small quarry-pits from which it was taken can sometimes be seen running at intervals along the line of the road. A central rib and kerbstones were provided to contain the surfacing material and help prevent erosion. This is usefully illustrated by the lengthy stretch of Roman road known as Wade's Causeway which crosses Wheeldale Moor in North Yorkshire, SE 793938–812988. The gravel metalling has been

Wade's Causeway: Roman road-surface across Wheeldale Moor, North Yorks

washed away to reveal the rough cobble foundation some 5 yards wide, for a length of one and a quarter miles. Gutters and drainage culverts passing beneath the road are still visible at the eastern end.

In iron-producing areas such as the Forest of Dean, South Wales or the Weald, the roads were commonly surfaced with iron slag or cinder waste. An example can be seen on an excavated section of the London to Lewes road at Holtye, near to where the Kent, Sussex and Surrey boundaries meet, TQ 461391. The

original impacted surface is now considerably weathered and broken up by frost, but the ruts made by heavy industrial waggons are still visible.

In swampy areas, as at the head of Windermere where the land is liable to flooding, 4-inch oak piles could be driven in to contain the foundation material. Or lengths of causeway were constructed from logs about a foot in diameter, laid transversely across the line of the road close together or at intervals of up to $2\frac{1}{2}$ feet, so as to make a 'corduroy' surface.

Shallow rivers could be forded. Scattered blocks of stone from a paved ford are still visible in the bed of the river at Iden Green, on the road from Rochester to Maidstone, Kent, TQ 802323. And another lay close to a fine paved stretch of road running through the industrial Forest of Dean from Ariconium to Lydney, at Blackpool Bridge, SO 653087. The remains of bridges survive next to two Roman forts along the line of Hadrian's Wall in Northumberland. At Chesters on the North Tyne, NY 914701, the embankment of a road can be seen leading to a massive masonry abutment on the east side of the river. Nowadays it stands high and dry because the river bed has shifted some yards to the west. Its north face bears the talismanic carving of a phallus. A corresponding abutment on the other side of the river now lies in the water and between them are the three stone piers which carried the timber superstructure (see p. 100). At Corbridge, lower down the Tyne, NY 982647, similar piers and the southern abutment can be seen half a mile upstream from the present bridge when the water is low during the summer.

As with Watling Street, major Roman roads often lie beneath modern roads, and so seem probably to have been in continuous use since they were first built. Especially where embanked, Roman roads would certainly form a prominent feature of the landscape in subsequent ages. They could be conveniently followed in defining the boundaries of fields and estates, and later parish or even larger boundaries. A seven-mile stretch of the Foss Way north of Malmes-

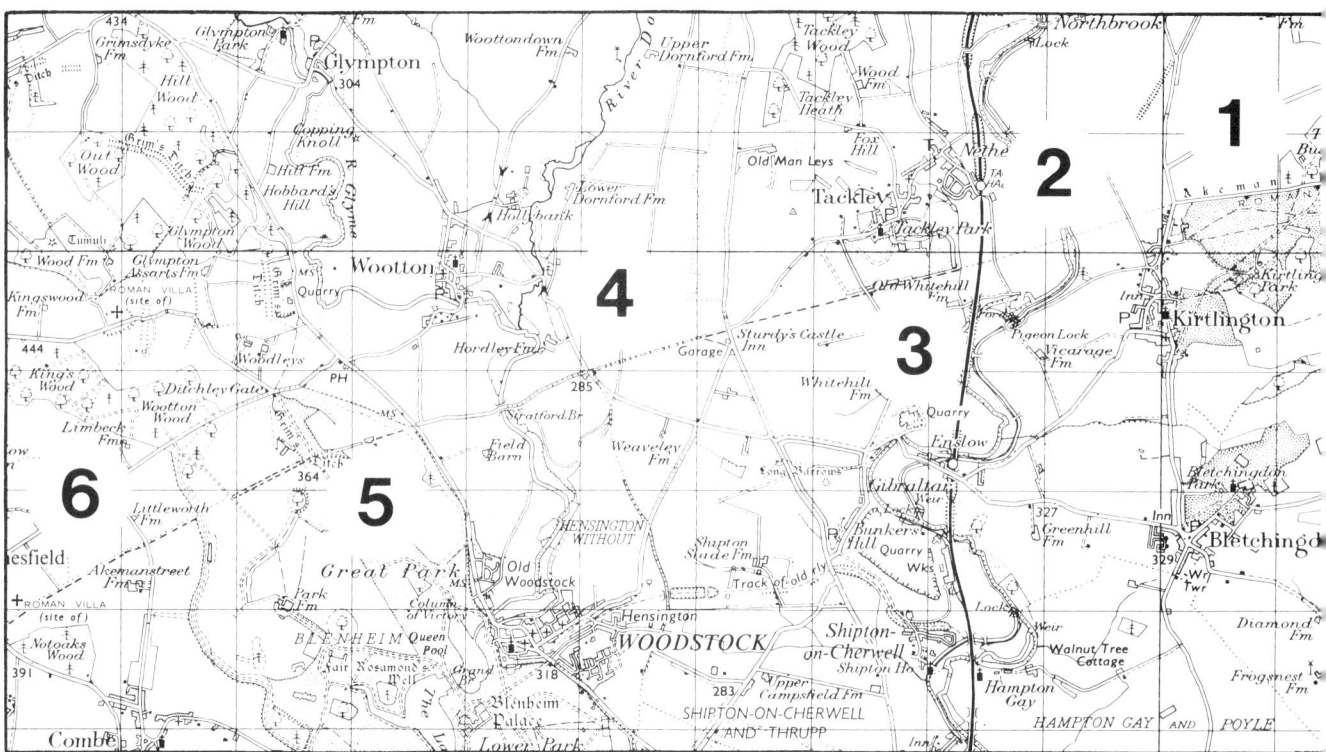

The line of Akeman Street Roman road north of Woodstock, Oxfordshire (based on Ordnance Survey 1-inch map). Akeman Street was a major east–west arterial route linking St Albans with Cirencester and Bath

(1) A modern metalled road clearly raised on the original embankment. (2) Crossing the valley of the River Cherwell, the route is marked by occasional hedgerows with slight traces of the embankment either side. (3) The line is picked up by estate boundaries (the southern wall of Tackley Park) and a footpath leading to Sturdy's Castle Inn. Along this stretch the embankment is 10 yards wide and 3 feet high. (4) Thereafter the footpath expands to a cart-track and then a narrow lane followed by Wootton parish boundary as far as Stratford Bridge. (5) The route continues as a bridleway through Blenheim Park (the embankment 18 yards wide), and cuts the line of Grim's Ditch boundary dyke. (6) Leaving the Park the line is again followed by a parish boundary and a field-path passing close to the site of a Roman villa

bury was used to divide the counties of Gloucestershire and Wiltshire, ST 896879–962971. Even where not followed by modern roads or bridle-paths, the walker can often trace the course of Roman roads for many miles through woods and across fields. The embankment, even where no longer obvious as such, is often followed by the line of a hedgerow. The course of a metalled surface can be recognised in a line of parched grass or stunted crops, or as a continuous strip of stony ground across a ploughed field.

Coastwise shipping and easily navigable rivers meant that water transport could supplement road communications. And in the East Midlands an important waterway system was developed linking the agricultural and industrial region of the Fens with military and other markets in the north. The major element in this system was the Car Dyke, an artificial canal constructed for over seventy miles. It leaves the River Cam just south of Waterbeach, TL 497641, and runs via sections of natural river to the Great Ouse near Earith, TL 394757. From here a direct link was probably made with the Nene at Peterborough, partly by natural watercourses and partly by artificial cuts. From the Nene the canal extends northwards for fifty-six

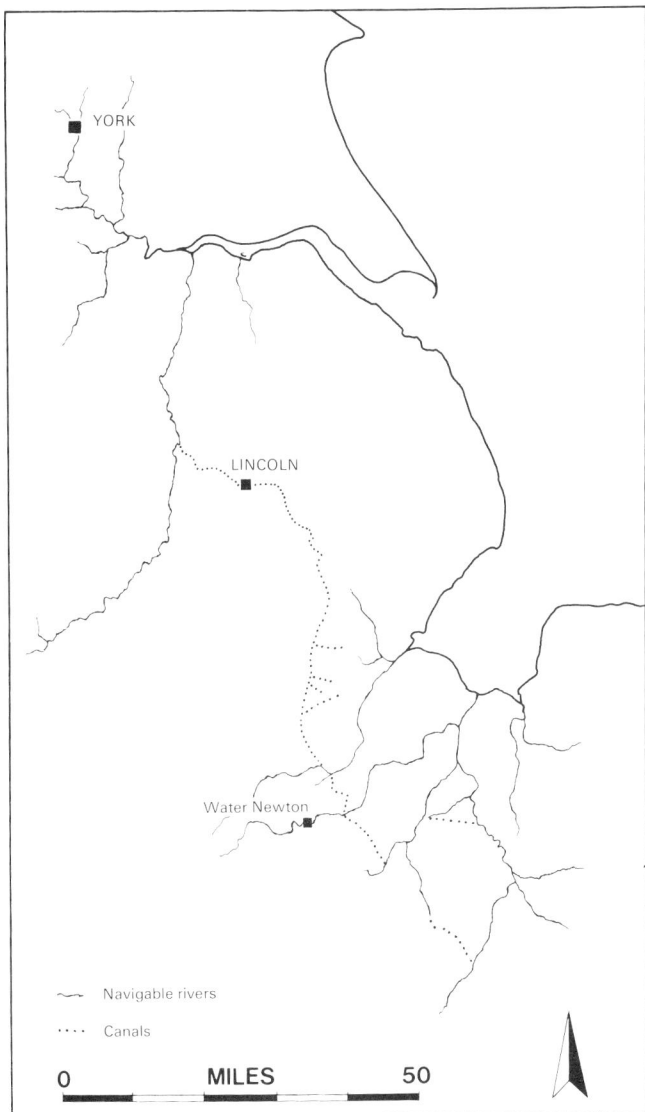

Roman waterway system in the East Midlands

miles, along the western edge of the Fens, to reach the Witham a mile or two east of Lincoln at Washingborough, SK 045714. Several short lateral feeder canals including Lark Slade, Reach Slade, Marsh Cut, Soham Lode and Colne Dyke, have been recognised extending eastwards into the Fens. Car Dyke itself is now little more than a land-drain. But excavation shows it to have been comparable to modern canals, cut about 8 feet deep, and wedge-shaped in section, 17 yards wide at the top tapering to 10 yards wide at the bottom. An easily visible and reasonably intact stretch lies beside the A10 at TL 485664.

From the River Witham at Brayford Pool outside the south wall of Lincoln, a connection was made with the Trent south of Torksey, SK 835782, by a further canal now called Foss Dyke. This is known to have been reconditioned in the reign of Henry I, and improved in the eighteenth and nineteenth centuries, and is still in use. Foss Dyke linked with the Trent–Humber river-system, thus allowing access to York and points farther north.

Roman engineers had considerable experience of canalising water for industrial and other purposes. I have already mentioned the aqueducts used to supply the gold-mining centre at Dolaucothi (see p. 52). Many towns were so situated that an adequate water supply had to be brought from a distance. At hilltop Lincoln, for example, water had to be raised about 70 feet from its source to one or more cisterns, embedded in the wall ramparts from where the town's complex system of fountains, public baths, drains and sewers could be served. The cisterns were fed by an underground pipeline built from 3-feet lengths of clay tile with a $5\frac{1}{2}$-inch bore, and sheathed in waterproof pink concrete. This tapped springs several miles to the north-east of the city. The pipeline lay underground for the most part, until, approaching the town, it rose on an embankment and then crossed the stream Roaring Meg by way of a raised aqueduct bridge, the piers of which have been found by excavation. The necessary head of pressure might have been

71

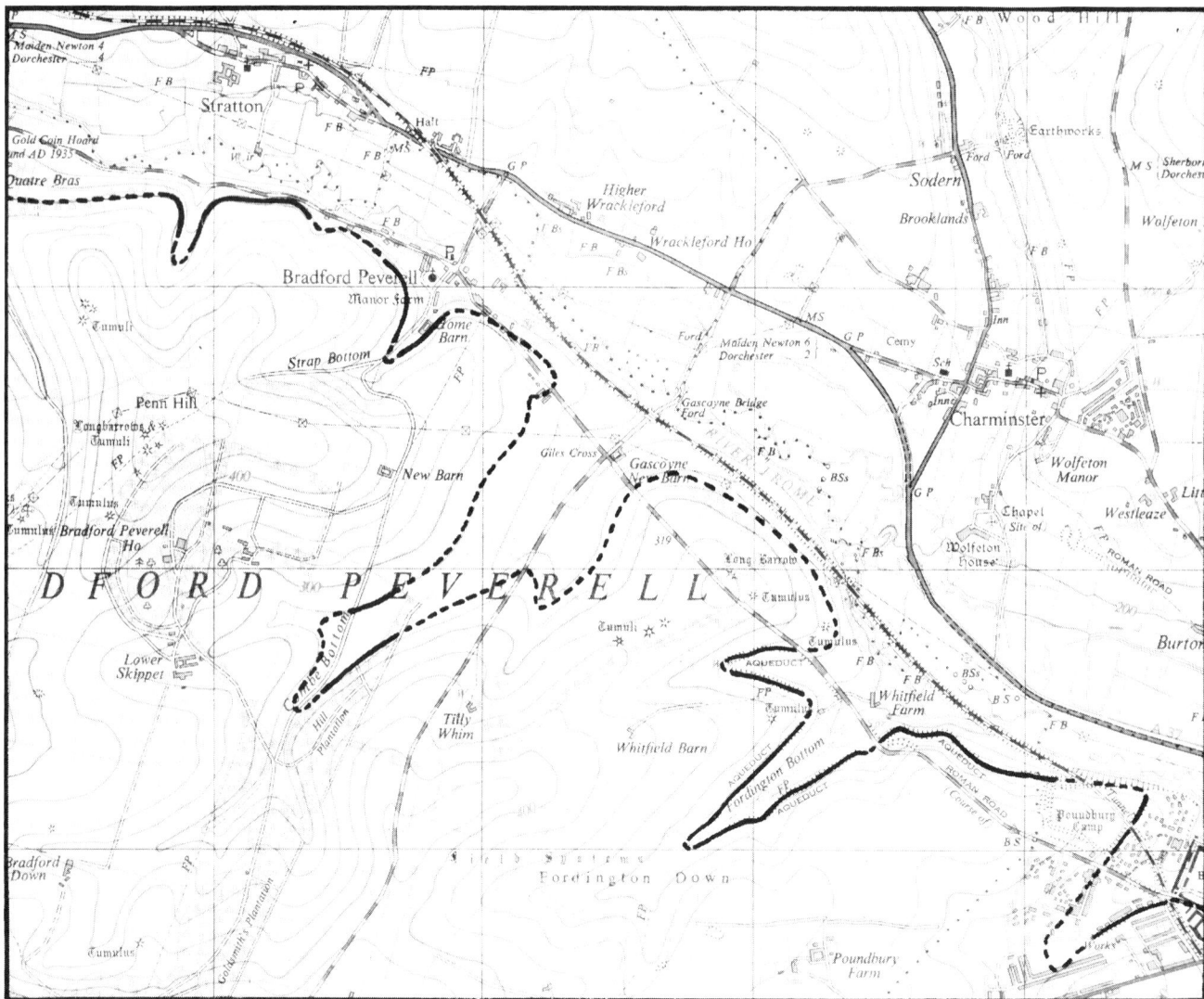

Plan of Roman aqueduct approaching Dorchester, Dorset (based on Ordnance Survey 2½-inch map)

raised by a hydraulic pump, although this presents certain mechanical problems. Otherwise it could only be provided from springs which lie twenty or so miles away to the north-east in the Wolds beyond Market Rasen.

Other towns which stood closer to the level of a good source of water, like Caerwent, Caistor, Cirencester, Silchester or St Albans, could rely on simple gravity-fed supplies carried in underground timber pipes joined together with iron collars. At Bath, near to the Mendip lead-mines, fine lead pipes could be used. None of these can be seen, of course, except where lengths of excavated piping are preserved in museums.

At Dorchester, however, the water was supplied in an unlined leat or channel cut into the chalk, which tapped the River Frome some nine miles to the west at Notton Mill, SY 609958. This channel was capable of supplying almost thirteen million gallons a day. It was cut some 3 feet deep, and wedge-shaped in section, 5 feet across at the bottom, and about 7 or 8 feet across at the top where the lip has weathered. The excavated material was dumped on the downhill side to form a terrace, and the route is now traceable as an embanked shelf along the side of the hill. It follows a winding course for twelve miles down the side of the Frome valley, just below the 300-foot contour, with a gradual fall of 25 feet overall. It passes the edge of the prehistoric fort of Poundbury to a point near the west gate of the Roman town.

The Romans had developed an advanced system of communications using fire beacons, smoke signals, and a sort of semaphore to transmit messages over short distances. The distance between signalling stations was dependent on the sight lines possible. A series of ten military signal stations were built along an eight-mile stretch of road on the Gask Ridge west of Perth, NN 917186–NO 022206. Typically the station consisted of a four-post watchtower $3\frac{1}{2}$ yards square set within a circular enclosure between 12 and 16 yards in diameter. A single entrance faced the line of the road. This enclosure took the form of a ditch, with the excavated material thrown up to form a bank on the outside, suggesting that it was intended for drainage rather than defence.

Signal stations built later in the period of Roman occupation when conditions were less secure, were much more strongly built. Thick-walled stone towers about 7 yards square continued the line of Hadrian's Wall westwards around the Cumbrian coast almost as far as Whitehaven. They were so situated as to command a good view of the sea, and occur regularly at every 540 yards.

A similar chain of stations has been found round the Yorkshire coast between Hartcliff and Filey. These were even stronger: stone towers up to 16 yards square, surrounded by a square perimeter wall with bastions and an outer ditch. They were still entered by a single gateway. These were built late in the Roman period, perhaps in response to the threat of Saxon pirates coming across the North Sea. Like the Cumbrian series, they look out to sea, and were probably intended to maintain communication with naval patrols. The outline of one example can still be made out on the very edge of the cliff east of Scarborough Castle, TA 051892. The remains of another at Goldsborough, NZ 835152, consists now merely of a prominent mound. Excavation here supplied dramatic evidence of the need for strong fortification in the last days of the Roman rule in Britain. The Goldsborough signal station had been subjected to a sudden attack, perhaps by invading Picts or Saxons from the sea. Skulls and other fragments of skeletons found around the site are a graphic witness to its violent end. The skeletons of two middle-aged men lay huddled in one corner of the tower; one lay face down across a hearth, his left arm twisted behind his back; another lay at his feet, sprawled across the skeleton of a powerful guard dog. This man had received several sword cuts in the skull, and was finally despatched by a crushing blow.

Other signal stations looked out over the Bristol

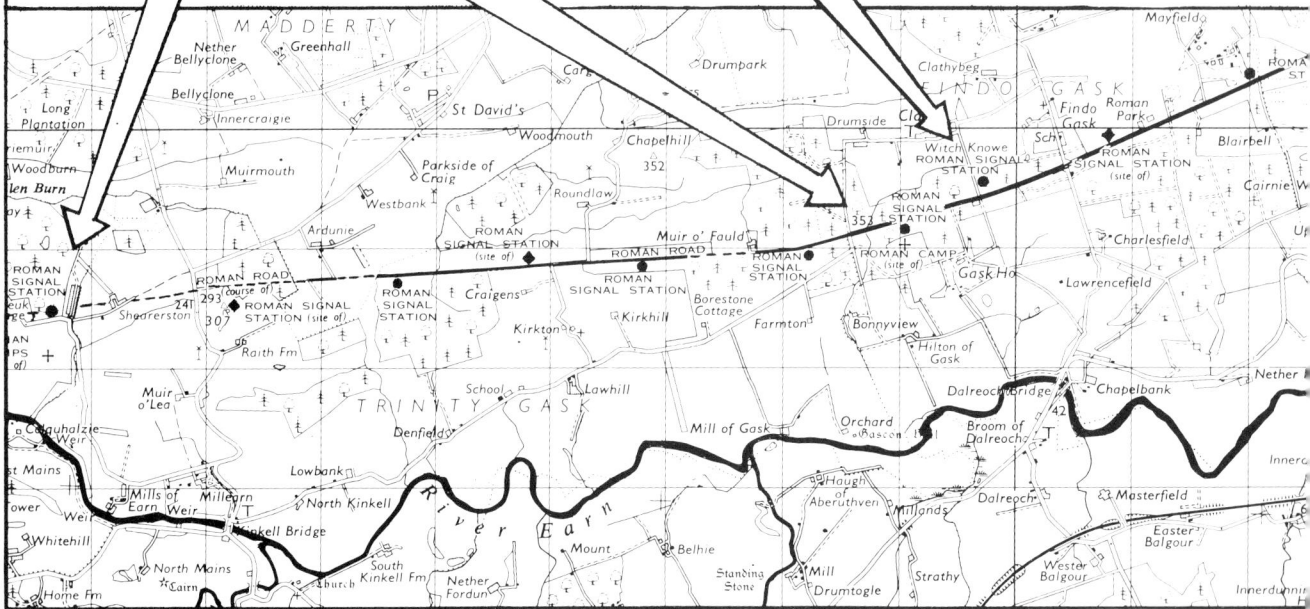

Plans and position of Roman signal stations along the Gask ridge, Perthshire (based on Ordnance Survey 1-inch map)

Channel from the north Devon coast at Martinhoe, SS 663493, and Old Burrow, SS 788493. Excavation shows these not to have been in contempory use. They are not known to have formed part of any continuous system, and must have served some more isolated function.

Only one example of a lighthouse proper is known from Roman Britain, standing now within the precincts of the medieval castle high on the cliffs at Dover, TR 326418. The outer face of dressed stone has almost entirely disappeared, and the flint rubble core presents a somewhat conical appearance. The original lighthouse tower was about 13 yards across at the base, octagonal in plan outside, and square inside. Only four of the original storeys survive, the fifth being a medieval reconstruction. It was probably designed to be about 80 feet high and to consist of eight storeys, each stage set back a foot so that it had a stepped exterior. It was entered by a door at ground level, and each stage was provided with windows, some looking out to sea. A second lighthouse, now represented merely by an undistinguished lump of masonry, lay on the western heights at the other side of Dover harbour. Ships were apparently guided into haven by setting a course exactly between the two. A similar structure formerly existed at Boulogne on the other side of the Channel. The Roman Channel Fleet was based at Dover and Boulogne, and these lighthouses were presumably constructed to facilitate night patrols.

Dover, Kent: Roman lighthouse

DEFENCES

The development of a surplus-production economy brought with it not only the luxury of professional services and specialist industries, but the threat of violent parasitism. As the fruits of agriculture and industry became ever more desirable, the demand for ownership of land and resources increased. And there were those who would take by main force what they had not the skill or inclination to produce. Eventually the prehistoric communities of Britain found it necessary to build for their protection. Because of the sheer size and massiveness of their construction, the defensive earthworks and fortifications they built are among the most impressive monuments to be seen.

As early as the end of the Bronze Age, perhaps some time about 850 BC, simple earthen defences were considered desirable. Probably the techniques were introduced to Western Europe by Bronze Age warriors from the East Mediterranean, where the urban defences of Mycenae and Troy were famous. In course of time further bands of warriors came from the East equipped with superior iron weapons. Evidence from their graves shows that the earlier waves rode in four-wheeled carts, and the later in fast two-wheeled war chariots. The remains of no less than three thousand hillforts and defensive enclosures survive from this period in Britain. These enormous numbers suggest that from about 500 BC until the Roman occupation Iron Age Britain entered a phase in which innumerable fragmented tribal units existed, among whom feuds, cattle raids and seasonal warfare were endemic. Successive waves of warriors introducing new methods of warfare necessitated more complex defences. Eventually the familiar pattern of offence and defence resulted in very elaborately designed fortifications.

Prehistoric hillforts vary greatly in size and plan. Most are very small, enclosing an area of three acres or less, and sometimes as little as one-twelfth of an acre. But many are much larger, and some of the largest cover an area of well over two hundred acres. Since their primary function was defensive, hillforts were situated so as to make access as difficult as possible for approaching enemies. An eminence or hill ridge might give an uninterrupted view of the surrounding countryside (the ramparts of hillforts often afford superb views), while the height would enhance the range over which defenders could hurl their missiles. Good advantage was taken of those natural features of the terrain which needed merely to be supplemented to provide a naturally defensible stronghold.

Around the coast, but especially in the south-west, rocky promontories surrounded on three sides by sheer sea-girt cliffs, could be converted into a stronghold merely by throwing a bank and ditch across the landward neck, effectively and rapidly isolating an

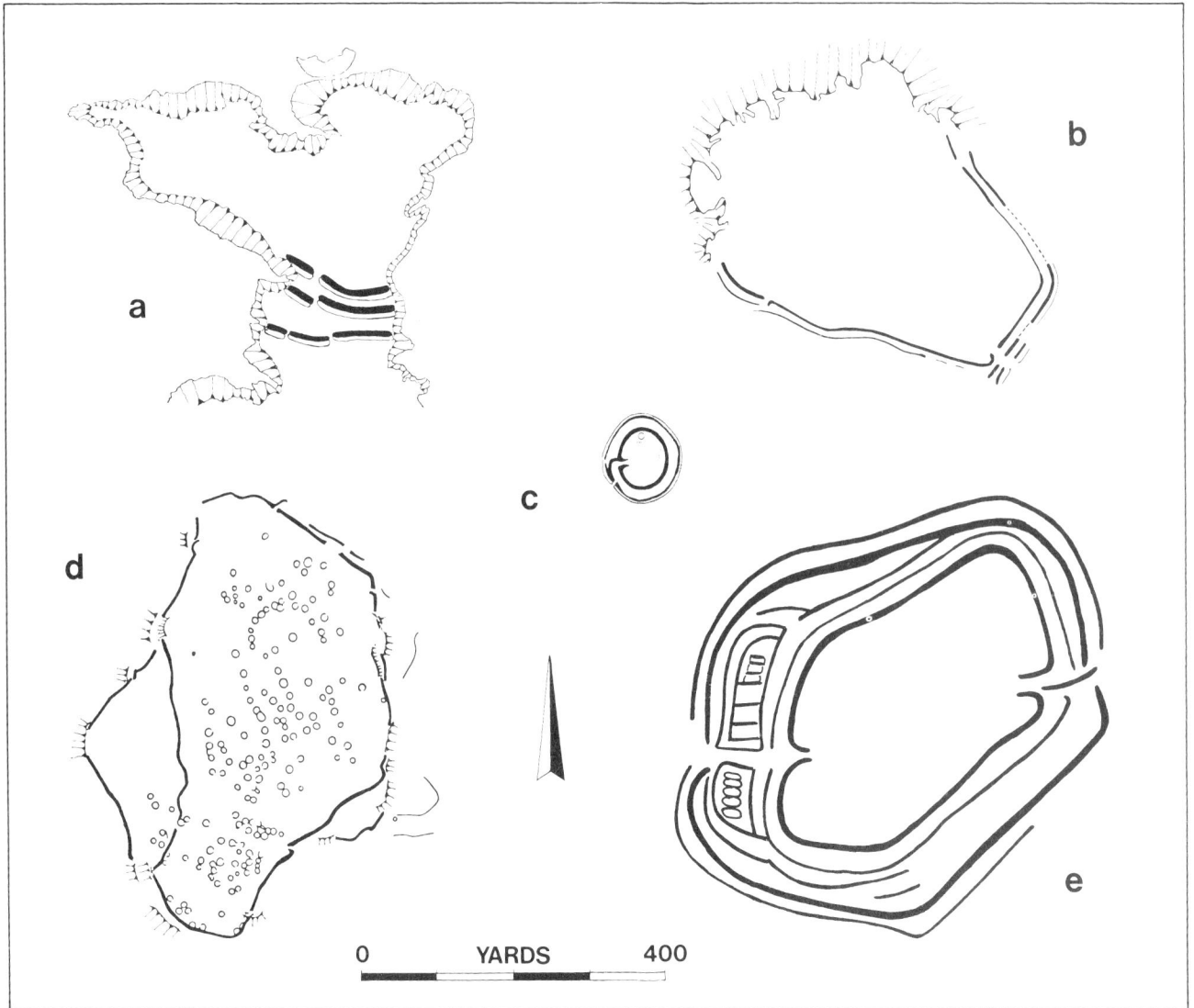

Comparative plans of Iron Age hillforts: (a) The Rumps, Cornwall; (b) High Rocks, Sussex; (c) Chun Castle, Cornwall; (d) Garn Boduan, Gwynedd; (e) Old Oswestry, Shrops

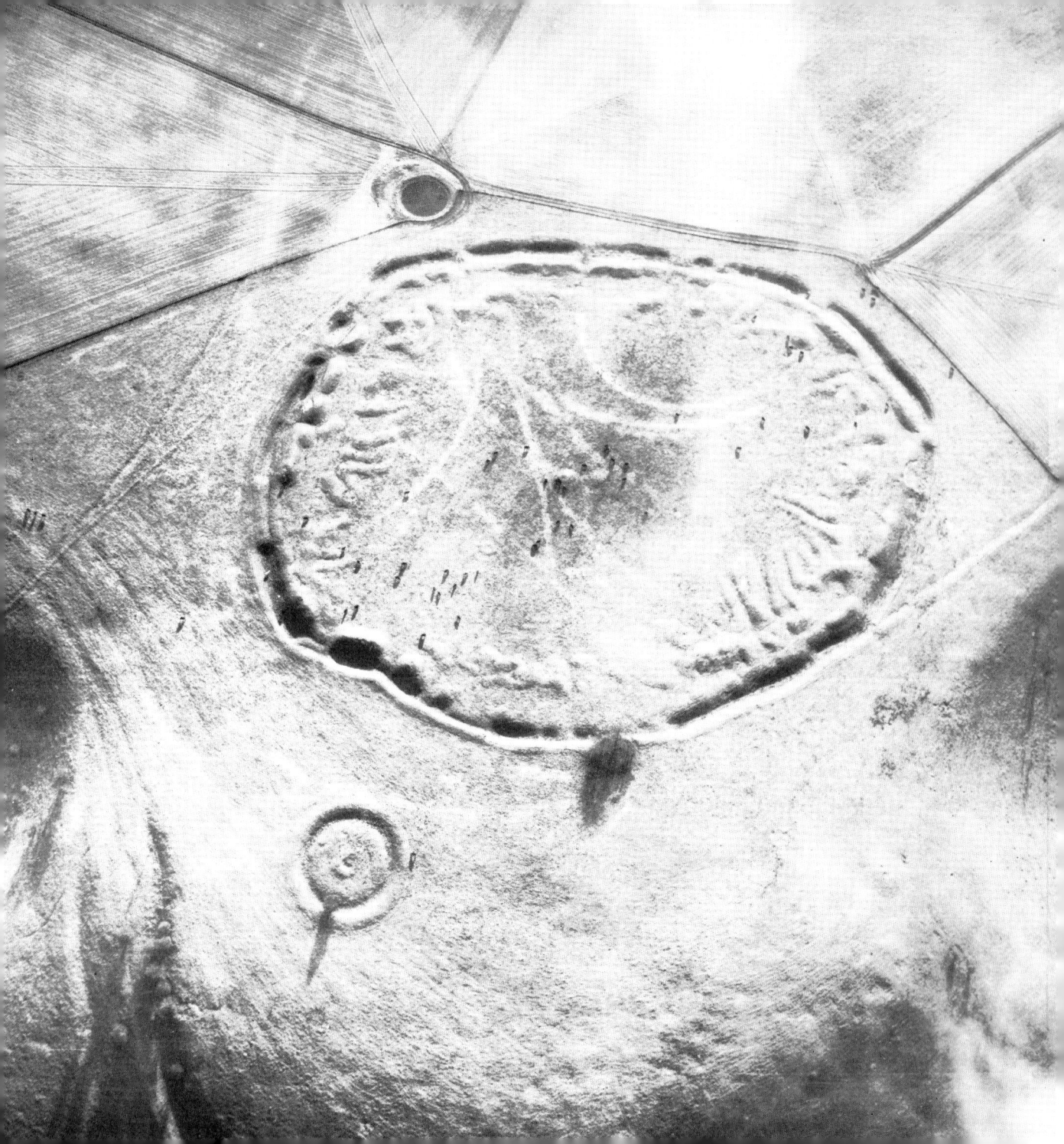

extensive area. There are forty such promontory-forts or 'cliff-castles' in Cornwall alone. A particularly fine example can be seen at The Rumps on the north coast at Pentire Head near Polzeath, SW 934810. A triple rampart cuts across the peninsula, isolating two separate headlands. The banks were built of weathered shale faced with boulders, the ditches cut up to 15 feet deep. The entrance passages were lined with timber and dry-stone walling, and were presumably provided with strong gates. Farther to the west on Trevelgue Head at Newquay, SW 827630, the promontory is defended by no less than six lines of ramparts, three on the landward side and three on an 'island' cut off by a sea gorge. The embankments still stand up to 8 feet high, and the ditches 12 feet deep.

Inland, especially in more broken hill country, it was often possible to rely on similar natural obstacles, so that not all sides of a stronghold needed artificial defences. At Lydney in Gloucestershire, for example, SO 616026, a steep-sided spur overlooking the Severn needed only to be supplemented to the north and east by a double bank and ditch. At Oldbury near Sevenoaks in Kent, TQ 582562, the steep hill required only a single rampart, and the western edge could safely be left unmodified, while at High Rocks near Tunbridge Wells, TQ 561382, the precipitous sandstone escarpment on the north-western edge required no additional defence. (In either case it was this sandstone overhang which Stone Age men used to shelter beneath, see p. 18.)

Ordinarily, however, it was necessary to build the entire defensive perimeter. The method of construction is well illustrated from one or two unfinished hillforts like those on Ladle Hill, Hampshire, SU 478568, or Elworthy Burrows in the Brendon Hills of Somerset, ST 070338. The outline of the fort was marked out around the most suitable contour, enclosing a more or less irregular plan depending upon the lie of the land. This might be set out with a shallow trench—probably little more than a plough furrow— or a low marker-bank of turves. Then separate gangs

of workmen began to cut sections of ditch, throwing up the excavated material into the interior. As the ditch grew deeper, solid blocks of chalk suitable for facings and internal revetments could be hewn out. At Ladle Hill this loose material—turf, topsoil and rubble—still lies around in disordered dumps, waiting to be built into a rampart on the inner edge of the ditch. It might have been consolidated with turf or timber and strengthened with wood, turf or dry-stone facing. But events seem to have overtaken the builders, since the project was abandoned when even the ditch was still discontinuous.

Even the simplest structures required a considerable investment of labour. A single rampart enclosing sixty acres near the flint-mines at Cissbury on the South Downs, TQ 139081, involved quarrying 35 thousand cubic yards of chalk, and the preparation of about ten thousand 15-feet main timber uprights, apart from other materials. Naturally much would depend upon the workforce available. But in an emergency the work could be done very quickly indeed. Experiments on Overton Down (see p. 8) show that using antler picks, shoulder-blade shovels and baskets for carrying, a man can loosen, dig and dump between one and one and a third cubic yards a day. So even using primitive implements of this sort, the earthwork at Cissbury could probably be completed by a labour force of one thousand in about a month. In fact Iron Age builders would have used much more efficient tools. Caesar describes how Celtic tribesmen built a rampart near Namur in Belgium in the winter of 54–53 BC; cutting the sods with their swords, lifting the earth with their hands and using cloaks to carry it, they built an embankment 10 feet high and a ditch 15 feet wide, three miles in circumference in less than three hours!

Although still massive, the present appearance of prehistoric ramparts often belies their formidable strength. They rarely now stand more than 10 to 20 feet high from the surface of the silted-up ditch to the top of the degraded bank. The smooth profiles

Iron Age rampart sections: artist's reconstructions of different types (after Coblenz)

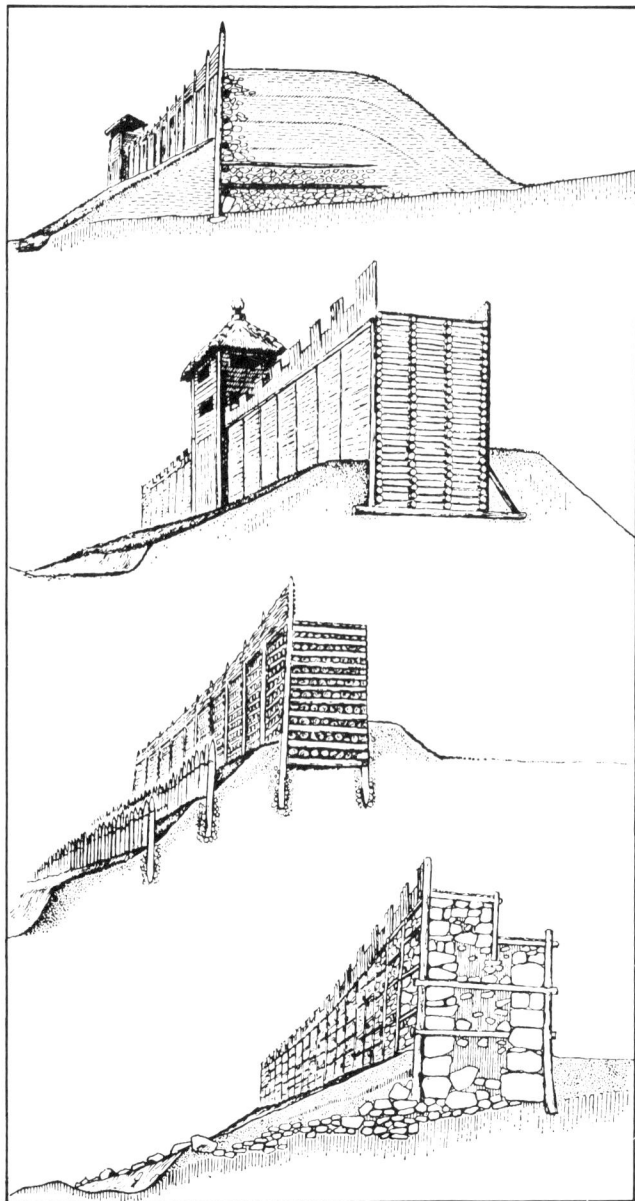

of these grassy downland embankments were originally brutally steep ditches confronting sheer walls crowned with wooden palisades. Tumbled scree often conceals the lower courses of strongly-built stone walls. The most straightforward way of constructing a rampart was simply to dump soil from the ditch on to the interior edge so that a steep slope or 'glacis' ran continuously from the bottom of the ditch to the top of the bank. Even without the addition of a palisade, this would present a considerable obstacle in itself, usually 30 or 50 feet above the ditch bottom. Loose material rarely has a natural slope of more than 35–40 degrees, but it was desirable that the obstruction confronting an attacker should be as steep as possible. The main problem was to prevent the soil from slipping back into the ditch. This could be done by stabilising successive layers with lines of turf or stone or lacing with horizontal timber struts. Alternatively, or in addition, the dump could be built up against the rear of a dry-stone or timber wall. If the rubble rampart were completely 'boxed' with timber or dry-stone walling, then the height possible using the same quantity of material was greatly increased, while presenting a more formidable vertical or near-vertical exterior face. In this case, however, a narrow level platform or ledge had to be allowed between the bottom of the wall and the lip of the ditch to prevent collapse. All ramparts were topped by a timber walkway from which the defenders were well positioned to fire accurately on those below. (In some places, especially in Scotland, the timber-work has been fired, resulting in the vitrifaction of surrounding areas of stone, but whether intentionally or by accident is open to question.)

In all fortification, entrances are potentially the most vulnerable points, and special attention was paid to strengthening these. The simplest kind of entrance, as found at Figsbury Ring, Wiltshire, SU 188338, consists merely of an open gap in a single line of defence, although presumably blocked by stout timber gates. Any degree of inturning in the line

Maiden Castle, Dorset: Iron Age ramparts

of rampart would form the entrance into a kind of funnel, in which an enemy would be vulnerable to attack either side from the rampart above, as at Old Oswestry in Shropshire, SJ 296310. At Uffington in Oxfordshire, SU 299864, a single loop in the rampart created a narrow passage no less than 40 yards long. Such a close passageway could easily be boxed into a timber tunnel if necessary. But at the very least a guardhouse might be set into the width of the rampart, with an inner and outer set of gates at either end of the passage. The floor was commonly cobbled since the passageway took considerable wear. Alternatively, or in addition, the entrance could be strengthened by a futher line of defence forming a barbican, thus exposing anyone forcing an entry to attack from the flanks. A good example of this occurs at Castle Dore near Fowey in Cornwall, SX 103548. Outworks of this kind could be duplicated so that the approach became more and more devious, overlooked at every

turn. At Maiden Castle in Dorset, SY 668885, the western entrance is particularly tortuous, a corridor 80 yards or more long threading between guardhouses and ramparts sheltering platforms for slingmen.

The most impressive and complex hillforts eventually consisted of numerous ramparts, covering many acres. Excavation shows this to have been a gradual series of developments in response to new conditions. The history of Maiden Castle is instructive in this respect. It lies on a broad saddle-backed ridge some thousand yards long, lying east—west about two miles south-west of Dorchester. The more easterly of the two knolls had been the site of a causewayed camp used by local Neolithic herdsmen. Then some time about 300 BC this hill was chosen by early Iron Age people for a simple univallate defence: a single rampart and ditch enclosing a roughly oval area fifteen acres in extent. In this first phase the V-shaped ditch

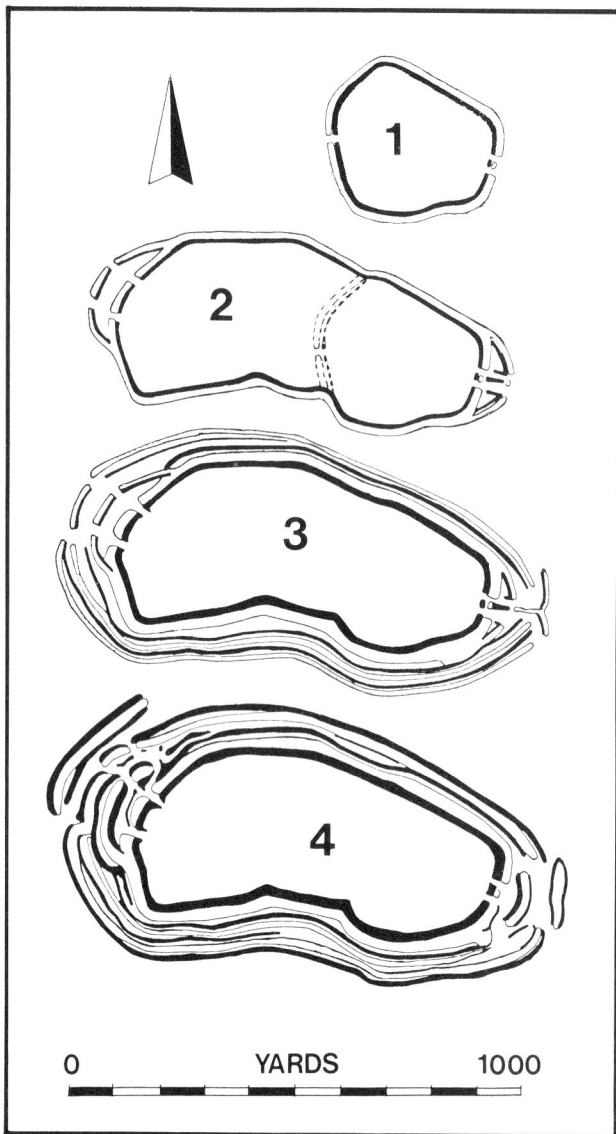

Maiden Castle, Dorset: stages in its development (after Wheeler)

was dug 17 yards across and 20 feet deep, separated by a 2-yard platform from an earthen rampart, 3 yards wide at the base and 7 or 8 feet high, revetted with timber at front and rear. There were entrances at opposing ends. That to the west was 5 yards wide, closed by a pair of heavy timber gates. To the east a double portal was divided by a 20-yard length of walling, and outside this an area about 100 yards square cobbled with flints probably served as a market place. Later this single rampart was extended westward to embrace the entire hilltop, enclosing an area of forty-five acres in all—three times its original size. The rampart design was modified, and from now on was of the simple glacis type with no platform separating the bank from the ditch. The entrances were further strengthened by outlying 'horn-works' enclosing a small barbican and screening the gate-

Maiden Castle, Dorset: aerial view

ways. ⟨...⟩ce ramparts presented vertical fronts with upright ⟨...⟩ber facing and dry-stone walling between. After an interval, and possibly in response to invaders from across the Channel, a third phase of construction was begun. Now the main rampart was massively enlarged to almost double its size, strengthened with internal revetments of limestone blocks, and with a flat walkway along the top. A second bank and ditch was added round the entire circuit and a third around its greater part, with consequent elaboration of the entrance designs. The development of multiple ramparts was apparently made possible by the introduction of the sling as a defensive weapon, having a range of about 100 yards—and rather more downhill. Ammunition dumps were found piled at strategic points round the interior, one heap containing some twenty thousand selected beach pebbles. A fourth and final phase saw the addition of one more rampart round the entire perimeter, while the entrances either end were made yet more convolute, with stone platforms (now buried) positioned so as to allow sling-men to command the avenues of approach.

With the arrival of the Romans, some native hillforts can be seen in a historical context. Caesar's second expeditionary force of 54 BC advanced inland from the Kentish coast and stormed a native hillfort which must almost certainly be identified with Bigbury Camp, two miles west from what is now Canterbury, TR 116576. The fort occupies a strategic position straddling the line of an ancient track (a branch of the so-called Pilgrims' Way), and standing on a gravel-capped hill commanding the Great Stour river crossing. The main rampart consists of a 9-foot bank and 7-foot ditch following the line of the 200-foot contour and enclosing an area of about ten acres, with a further seven-acre annexe to the north, probably intended as a compound for cattle or horses. There are entrances to both east and west, the former approached by a hollow way. The interior has been disturbed by gravel-working, but on the north side especially the slopes are still heavily wooded as they were in Caesar's day. Hillforts were commonly built on densely wooded sites since this in itself represented a considerable obstruction to any attacker. The presently wooded slopes of many hillforts may therefore closely correspond to their original appearance. Excavation at Bigbury recovered a good range of domestic finds, including iron saws, ploughshares, cauldron hooks, horse bits, fine firedogs and a slave chain with its padlock. Caesar's report of the attack on Bigbury represents the first account of any battle fought on British soil. He had landed near Sandwich and learned from prisoners of the whereabouts of the native forces. A night march inland of about twelve miles brought him in sight of the enemy, whose chariots and cavalry were advancing from higher ground towards the river. Repulsed by Roman cavalry, they fell back to the woods and occupied a position strongly defended by natural and artificial features. This fortification seemed to have been a recent construction, probably the result of internal warfare, since the entrances were blocked by masses of tree trunks placed close together rather than with a properly constructed gateway. The Roman attack was at first hampered by sorties of skirmishers, sallying out from the woods. But then men from the 7th Legion, advancing in a column with shields locked together and lifted up, managed to fill part of the ditch with a ramp of earth or brushwood, and thus breached the defences. The occupants retreated. Next day Caesar learned that the Roman fleet had been badly damaged by a storm and he was obliged to retire.

Excavation provides equally graphic evidence for the violent end of some other hillforts. On Bredon Hill in Worcestershire, SO 958402, the northern end of a limestone ridge had been turned into a small but strong promontory fort by the construction of a double rampart. In and around the entrance was found evidence for a wholesale massacre. The remains of sixty or seventy bodies—mainly of young men—had been savagely hacked to pieces, the

PILGRIMS' WAY

OLD ROUTE

GRAVEL PIT

SCARP PLOUGHED OUT

0   YARDS   300

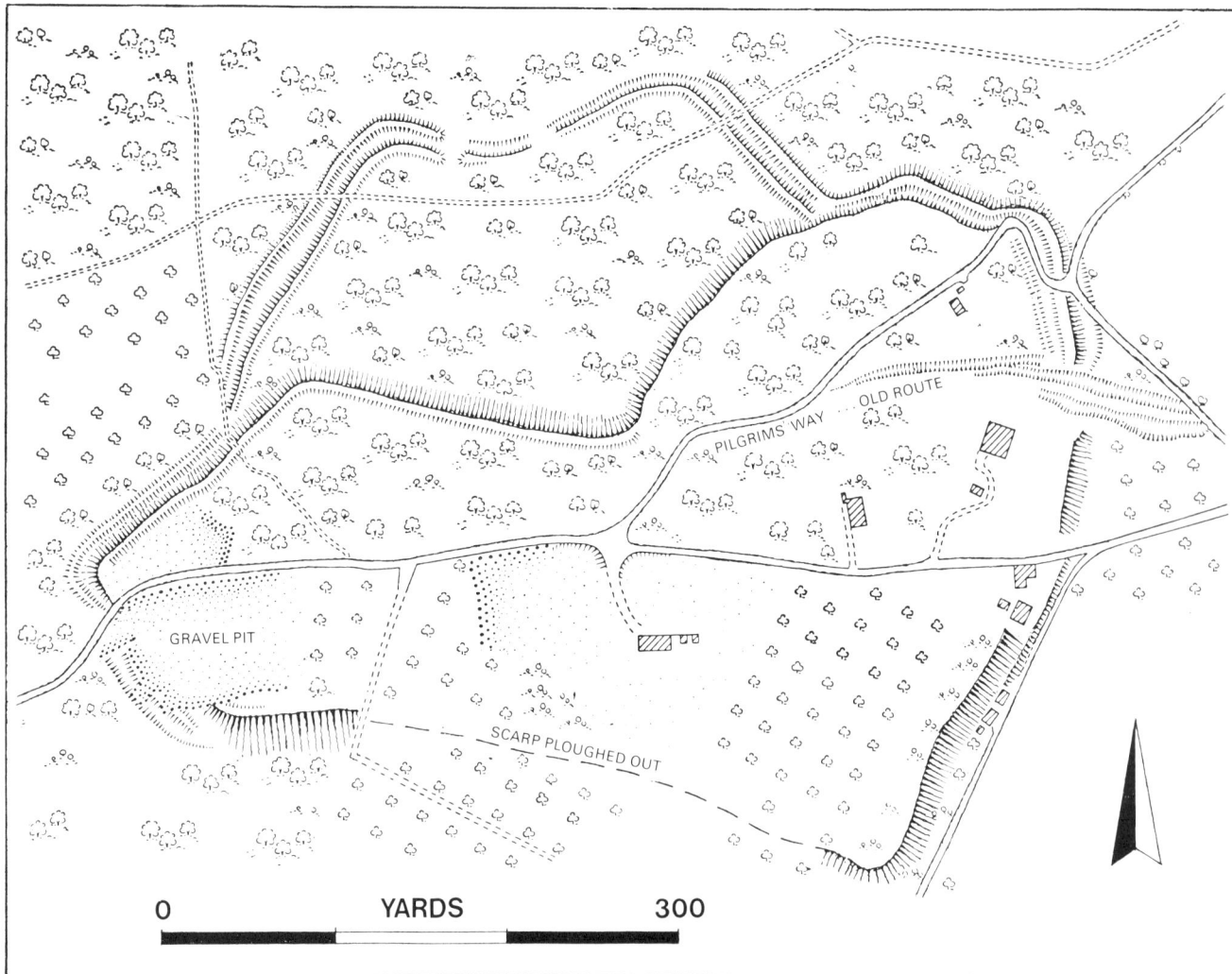

Plan of Bigbury hillfort, Kent

bodies, many limbless or headless, lying where they fell. Possibly it was a case of revenge by a neighbouring tribe; certainly the inhabitants of the Bredon Hill fort were equally violent. They had been accustomed to hang war-trophies—the heads of their enemies—over the main entrance. A row of six skulls was found among the ashes where the gateway had been burnt down.

Prehistoric hillforts were not military defences in the usual sense of the term. Unlike later Roman or medieval castles, they were part of no co-ordinated defensive system, but isolated entities unrelated to one another and reflecting purely local strategy, meeting the needs of individual communities rather than that of an entire nation. It was this independence which resulted in their relatively easy subjection at the hands of the Romans. The smallest hillfort enclosures may have been little more than the defended homesteads of local chieftains. Perhaps many larger hillforts began as temporary wartime refuges for those who normally lived elsewhere in the vicinity. The large acreage could be accounted for by the need to shelter flocks or herds in an emergency. But the sophisticated engineering and very considerable investment of labour involved suggests more permanent occupation.

By the time of the Roman invasion proper, the most elaborate of these fortifications must have housed relatively large communities living in permanent or semi-permanent quarters. But even the most impressive defences were unable to resist the might of the Roman military machine. Maiden Castle was merely one of more than twenty 'towns' which fell to the 2nd (Augusta) Legion under General, later Emperor, Vespasian during his advance westwards in the mid-40s AD. Dramatic evidence for the fall of Maiden Castle was brought to light by the discovery outside the main eastern gateway of a large war grave. About forty men and women had been hastily buried in a shallow grave cut through the ashes of burnt-out houses. Many of the skulls had multiple sword-cuts, and one skeleton had a Roman artillery arrowhead embedded in the spine. After the fort had been taken, the main gateway was demolished, and a few years later the inhabitants moved down to the newly established town of Dorchester.

The few hillfort interiors so far excavated suggest more than sporadic occupation, with a large number of huts and grain-storage pits. In rocky regions of the north and west hut-circles are often readily visible.

Tre'r Ceiri, Gwynedd: aerial view

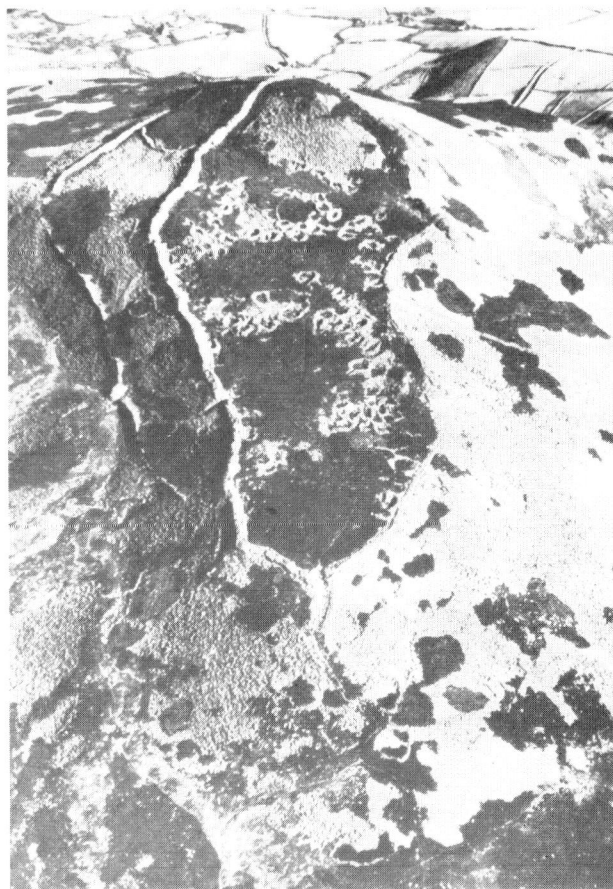

The thirteen-acre interior of Yeavering Bell in Northumberland, NT 928294, contains about 130 hut-circles, while at Garn Boduan in the Lleyn Peninsula, Gwynedd, SH 310393, covering an area of twenty-seven acres, it is possible to trace the remains of some 170 round huts, which may possibly represent a regular population of 700 or so. Other such 'towns' include Tre'r Ceiri just five miles north-east of Garn Boduan, SH 374447, Carn Brea west of Redruth in Cornwall, SW 686407, and Eildon Hill, a mile south of Melrose, Roxburghshire, NT 554328, 1300 feet above sea level, and the largest hillfort in Scotland, enclosing an area of some forty acres, with more than 300 hut platforms still discernible.

There is a marked absence of hillforts of any kind east of the Pennines. It is perhaps natural that few if any should be found in the flat lands of the East Midlands and East Anglia, but their absence from the Wolds of North Lincolnshire and East Yorkshire is puzzling. It may be significant that this coincides with the distribution of Iron Age chariot-burials (see below, p. 135). Perhaps the native tribes of these parts favoured a more open, mobile kind of warfare at this time. Certainly the curious series of parallel lengths of running ditches found in this region, seem well suited to obstruct chariot warfare. Scamridge Dykes, to the north-east of Pickering on the edge of the North York Moors consist of no less than seven parallel ditches covering a strip of land 150 yards wide running for two and a half miles or more, SE 882852–915867. Similar systems lie within a mile or so either side. Farther south, Huggate Dykes on the East Yorkshire Wolds, SE 852556–893576, consist of only five such parallel ditches.

Linear earthworks, usually consisting of a bank and ditch, are to be found in all parts of the country, some only a few yards in length, others covering many miles. Some large cross-country dykes seem to have been frontier works, like Beech Bottom Dyke near St Albans in Hertfordshire, best seen at TL 150091. Thirty feet deep and 30 yards wide, it crosses open ground between the Rivers Ver and Lea. A bank 28 yards broad lies on the southern side and presumably therefore this earthwork 'faced' northwards. Others are so sited as to lie across routeways, and rest their flanks on natural obstacles either side. A classic example is Ponters Ball, a half-mile length of rampart, 12 feet high and 10 yards wide with a 12-foot ditch on the eastern side, which straddles the causeway linking the marsh-girt Isle of Glastonbury with higher ground to the east, ST 533377. Others control movement along major routes, like those which lie on the Icknield Way, running from marshy fenland on the south-east to originally forested land on the north-west. The most remarkable of these, and perhaps the most impressive earthwork in the country, is the Devil's Ditch, which straddles the Icknield Way as it crosses Newmarket Heath in Cambridgeshire, running for a distance of seven or eight miles from TL 568660 to 653583. On the borders of Hampshire, Dorset and Wiltshire lies Bokerly Dyke, SU 022198–063168. Three and a half miles long, 6 feet high in places and 11 yards across, with a 10-feet rock-cut ditch now silted up, this effectively controlled movement along the line of Ackling Dyke, the Roman road from Dorchester to Salisbury.

The majority of the larger hillforts are situated in the broad downlands of southern England. The more broken terrain, and possibly more fragmented communities, of the north and west favoured much smaller defences for the most part. These are characteristically circular or sub-circular in plan. Typical is Castle Dore in Cornwall, SX 103548, commanding the line of an ancient transpeninsular route from the northern coast as it approaches the natural southern harbour on the Fowey estuary. It consists simply of two ramparts enclosing an area of rather less than an acre. The outer rampart diverges so as to form a barbican, through which ran a metalled roadway commanded by guardhouses. In the far west a particularly strong fort at Chun Castle, just inland from Morvah, dominates much of the Land's End district, SW 405339.

Its stout dry-stone granite walls are still impressive, standing 10 feet high in places. The perimeter wall was doubled and its entrances staggered, so that those entering had to follow a zigzag route inside. In its external appearance this must have closely resembled the contemporary stone-built forts of Scotland.

In Scotland there developed the type of small stone-walled fort known as a 'dun', in which the massive walling, anything between 3 and 6 yards thick, is disproportionate to the small area enclosed. They are rarely more than 20 yards in diameter, and usually much less. The massive wall is narrowly pierced with a single entrance passage, often with a guardhouse set into the thickness of the wall. In many the dry-stone walls are sufficiently thick to contain passages with steps leading up to an open parapet on the top. Alternatively the top could be reached by steps built against the inner face of the wall. The main concentration of these duns is found in the coastal region of south-west Scotland. Many are located on more or less inaccessible islands. But a particularly fine example can be found on the summit of a rocky knoll overlooking the sea at Kildonan, a few miles north of Campbeltown in Argyll, NR 780277. Others found on the shore-line of the Isle of Skye include: Dun Ardtreck, Dun Ringill and Dun Beag, NG 335357, 562171, 575199. A good example on the coast of Tiree can be found in Dun Mor Vaul, NM 042493.

In the farther north of Scotland and in the Western Isles there developed an impressive tower-like variant, known locally as a 'broch'. Brochs are more compact and more systematically planned than duns. The lowest stage closely resembles the dun: walls 4 or 5 yards thick containing one or more flights of stone steps. But these lead to a series of narrow galleries, one above the other, ventilated by tiers of windows looking into the interior. Externally the tower sloped inwards, slightly conical, representing a truncated cone. Originally the walls stood 50 feet or more high, providing a considerable defence against missiles.

Most brochs are now sadly ruined, but many are still impressive even in their ruined state. Some five hundred or more brochs are known in all, mostly concentrated in Orkney, Shetland and the northernmost mainland of Caithness. Probably the finest extant example is that standing on the rocky shore of the small island of Mousa in the Shetlands, HU 457237. The walls stand 44 feet high, tapering from about 17 yards across at the base to 13 yards diameter at the top. A single entrance on the seaward side, little more than a yard across and 5 yards long, leads to an interior space 7 yards in diameter. Along the entrance passageway the slot for a strong barrier can still be seen. Ranged round the interior at ground level are three recesses and three larger rooms lying in the thickness of the walls, which are otherwise solid for

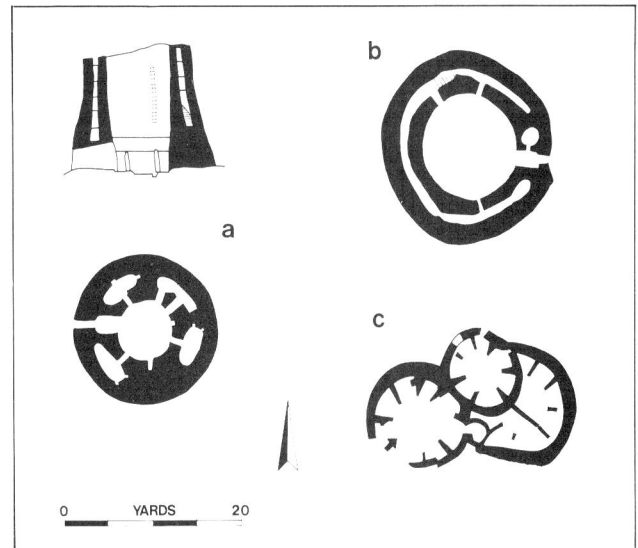

Comparative plans of duns and brochs: (a) Broch of Mousa, Shetland; (b) Dun Mor Vaul, Tiree; (c) Sequence of wheelhouses at Jarlshof, Shetland

Broch of Mousa, Shetland

the first 12 feet. Two stone ledges running round the wall would have supported timber galleries or half-floors, 7 feet and 12 feet above ground level respectively. From this point upwards the walls are hollow, containing six circular galleries, rising one above the other to the existing height of the tower. A narrow stairway, no more than a yard in width, winds clockwise up through these galleries to the wall-top. Tiers of small windows look into the interior.

Two other fine, but partly collapsed brochs, Dun Telve and Dun Troddan, can be seen just a quarter of a mile apart south of Glenelg on the west coast of Inverness, NG 829172, 834172. The latter when excavated revealed a pattern of postholes on the interior suggesting support for a wooden floor. In Orkney the Midhowe broch on Rousay, HY 371308, is one of an original three in a quarter-mile radius: built on a spur of rock lying between two creeks, and thus protected by water on three sides at high tide, and supplemented by further defensive walls. The Broch of Gurness on the shore at Aiker Ness, HY 383268, stands now only 10 feet high, but was just one of a dozen in the immediate vicinity.

Whereas in the south of Britain the Roman conquest resulted in native forts being slighted and abandoned, in the far north there was no such interruption, and many sites like Jarlshof (see p. 22), or Clickhimin on a promontory outside Lerwick, HU 464408, witnessed a continuous history of occupation from Neolithic into Medieval times. The Broch of Mousa itself figures as a stronghold under siege in the Viking *Orkney Saga*.

The invasion of Britain by the Roman legions in AD 43 proceeded fairly rapidly. The rich lowland zone south-east of the line from the Severn to the Trent was more or less secure within seven years and could be relinquished to civilian rule. But further advances north and west into the broken hill country were less easy. The native tribes were more hostile, the terrain more difficult; and this continued a military zone for the entire period of Roman occupation. It took a

further thirty years or so for the legions to fight their way to the edge of the Highlands beyond the Clyde. Then in AD 84 they halted. North of the Forth–Clyde line the native tribes were never subdued, despite occasional punitive expeditions sent into the interior. One legion, the 9th, disappears from the army list altogether; perhaps it marched north and was annihilated, or possibly it was defeated so discreditably that it was disbanded. Its base at York was taken over by the 6th (Victrix) Legion. Further advance was either impractical or unrewarding, and after about fifteen years the legions withdrew to a more defensible line from the Tyne to the Solway Firth, where finally in about AD 120 the Emperor Hadrian ordered the construction of a permanent frontier wall.

During the course of campaigning, Roman soldiers constructed temporary 'marching-camps', built in conformity with military manuals. A trenching-tool and one or two palisade stakes were standard issue to every soldier. Even overnight bivouacs were surrounded by a V-shaped ditch anything between 2 and 6 feet deep and an earth embankment 5 or 6 feet high crowned by a palisade. The commanding officer's tent was pitched in the centre, surrounded by other tents in rows. The variable terrain on which it was necessary to camp resulted in occasional modifications. But ideally a rectangular plan was aimed at. Roman marching-camps have a characteristically playing-card plan: straight sides with slightly rounded corners, and two, four or more gates depending on their size. They were expected to house three hundred men to the acre, so that a full legion could be accommodated in a camp about 300 yards square. The larger the area enclosed, the less rampart per capita was required. At Rey Cross (see below), it worked out at about only 7 inches a man. Entrances could be defended either by a short piece of rampart set a yard or two in front of the gap, and intended to divert the direct charge of an enemy while allowing sudden sorties to counterattack, or a small hook-like extension of the rampart either inside or outside the line.

Many temporary camps are known from aerial photographs to have existed in southern Britain, but the sole visible examples are found on unploughed moorland in the mountainous military zone. Good examples can be seen at Y Pigwyn, in a desolate situation 1350 feet above sea level in the Brecon Beacons, SN 828313. One three-and-a-half-acre camp had been built big enough to hold a legion, and later a second smaller one was built within the line of its predecessor. At Rey Cross on the summit of the Stainmore Pass across the back of the Pennines, on the border of County Durham and Cumbria, NY 902124, an eighteen-and-a-half-acre camp had been constructed capable of holding six thousand men in all. A ditch was only dug on one side, since elsewhere the natural rock close to the surface made trenching impractical. But a substantial rampart was built, up to 6 feet high in places and almost 7 yards across. Later the line of the major trans-Pennine Roman road passed through this camp. At Chew Green on Roman Dere Street where it crosses the Cheviots into Scotland, NT 787085, four successive camps were constructed, overlapping in plan, and decreasing in area, until the last and smallest seems to have taken a more or less permanent form. Probably this was a base for patrols accompanying convoys of wagons across this wild country.

In training, small practice camps were built, and these can sometimes be found in numbers close to base camps. Outside Llandrindod Wells in Powys, SO 054602, the remains of fourteen or more can be traced, between 15 and 30 yards square. These were probably built by troops sent out from the permanent fort at Castell Collen a mile-and-a-half to the north, SO 055628. Others on the Wheeldale Moor Roman road at Cawthorn, North Yorkshire, SE 785900, were almost certainly built by men from the 9th Legion stationed at York. At Burnswark, south-east of Locherbie in Dumfriesshire, NY 186788, there is graphic evidence for the Roman army on manoeuvres. Troops from the fort south of Middlebie, NY 218753, were sent three miles north-west to stage a mock attack on an abandoned British hillfort. They constructed a large rectangular siege camp either side of the hillfort (that to the north never finished), and three large circular platforms for machine catapults, which were used to lay down an artillery barrage, the lead and clay bolts of which have been found by excavation in the interior of the fort.

Once the conquest of the province was complete, forts of a more permanent nature could be planned and built by military engineers. Unlike the native defences, Roman forts were conceived as interrelated elements in a highly organised system of military occupation, linked by road and sea communications both with each other and with a rear base, and ultimately with provincial and imperial headquarters. Now that the nature and extent of the new province was known, the legions themselves, the corps d'élite of the imperial army, 6000-strong infantry units composed of Roman citizens, garrisoned permanent bases at York, Chester and Caerleon. These were strategically disposed to the rear of the forward line. They each lay on navigable rivers giving access to the sea, which not only facilitated provision and reinforcement direct by sea, but ensured additionally secure communication-routes. Previous legionary fortresses at Lincoln, Gloucester and Wroxeter were relinquished and became the sites of thriving civilian towns. Impressive stretches of stone perimeter wall can still be seen at York and Chester, where they were kept in good repair as part of the medieval town walls. But although excavation has revealed some part of the interior plan of these forts, little or nothing of any significance is now visible. At Caerleon, ST 339906, which was only partly built over in later ages, the fifty-acre fort was surrounded by an earthen rampart, later given a stone facing, although this is now somewhat degraded. The south-west section of the interior has been excavated to reveal four out of an original sixty-four rectangular barrack-blocks, together with associated square cookhouses and ovens. Outside the fortress the

Caerleon, Gwent: aerial view of the military amphitheatre (ludus)

foundations of a large bath-house stands to the south-east; and to the south-west in a remarkable state of preservation lies the military 'ludus', an amphitheatre-like arena used for weapon-training. It was an oval area, 75 by 90 yards, and could accommodate about 6000 spectators, i.e. the whole of the 2nd Legion, on embanked seating. Unlike civilian amphitheatres, the proportion of arena to auditorium is large. Seating was ranged around a stone-faced earthen embankment, pierced by eight symmetrical entrances. A 'box' was provided for senior officers, and a domed recess probably represents a shrine containing a statue of Nemesis, goddess of Fate. Chester boasted an even larger ludus with plastered walls painted to imitate marble. But it has been possible to reveal only half by excavation outside the south-east angle of the fort.

Plans of Roman earthworks: (left) manoeuvre earthworks either side of a native hillfort at Burnswark, Dumfriesshire; (right) sequence of marching-camps at Chew Green, Northumberland

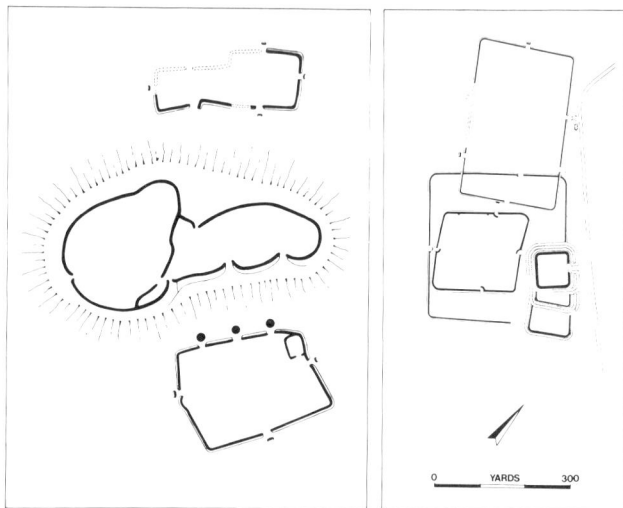

Potentially much more rewarding for the archaeologist was the site of an abandoned legionary fortress at Inchtuthill in Strathtay on the edge of the Highlands, NO 125397. Construction began in AD 84 when the legions began their abortive advance into the Highlands, and was still incomplete when four years later the order came to withdraw. The site was never built over and thus remained to reveal its full history to the excavator. The fort was square in plan. The earthen ramparts were faced with stone brought from quarries at Gourdie Hill two miles to the north and others two and a half miles to the south at Innernytie. A gateway flanked by timber towers lay in the centre of each side. All buildings on the interior were wooden, although the bath-house outside the wall was necessarily built of stone. The interior was quartered by roadways leading from the four gates. At the centre, close to where they crossed, lay the headquarters building, one room of which normally served as a chapel or shrine where the military standards were lodged. Barrack blocks in groups of six were ranged round the outside, with the centurions' quarters, rather more spacious and with tiled rather than shingled roofs, lying closer to the rampart. Six large granaries had loading-bays front and rear. Workshops were ranged round four sides of a square. And a large military hospital with sixty-four wards corresponding to the sixty-four centuries that made up the legion, was also ranged round an open court-yard to allow fresh air and peace away from the bustle elsewhere. A drill-hall with attached classrooms allowed arms practice in wet weather. To the south of the headquarters building, four out of six quarters had been built for the senior officers. The commandant's house itself was not begun when the order came to withdraw to a more practical defensive line farther south. Then the site was systematically laid waste so that nothing whatever of value should fall into enemy hands. The stone wall facing was broken down and the bath-house demolished. Foundation trenches were filled with bent nails from dismantled timber

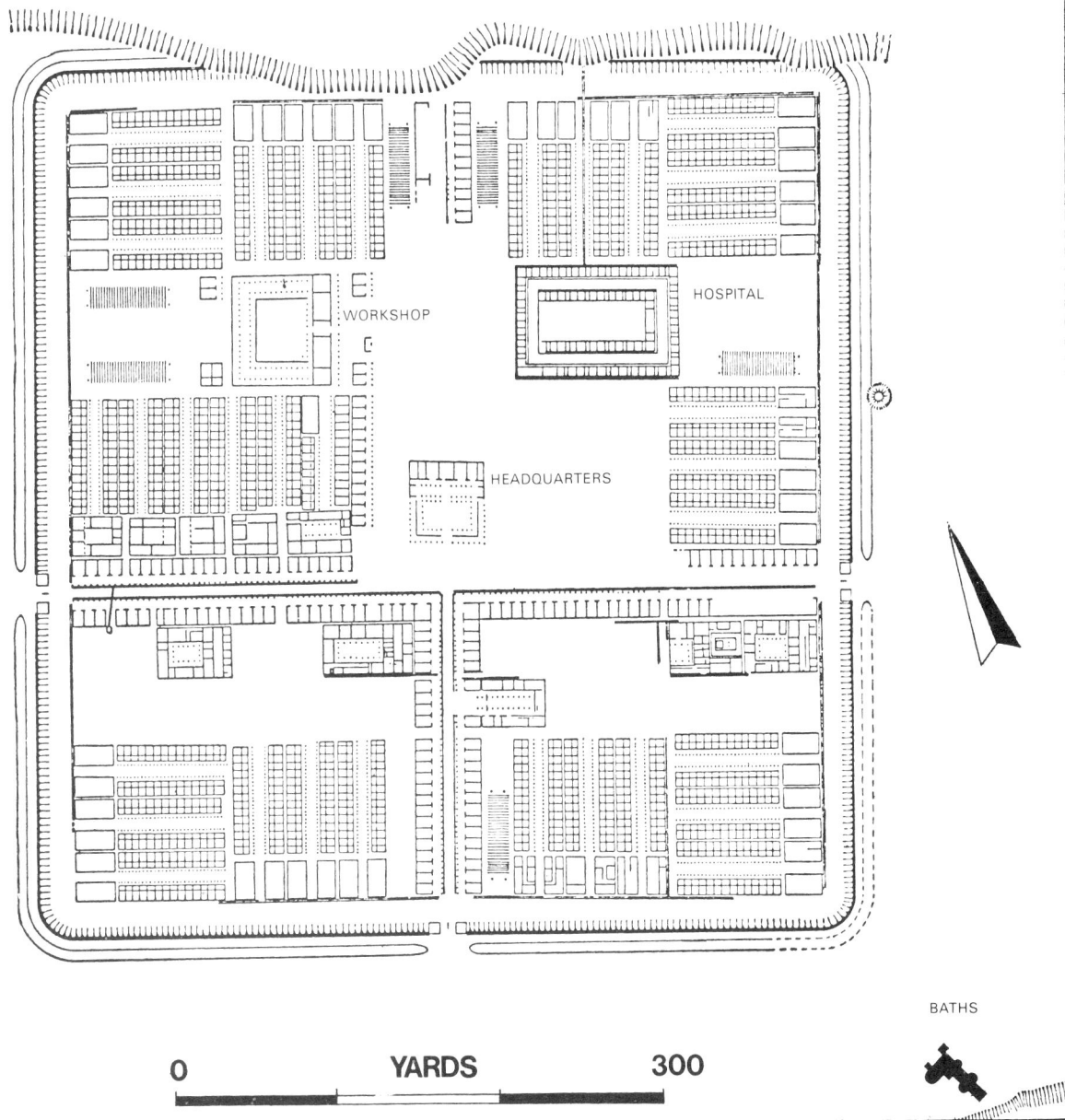

WORKSHOP

HOSPITAL

HEADQUARTERS

BATHS

0   YARDS   300

Inchtuthil, Perthshire: excavation plan of legionary fortress (after Richmond)

93

buildings. The hospital drains were blocked with gravel. Roughly a million unused nails, weighing some twelve tons and too heavy to cart away, were buried beneath the workshop floor. Glass and pottery were smashed to smithereens. The garrison itself, the 2nd (Adjutrix) Legion, was transferred to the Danube frontier.

Nothing now remains to be seen at Inchtuthill except the outline of rampart and ditch. But many good examples of smaller forts remain, built on much the same principles by the same military engineers. These were largely positioned in forward parts of the line and were occupied by smaller auxiliary units of infantry and cavalry recruited from tribes elsewhere in the Roman Empire. These troops were intended to bear the main brunt of any attack, so that the crack legionaries could be held in reserve.

One good example of an auxiliary fort may be seen on the outskirts of Caernarvon, overlooking the Menai Strait towards Anglesey, SH 485624. Like the nearby medieval castle, this five-and-a-half-acre fort commanded a strategic position at the mouth of the river. Its Roman name was Segontium, i.e. 'The Powerful River'. It was garrisoned at one time by a German infantry unit recruited from the tribe of the Sunici. The site is now cut through by a modern road, but much of the stone perimeter wall remains, and the stone foundations of many of the interior buildings have been excavated. There are barracks, workshops and a granary, recognisable by stout walls buttressed and pierced by ventilation holes at the base to allow air to circulate beneath the damp-proof floor. The commandant's fine house was designed with four ranges of rooms looking onto a central courtyard. An interesting feature of the headquarters building was the construction of an underground strongroom or vault, presumably for the use of the unit paymaster.

Substantial remains of another auxiliary fort are visible at Hard Knott, guarding the head of Eskdale in Cumbria, NY 218015. Built on the mountain edge, this two-and-three-quarter-acre fort commands

spectacular views in all directions. The perimeter wall still stands 8 or 10 feet high in places. In the interior there can be seen foundations of the headquarters and commandant's house, and two granary blocks. The remaining barrack blocks and other buildings were probably made of timber. The bath-house lies below the fort to the south and a parade ground stands on an artificially levelled shelf 200 yards outside the east gate. This fort was garrisoned by Yugoslavian infantry.

At the Lunt Roman fort on the southern outskirts of Coventry, SP 344752, reconstructed lengths of earth and turf rampart together with timber towers, gate and walkways, demonstrates how very effective these defences could be. Among the internal

The Lunt Roman Fort, Coventry, Warwicks: reconstruction of rampart and gateway

Porchester, Hants: south wall of the Saxon Shore fort showing semi-circular bastions

structures also undergoing reconstruction here, is a remarkable 'giro', a circular arena, 34 yards in diameter, cut 3 feet into the subsoil, which was used as a cavalry training ground.

Originally these auxiliary forts were intended as a base for soldiers trained to fight in the open, and were therefore designed with broad, sometimes double, gateways to allow rapid sallies out into open terrain. Later, however, they acquired an increasingly defensive rather than offensive role. The gateways were remodelled and made narrower and more defensible, while the rampart was no longer merely a patrol walk, but a fighting-platform, supplied with bastions to allow flanking crossfire on an enemy attacking the walls and to act as platforms for permanently-mounted artillery machines: large mechanical slings and cross-bows powered by twisted sinew. The latest Roman forts were all of this type.

Towards the end of the Roman period, the most vulnerable area was found to be the hitherto peaceful south-east, which was increasingly subject to depredations by German pirates and raiding parties crossing the North Sea and the Channel. Massive, usually four-square, forts were built around the 'Saxon Shore' at intervals from the Wash to Southampton Water. Because of their size, these are among the most impressive monuments of Roman Britain. Their walls, 3 yards thick, often still stand 30 feet high. Their strength was recognised by later medieval castle-builders, who used them as the perimeter walls for their own defences. Medieval keeps are found snugly sheltering in the angles of Roman forts at Porchester

on Portsmouth Harbour, Hampshire, SU 625046, and at Pevensey, Sussex, now a little inland, TQ 644048. And we know that in the last century another was cleared from inside the fort at Burgh Castle in Suffolk, TG 475046. At Lympne near Hythe in Kent, TR 117342, all that remains to be seen is massive masonry blocks tumbled down the hillside below a later medieval castle. Twenty miles away at Rich-borough, however, TR 325602, excavation has cleared the interior of the best-known of these Saxon Shore forts. This lay at one end of the channel which cut the 'island' of Thanet from the mainland. Walls 4 yards thick, and still standing 25 feet high on three sides, enclosed an area of six acres. Richborough was the main point of entry into Roman Britain from the Continent. It had been the site of the original invasion bridge-head of the Roman legions, and at one time contained a magnificent four-way triumphal arch commemorating the conquest of the province. It probably towered 90 feet high, adorned with bronze statues and marble imported from Italy. But it was dismantled before the Saxon Shore fort was built and now only its enormous cruciform foundation remains. Richborough is now stranded inland as the sea line has receded; but at the other end of the Thanet channel on the north Kent coast the remains of a similar fort at Reculver, TR 227693, have been cut in half by the encroaching sea, and occasionally fragments of pottery and tile can be picked up on the shore at low tide.

In the west of Britain at least one fort of this type was built at Cardiff, ST 181766, to protect the Gla-morgan plain from Irish pirates. It was largely recon-structed at the turn of the century, and gives a good idea of how formidable these forts must have been in their heyday.

However, the best-known and most instructive series of Roman forts are those associated with Hadrian's Wall. This defensive frontier work took the form of a chain of fortified posts linked by a con-tinuous barrier sufficient in itself to form a physical obstacle to enemy troops. It would serve as a customs barrier and as a protection against cattle-rustling. But most important of all, it hindered collaboration between the still hostile tribesmen of the northern Pennines and their traditional allies in southern Scot-land. Its planning was a feat of imagination, and wit-nesses to the supreme confidence of Roman military engineers. The course chosen took the most strategic and naturally defensible line. It is set amid often spec-tacular scenery, so situated that the view to the north is as extensive as possible. From Newcastle in the east it gradually climbs to the northern rim of the Tyne valley, descending only to cross the river at Chesters (see above, p. 69). The middle section from Sew-ingshields to Greenhead runs along the Whin Sill crags, a volcanic rock cliff 200 feet high in places. Then crossing the River Irthing downstream from Gilsland, it gradually drops into the marshy Cumbrian Plain, crossing the Eden at Carlisle, and skirting the Solway Firth to Bowness. From Wallsend in the east to Bowness in the west is a distance of seventy-five miles. The sheer magnitude of the undertaking cannot fail to impress. Over a million cubic yards of stone needed to be quarried, transported and then built in position. The wall alone required forty thousand tons of stone per mile, not counting that used for ancillary structures like forts.

The construction work was allotted to military working parties, each responsible for a length of about 45 yards. The stretch was marked at each end with small roughly-cut inscriptions set in the face of the wall, giving the name of the unit responsible. The wall was designed with a width of 10 Roman feet (i.e. about $9\frac{1}{2}$ feet in modern measurements). Although today it nowhere stands higher than 9 or 10 feet, originally it must have stood 15 feet high to the walk-way, with a defensive parapet and battle-ments in front rising a further 5 or 6 feet. The wall was composed of a rubble core faced with uniform blocks of dressed stone. Good freestone could be quarried for the first forty-five miles of its length. But

Firth of Forth

R. Forth

Loch Lomond

Rough Castle

R. Kelvin

Castlehill

Firth of Clyde

Clyde

R

R. Almond

THE ANTONINE WALL

HADRIAN'S WALL

North Tyne

Birrens

Irthing

Housesteads

Carrawbrough

Chesters

Wallsend

South Shields

Corbridge

South Tyne

Newcastle

signal stations

Bowness

Carlisle

Stanwix

0   MILES   30

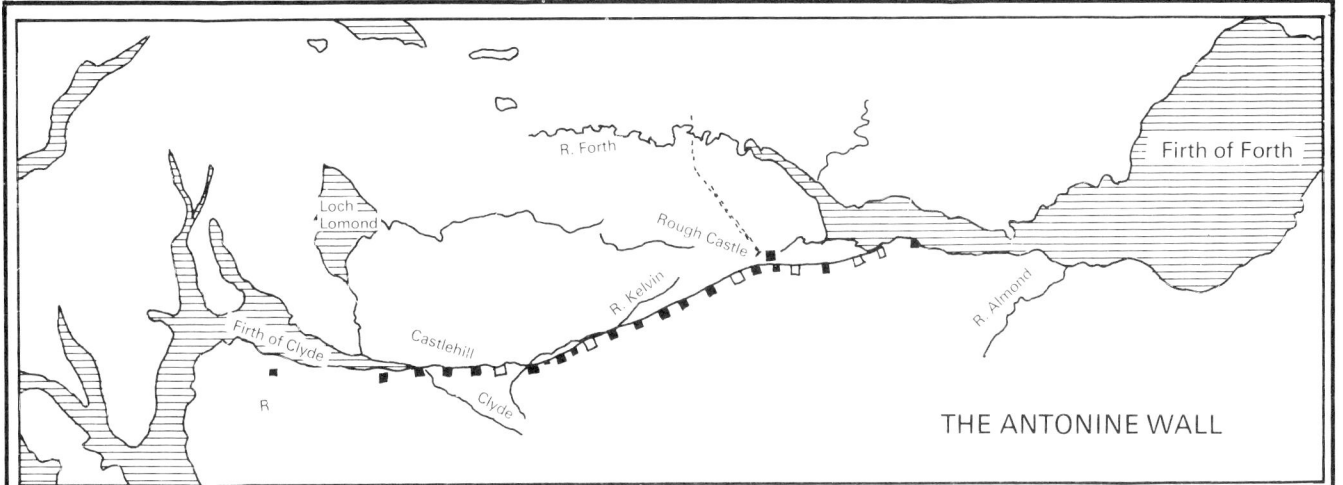

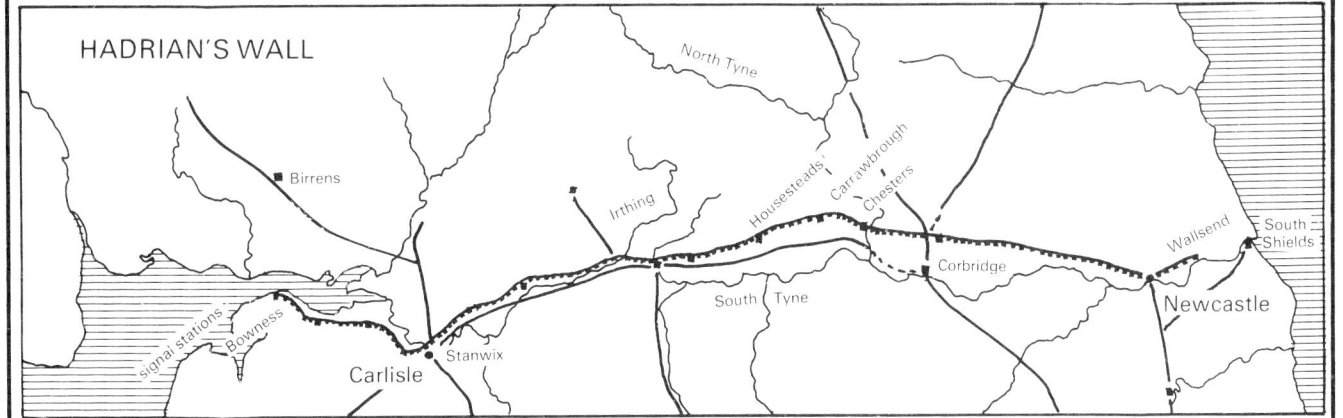

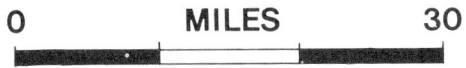

Plans of the Antonine Wall and Hadrian's Wall

Hadrian's Wall along the Whin Sill Crags, Northumberland

west of the Irthing limestone gives way to a soft sand-stone unsuitable for building. However, the wet climate ensured plentiful supplies of good Cumbrian turf, a sturdy building material approved by the military manuals. And for a further thirty miles the wall and its associated forts were first built of sods, and only later faced with stone.

Seven yards or so in front of the wall a large V-shaped ditch was dug about 9 yards wide and 9 feet deep. The spoil was spread in a low bank on the outer lip so as to deepen the ditch without affording cover for an attacker. In places this ditch had to be cut through solid rock. On Tepper Moor just west of Chesters, NY 875717, large blocks of volcanic rock still lie in the bottom of the ditch, drilled for wedges but never broken up for clearance. This ditch runs for the entire length of the wall, except where the sea or high crags made it unnecessary. Rearwards of the wall, usually 30 or 40 yards to the south, sometimes more depending on the terrain, was constructed a more elaborate earthwork known as the 'vallum'. This consisted of a flat-bottomed ditch, about 10 feet deep, 3 yards wide at the bottom and 7 yards at the top. On either side a flat 10-yard platform separated this ditch from a turf bank 7 yards wide and usually about 6 feet high. The whole system occupies a strip of ground 40 yards in depth, and was presumably in-tended to keep unauthorised personnel from approaching the frontier. Gaps in the vallum opposite each fort allowed traffic to pass at recognised check-

points. A military road ran between the vallum and the wall.

Along the line of the wall itself at intervals of one Roman mile (1620 yards) small squarish fortlets were built. They measured about 23 by 18 yards internally, and provided accommodation for between thirty and fifty men. Each had two gateways about 3 yards wide, one to the south and one to the north passing through the line of the wall itself. Between each of these 'mile-castles', lay two stone turrets, about 7 yards square and with walls a yard thick. These were presumably used as watchtowers for surveying enemy territory to the north, and signalling along the line of the wall and to the rear in case of attack.

The most interesting and spectacular stretches of wall can be seen either side of Housesteads, along crags overlooking Crag Lough and Broomlee Lough, NY 784681, and farther west along Walltown and Peel Crags, NY 677666, 755677. Unlike the rampart of a hillfort or medieval castle, the wall was not intended for use as a fighting-platform, but merely for foot patrols. The large number of broad gateways provided were specially designed to facilitate the kind of open offensive warfare favoured by the Roman army. Forts lay on or astride the wall. At Chesters not just one but three separate gates lie on the northern side, allowing the rapid deployment of cavalry squadrons to the fore. Later, however, when the wall assumed a more defensive role in common with other Roman fortifications, these gates were narrowed. The double-leaved doorways of the mile-castles were reduced to small posterns or blocked altogether.

Some sixteen forts were added to the line of the wall. At Chesters, where the wall crossed the North Tyne, NY 912701, a lovely spot in the water-meadows was chosen for a large cavalry fort manned, during the third century at least, by a detachment of Spanish horsemen from the Asturias. A fine example set amid dramatically rocky scenery can be seen at Housesteads, NY 784681. The Roman name of this fort was Vercovicium, i.e. 'Hill Station'. During the third century it was garrisoned by a thousand-strong unit of Belgian infantry. Farther west, on a promontory overlooking a bend in the River Irthing, is the fort of Birdoswald, NY 615663, its original name Camboglanna, 'The Crooked Bend'. When fully manned, the wall garrison probably amounted to some twelve thousand men made up from various auxiliary units and commanded from a large cavalry fort at Stanwix, now lying beneath the northern suburb of Carlisle. Taking into account the line of signal stations which continued the line of defence around the Cumbrian coast, the Stanwix headquarters lay not at one end, but in the very centre of the frontier system, and gave additional strength at a point where the low lie of the ground rendered the frontier more vulnerable to attack.

Behind the line of the wall lay supply depots. At Corbridge, straddling the Stanegate road, NY 983648, a supply-base and arsenal with store-houses, granaries and workshops, was manned by a 500-strong cavalry unit from the headquarters at Stanwix. To the far east at the mouth of the Tyne the fort at South Shields, NZ 365679, allowed provisioning by sea. At one time this depot contained no less than twenty-two granary blocks, although later some of these were divided with partitions to convert them into living quarters. The garrison was made up at least in part of a detachment of boatmen from the River Tigris in Mesopotamia, presumably brought in because of their skill in navigating the shoals of the undredged Tyne.

Tradesmen and others found the military garrisons profitable, and civilian settlements often grew up outside the main gates of Roman forts, offering taverns, shops, brothels and other services to off-duty servicemen. From about AD 200 serving soldiers were allowed to marry officially, and no doubt these towns could provide some sort of accommodation for wives and families.

For a brief period under Hadrian's successor Antoninus, from about AD 140–162 the frontier was

WALL

BATHS

RIVER
NORTH
TYNE

0   **YARDS**   400

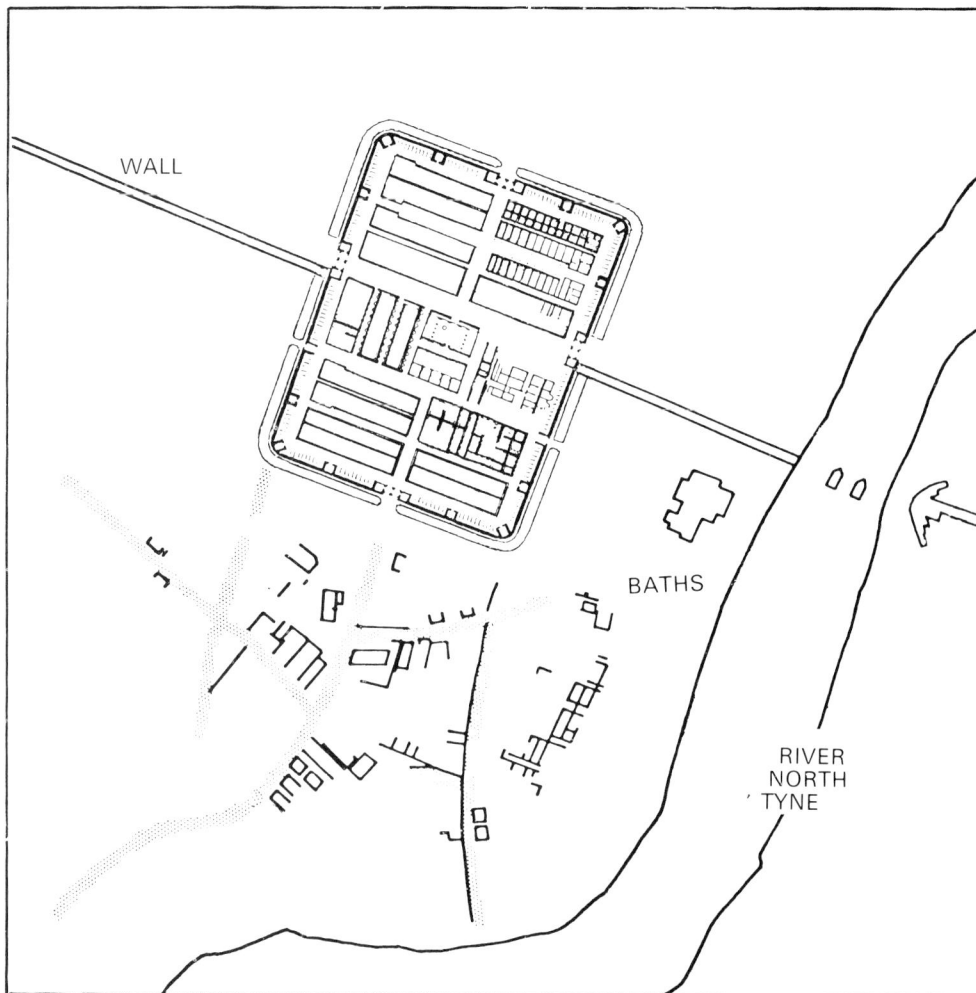

Chesters, Northumberland: plan of the Roman fort, showing its relationship to the bridge and (revealed by air photography) the area of civilian settlement outside the south gate.

advanced farther north to a line running between the estuaries of the Forth and Clyde. A further wall was built running for thirty-six miles along the brow of a more or less continuous range of hills overlooking level and often swampy land to the north. It runs not along the crest of the hills, but on the forward slope, with accompanying forts on the hilltops wherever possible. The Antonine Wall was provided with a good heavy rubble foundation, drained by culverts. But the wall itself was constructed entirely of turf. It is less than 5 yards wide at the base with faces sloping inwards about 70 degrees. Originally it was probably little more than 10 feet high, with an additional wooden breastwork supplied at the top. Now badly degraded, it stands little more than 5 feet high. But if the wall itself was less formidable than that farther south, the fronting ditch was very much stronger, and is the most obvious feature of the defence at the present day. It lies 7 yards or more in front of the wall, 13 yards wide and usually 12 feet deep, although sometimes very much less where it had to be cut through solid rock. There was no vallum to the rear. Particularly good stretches are preserved south and west of Falkirk, NS 834798–857798.

The forts are smaller and more closely spaced than those on Hadrian's Wall. On average they lie only two miles apart; and between them there is evidence of smaller patrol posts or signal stations, although the visible remains of these are negligible. Like the wall itself, the ramparts of the forts are built for the most part with turf. And although the headquarters buildings and granaries were invariably given stone foundations, all other buildings seem to have been entirely wooden constructions. The forts were regularly surrounded by double or triple lines of defensive ditches. Of an original eighteen or so forts, the best preserved is the smallest: the one-acre fort of Rough Castle, west of Falkirk, NS 843799. This fort was garrisoned by a detachment of Belgians under the command of one Flavius Betto, a centurion seconded from the 20th Legion. He had overseen the construction of the headquarters building, and it was probably this man who was responsible for having dug 20 yards north of the ditch the defensive system known to the military manuals as 'lilies'. An early equivalent of a barbed-wire entanglement, this consisted of ten rows of small oval pits, $2\frac{1}{2}$ feet deep, with pointed stakes at the bottom, and concealed with brushwood. (One or two are left open to inspection.) The best kind of committed soldier, Flavius Betto had erected an altar in honour of Victory, now to be seen in Edinburgh Museum.

The Mile-Castle at Cawfields, Northumberland. NY 729669

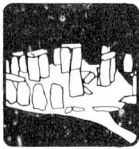

SACRED AND CEREMONIAL SITES

Like their contemporaries in southern France and northern Spain who executed the extensive cave-paintings, we may assume that the earliest inhabitants of Britain engaged in some sort of ritual or ceremony to ensure the fertility of both themselves and the herds of animals on which they depended. Perhaps sacred places were recognised, but the nature of their economy was not such as to allow for the construction of any substantial ceremonial structures.

Although the Neolithic revolution gave man a greater degree of control over his environment, he was still subject to the vagaries of natural phenomena. Good seasons were necessary to the farmer; and like cattle, the flint-mines could prove sterile. But Mother Earth, the womb from which he came, and back to which he would be given at death, could ensure his sustenance by its fertility. From this time onwards we find that society devoted considerable effort to the construction and maintenance of sacred structures which include some of the best-known monuments of early Britain.

Archaeology provides evidence for some early shrines of a purely local character, intended to placate Nature in a detailed way. For instance, at the Grimes Graves flint-mines one shaft had failed to produce nodules of a good quality; but before finally abandoning it, the miners had resorted to sympathetic magic in an attempt to restore its fertility. On a ledge in front

of the entrance to one of the tunnels, they stood a small 4½-inch chalk statuette of a heavily pregnant woman, in front of which they heaped a pile of flint nodules, a stack of antler pickaxes and a carved chalk phallus—a universal generative symbol. (Similar phalluses have been found in flint-mines elsewhere at Blackpatch and Cissbury in Sussex.) A roughly-carved wooden idol, 6 inches high and prominently phallic, had been placed in a simple wooden enclosure constructed of pegs and horizontal sticks, at the base of one of the Neolithic wooden trackways crossing the Somerset Levels. Presumably this was a foundation-deposit intended to secure its stability. (One is reminded of the phallus carved on the Roman bridge at Chesters, see p. 69).

Of conventional communal 'temples' of this date, only one possible example is known: at Stanydale in Shetland, HU 285502. This is a massive stone building, heel-shaped in plan, with walls 4 yards thick enclosing a large oval interior chamber measuring 13 by 7 yards. The walls probably stood no more than 6 feet high, and the entire structure had been roofed with timber and thatched. A single entrance is located in the centre of the flattened edge of the heel. Facing the entrance on the farther interior wall are six shallow recesses, perhaps intended to house stone or wooden idols of the Grimes Graves/Somerset Levels kind. Although it has something in common with local

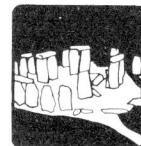

heel-shaped tombs, the forecourts of which seem to have been used for ceremonial purposes, the structure is quite unparalleled elsewhere. We are unlikely ever to know for certain what function it served. But it may be related to an arc of several standing stones situated some 14 or 15 yards to the south.

However, the most significant innovation of Neolithic times was the development of the large circular ritual or ceremonial enclosure known as a 'henge', the most celebrated and complicated example of which is Stonehenge on Salisbury Plain. Their construction was a large-scale undertaking, implying the existence of a society rich enough to devote considerable resources of manpower under the direction of centralised authority of some kind. This seems to have been an insular development, since nothing of the kind is found on the Continent. Between eighty and ninety henge monuments are visible in Britain, varying enormously in size and present condition. Basically the henge consists simply of a huge circular enclosure formed by a bank, and internal ditch, breached by one or two entrances. Many of these enclosures contained timber structures, some of which were later replaced by more or less elaborate stone settings. The surrounding embankment was patently not defensive in any way. It served to define a level arena and provide a stand for spectators to watch whatever ceremonies were being enacted inside. The internal ditch (found on the exterior only in the case of Stonehenge), actively separated the spectator from the participants, suggesting a distinct priestly caste within a reserved sacred precinct. Sometimes these enclosures contained merely a series of small ritual pits, which excavation has shown to contain cremations or votive offerings of valuable objects like stone axes. At Maumbury Rings outside Dorchester (a henge later converted into a Roman amphitheatre), SY 690899, chalk phalluses were found. And at Barford in Warwickshire (a monument now no longer visible from the surface), SP 289629, a pit dug outside the entrance contained no less than seven quern-stones.

Other henges contained settings of great timber posts or upright stones, some simply, others elaborately arranged. Although timber structures have left no surface remains, they have sometimes been discovered by aerial photography and subsequently excavated. The classic example is a site known as 'Woodhenge', which lies on the A345 just two miles north-east of Stonehenge in Wiltshire, SU 150434. This consists of a ditch cut about 6 feet deep and 4 yards across, surrounded by bank, now sadly degraded and partly ploughed out, the whole having a diameter of about 75 yards. There was a single entrance to the north marked by four post-holes indicating a squared timber gateway. On the interior were found six concentric circles of closely spaced postholes (now marked in concrete). Possibly these should be interpreted as an enormous ring-like timber building, the largest posts supporting the roof-ridge, while the lesser supported the roof as it sloped outwards. A small open space must be assumed at the centre of the plan. Alternatively, it may be imagined as a timber equivalent of Stonehenge, consisting of circles of free-standing posts, with some of the larger ones supporting lintels. At the very centre, now marked by a small cairn of flints, was found the crouched burial of a three-year-old infant who had been killed by a blow which split the skull in two. This must clearly be regarded as a foundation-sacrifice, buried at the heart of a temple whose other rituals and ceremonies we can only guess. It is one of the few pieces of evidence we have for human sacrifice in prehistoric Britain.

Just a 100 yards to the north of Woodhenge, lies the massive site of Durrington Walls, the second largest henge monument in existence. More than 540 yards in diameter, it encloses some 35 acres lying either side of the A345. The flat-bottomed ditch, originally 18 feet deep and 20 yards wide, would have taken an estimated 900 thousand man-hours to complete, which is witness of enormous social motivation at so early a date. The embankment, now largely

103

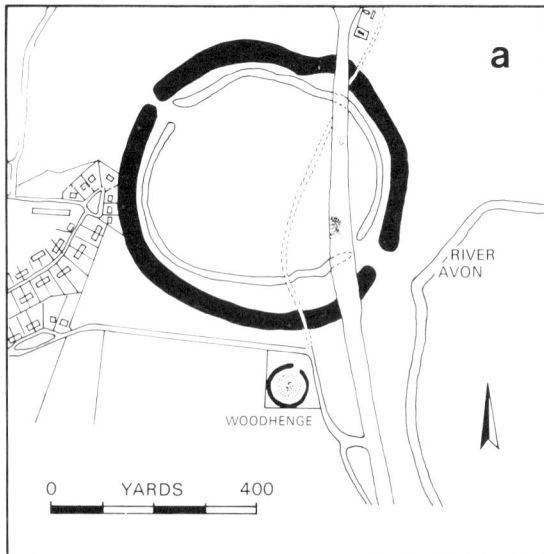

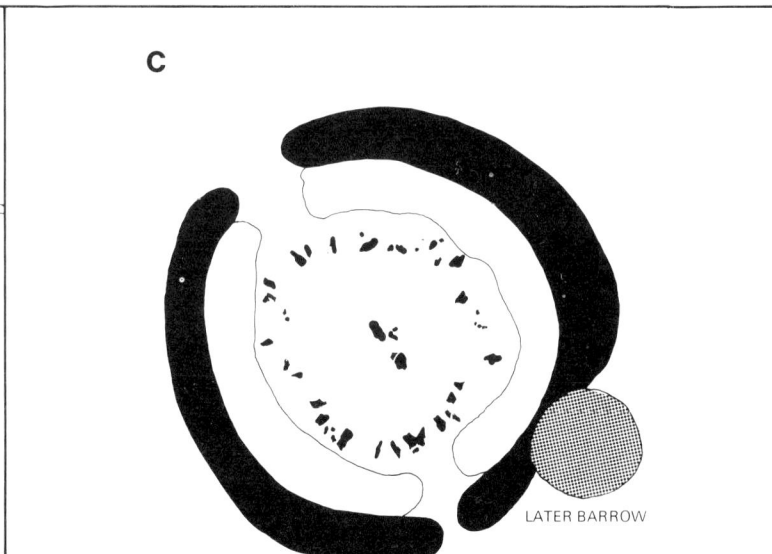

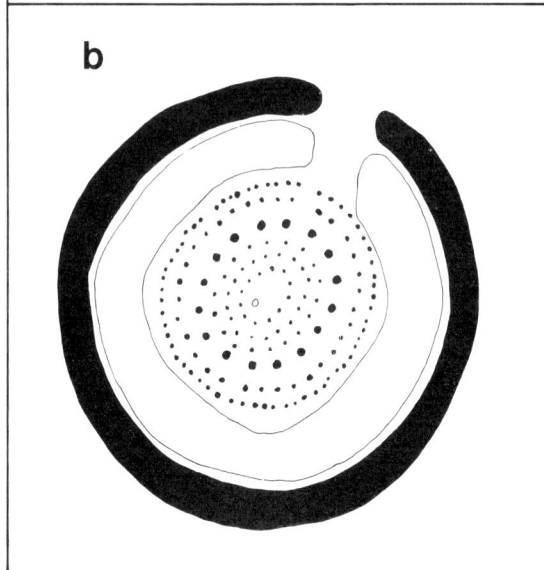

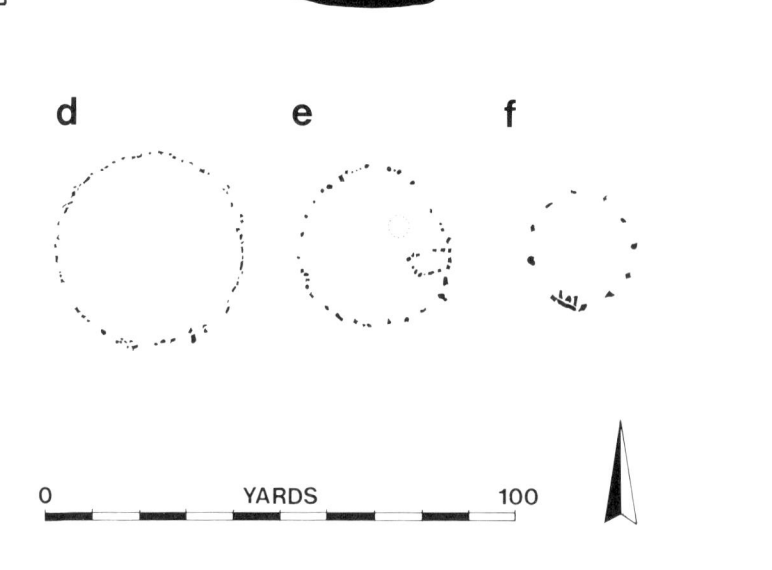

Comparative plans of henge monuments: (a) Durrington Walls with Woodhenge, Wilts; (b) Woodhenge, Wilts; (c) Arbor Low, Derbys; (d) Rollright Stones, Oxfordshire; (e) Castlerigg, Cumbria; (f) Easter Aquorthies, Aberdeenshire

ploughed out, was breached by two opposing entrances. On the interior lay two timber settings of the Woodhenge type, a larger one of six concentric circles 44 yards across, and a smaller one of only two circles 17 yards in diameter. They were connected by an avenue of posts. These two circles were destroyed during the building of the A345, but aerial photographs have revealed the existence of further timber structures within the enclosure, which must have represented a particularly important and complex cult centre for the region.

Similar henge monuments exist in other parts of the country. At Arminghall in Norfolk, TG 240060, two concentric ditches with a bank between, are breached by a single entrance, facing which stood an open horseshoe arrangement of eight massive oak posts. To judge from the depth of their sockets, these tree-trunks, 3 feet in diameter, must have stood 20 or 30 feet high. The posts had been stripped of their bark, and may possibly have been painted or carved in some fashion. Aerial photographs reveal that, as with other such sacred sites, a cluster of prehistoric burials accumulated around the Arminghall henge over the centuries.

At Thornborough in North Yorkshire three henge circles, each about 270 yards across, are laid out at equal intervals in a straight line almost a mile in length, SE 281801–289789. Excavation suggests that originally the 10-feet banks were coated with a deposit of gypsum crystals, perhaps in imitation of the brilliant white chalk henges of the southern downland. On the Mendips in Somerset near Priddy, ST 540527, stands an alignment of no less than four 200-yard circles extending over a distance of three-quarters of a mile. Like Arminghall, both the Thornborough and Priddy henges were associated with barrow cemeteries. The association of religion and death is almost inevitable. And although these monuments are not themselves primarily sepulchral, it is natural that men should choose to be buried in the vicinity of their sacred sites.

At 'The Sanctuary' lying beside the A4 as it crosses Overton Hill west of Marlborough in Wiltshire, SU 118679, a Woodhenge-like structure of six concentric timber circles was demolished in favour of just two larger circles of upright stones. (These were removed in the last century, but are now set out with concrete markers.) From here two parallel rows of stones form a ceremonial avenue following roughly the line of the B4003 road northwards. It is best seen at West Kennet, SU 112684. The avenue consists of roughly a hundred pairs of stones, about 10 feet high and 16 yards apart, erected at intervals of about 28 yards. Contemporary graves have been found against two of the stones.

The Kennet avenue traces a relatively sinuous course for one and a half miles north-west from The Sanctuary towards Avebury, where lies the most stupendous of all henge-monuments in Britain, SU 103699. One of the largest ceremonial monuments in Europe, it contains within its twenty-eight-and-a-half-acre enclosure the greater part of the present-day village of Avebury. The seventeenth-century antiquary John Aubrey said that comparing Stonehenge with Avebury was like comparing a parish church with a cathedral! The perimeter consists of a massive circular embankment of chalk, about 470 yards in diameter, still 20 feet high and 25 yards across, quarried from a flat-bottomed inner ditch, now half-silted up but originally 30 feet deep and 14 yards across. There were four original entrances: north, south, east and west, through which modern roads now run. Around the inner edge of the ditch stood a circle of some hundred massive upright sarsen monoliths. These are natural sandstone blocks hauled from the nearby Marlborough Downs, the largest weighing over 40 tons. Many have been cleared away by farmers during the last few centuries, but thirty still remain in place, and the position of others has been determined by excavation. On the interior there are the remains of two smaller stone circles, each about 115 yards in diameter, one of which enclosed a separ-

Avebury, Wilts: henge monument

ate horseshoe setting. Other sarsens were erected at the entrances.

Most henge-monuments are very much smaller. A good example is that at Arbor Low in the Peak District of Derbyshire, SK 160636. Eighty-four yards in diameter, the embankment stands to a height of about 7 feet, built of limestone quarried from the inner ditch, 10 yards across and originally some 6 feet deep. Fifty or so large stones form a circle, containing within it a small horseshoe setting. All the stones are now recumbent. No sockets have been found, and it must be assumed that they were originally held upright by small blocking stones. Another fine example is to be found 1000 feet above sea level at Cairnpapple Hill, West Lothian, NS 987717. Excavation reveals a complex history for this site. It had always been associated with burials, and was eventually dominated by an enormous cairn lying eccentric within the henge and overlapping part of the circle of stones. Farther to the north in the Orkneys two impressive, albeit ruined, examples stand facing each other on the rocky shore of the Loch of Stenness. In the Ring of Brodgar, HY 294134, almost half the original sixty stones remain. In the Ring of Stenness, HY 306126, although

only four stones survive, they form an impressive ruin, the largest stone standing some 17 feet high.

In addition to these true 'henge' monuments there are some seven hundred smaller stone circles in Britain without any surrounding ditch or embankment. Their relationship to the henges is uncertain. They seem to be rather later in date, ascribable to the Bronze Age for the most part, and perhaps represent local religious centres built in general imitation of the henge. They have a rather different distribution from the henges. All are found in parts of the country where stone is easily come by; none occurs in the southeast or in East Anglia, and only the rare example in the Midlands. They vary greatly in size from a mere 3 or 4 yards across to 130 yards in diameter. Very often they are ruined, with just one or two stones remaining, the others having been broken up by farmers to make cultivation easier. In upland areas the subsequent build-up of peat reduces the apparent height of many. During the eighteenth and nineteenth centuries, some circles were reconstructed faultily by landowners with a romantic taste for 'druidical' antiquity. And some altogether new stone circles were erected at this time, like the Regency 'Druid's Temple'

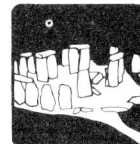

folly built on the fells near Masham in the North Riding, SE 174787, under the direction of William Danby of Swinton Hall.

Many stone circles stand in isolation, apparently unrelated to any other monument. Others are associated with burials, and some are parts of complex arrangements of circles, rows and avenues or single monoliths, suggesting elaborate cult centres. One such complex is found at Stanton Drew in Avon, ST 601634. It consists of an alignment of three stone circles, two with the remains of stone avenues merging as they proceed northwards towards the River Chew, and a monolithic horseshoe setting built of two large uprights with a third recumbent stone between. The largest circle is 120 yards in diameter, and twenty-seven of its original thirty stones are still visible. The other circles, 33 and 46 yards in diameter, are less complete. The three circles seem to have been aligned with Hautville's Quoit, a large monolith standing 500 yards to the north on the opposite side of the river.

Four miles north-east of Liskeard on the eastern flank of Bodmin Moor lies another important group known as The Hurlers, SX 258714. This consists of three almost contiguous stone circles aligned north-east/south-west. They have diameters of 37, 45 and 35 yards respectively. The stones were shaped, and excavation shows that care was taken to ensure that their tops were all at the same level above ground—achieved by setting them in pits of different depths. The interior of the northernmost circle was paved with granite, and a rough pavement, 6 feet wide, ran between that and the centre circle.

Other good examples of circles in the region include that at Fernacre, close to the Bronze Age settlement on Rough Tor, SX 144800; and in the farthest south-west of the peninsula the Merry Maidens, SW 432245, with two large monoliths known as The Pipers standing in alignment about 400 yards north-east. Many stone circles, rows and isolated monoliths can be found on Dartmoor, notably on Shovel Down,

SX 660860, and south-west of the Grimspound settlement at Merrivale, SX 553746. In Dorset the best example to be seen is probably the Nine Stones Circle, a small ring of only nine stones just 8 yards in diameter, standing by the side of the A35 west of Winterbourne Abbas, SY 611904.

In the Midlands the sole example visible is the Rollright Stones, lying beside the ancient ridge track where it forms the Oxford–Warwickshire border, SP 296308. This is a circle of about 33 yards diameter, containing in all seventy weather-worn sarsens. (It should not be confused with the Whispering Knights, the remains of a chambered tomb close by, see p. 126.) A few yards to the east stands the King Stone, an isolated monolith, $8\frac{1}{2}$ feet high and 5 feet in width. In the frequent juxtaposition of 'male' monoliths with 'female' circular elements, a basic symbolism, conscious or unconscious, can be discerned. Perhaps they were thought to evoke some regenerative function in the universal task of sustaining life.

Very many stone circles occur in all parts of northern Britain. In Cumbria the Castlerigg circle has a particularly spectacular setting on the fells just above Keswick, NY 292236. About forty stones are laid out in a somewhat pear-shaped setting, with a maximum diameter of some 37 yards, with a further rectangular setting of ten stones touching the inner circumference on the eastern side. Farther to the east beyond Penrith, Long Meg and her Daughters, NY 571373, consists of an oval setting of sixty out of an original seventy stones, with a maximum diameter of 120 yards, and an outlying monolith 12 feet high (Long Meg), standing 20 yards to the south-west. Seven hundred yards north-east a smaller circle of just eleven stones (Little Meg) originally surrounded a barrow burial.

Of the numerous stone circles found in the Western Isles, a particularly complex series of four lie within a radius of 2 miles at Callanish on the shore of Loch Roag in Lewis, NB 213330. The major ring, 14 yards across, encloses a burial cairn 8 yards in diameter;

Castlerigg, Keswick, Cumbria, stone circle

Callanish, Hebrides: aerial view of stone circle with alignments

and extending from it in a cross-like formation can be seen the remains of no less than four stone alignments: an avenue to the north, and single rows south, east and west.

In the north-east of mainland Scotland, in Aberdeen, Banff and Kincardine, is found a distinct regional type of monument known rather misleadingly as a 'recumbent' stone circle. That at Easter Aquorthies near Inverurie, NJ 733208, is a typical example. Nine stones form a circle 20 yards in diameter. But instead of being more or less equal in size and height, a 'focus' is formed from two particularly large stones between which lies one prostrate monolith, while the remaining stones gradually lessen in height as they lie farther away to the opposite side of the circle. A short distance to the north, a similar monument can be seen at Loanhead of Daviot, NJ 747288, with a Bronze Age burial cairn on the interior.

Easter Aquorthies, Aberdeenshire: 'recumbent' setting in stone circle

All sorts of isolated monoliths or 'menhirs' can be found marked on Ordnance Survey maps, apparently quite unrelated to any stone circle or other monument. Some may themselves represent the surviving vestige of a stone circle or chambered tomb. But they are impossible to date, and their precise significance is elusive. Bronze Age burials have occasionally been found at the base of some. Others have been erected in relatively recent times to act as boundary marks or as rubbing posts for cattle. As late as early medieval times, superstitious people were said to have worshipped stones like these, as such. The most impressive examples seem all to come from north Yorkshire. Close to the A1 at Boroughbridge, SE 391666, stand the Devil's Arrows, a row of three roughly aligned stones, between 18 and 22 feet high, brought six miles from the south from a quarry near Knaresborough. Another, called Wade's Stone, stands close to the presumed end of the Wade's Causeway Roman road near to the Goldsborough signal station, NZ 829144. In the churchyard at Rudston, TA 097677, stands the tallest monolith in Britain, $25\frac{1}{2}$ feet high and roughly 6 by $2\frac{1}{2}$ feet at the base. A further part must lie buried beneath the ground. This was apparently quarried some ten miles to the north on the coast at Cayton Bay. These are all gritstone monoliths, the surface of which seems to have been at least partially dressed. The vertical fluting that is now a characteristic part of their appearance is simply due to weathering.

Monoliths like these occasionally bear small areas of 'cup-and-ring' markings: groups of simple saucer-like depressions, often surrounded with one or more concentric grooves. Some are visible on the north face of Long Meg, for example. They also occur on natural outcrops of rock. There are several splendid examples to be found within a mile of each other near Wigtown in south-west Scotland at: Drumtroddan Farm, NX 363447, Big Balcraig, 374440, and Clachan, 376445. Many occur in Northumberland, perhaps most spectacularly at Roughtinglinn, four or five miles

north of Yeavering Bell hillfort, where an area of rock 20 by 13 yards is covered with several dozen markings. The fact that similar markings occur on chambered tombs suggests that they should be attributed to the Bronze Age. That they are clearly significant in some way is obvious, but their exact function is obscure. Many occur on vertical or even overhanging surfaces, so they could never have held liquid—let alone blood, as sometimes supposed! But they could well have been painted. It has been argued that they are set out with a degree of geometrical sophistication which relates them to the design of some of the greater standing circles (see below, p. 113).

Excavation shows that, like medieval cathedrals, the great stone monuments often had long and complex histories of modification and rebuildings. The most famous and complex of them all is the case of Stonehenge in Wiltshire, SU 123422. What we see now is just the ruin of merely the last of five building phases. The earliest structure, built in Neolithic times around about 2600 BC, was a relatively simple henge monument. This consisted merely of an earthen bank, originally about 5 feet high, surrounded by a ditch and breached by a single entrance gap to the north-east, outside which stood a single stone, an unshaped block of sarsen standing 15 feet high (the 'Heel Stone'). Two smaller stones set in the entrance possibly formed a gateway of some kind. Immediately inside the bank was dug a circle of fifty-six pits, the position of which is marked today in white chalk. They lay about 5 yards apart, varying in size from $2\frac{1}{2}$ to 6 feet in diameter, but regularly dug about $2-3\frac{1}{2}$ feet deep. Their purpose is obscure, although it seems clear that they were not intended to hold posts. They seem to have been filled with chalk rubble, and then reopened from time to time to receive the remains of cremations: burnt earth and human bones, either scattered or held together as if contained in bags. No cremation site has been found and perhaps they were brought from some distance at recognised festivals.

Just possibly there may have been a small central timber structure at this earliest phase.

Then about five hundred years later, at the opening of the Bronze Age, significant alterations were put in hand. Now the first stones were erected: a double horseshoe 25 and 29 yards across. These were made from about eighty blocks of distinctive dolerite ('bluestone'), brought for the purpose from the Prescelli Hills of Pembrokeshire (see p. 49), and each weighing some four tons when shaped. The original gateway stones were dismantled and the entrance-gap widened. A ditch and bank was constructed either side of the Heel Stone, to form a broad avenue 13 yards across, running for some two miles to the banks of the River Avon near West Amesbury. Only the stretch of the Avenue closest to Stonehenge is visible from the surface; the remainder has been obliterated by cultivation although the ditches can be seen easily enough from the air. It has been suggested that this avenue was specially constructed to mark the triumphal final stage of the bluestones' 240-mile journey. Certainly their presence at Stonehenge is witness of a powerful religious or social motivation, and a processional arrival is not out of the question.

Possibly the double-horseshoe shape was fortuitous. Perhaps it was intended to form a full circle. Certain it is that shortly afterwards the bluestone monument was dismantled and replaced by a number of massive sarsen stones, averaging about 20–30 tons apiece, brought from the Marlborough Downs twenty miles to the north. These were carefully shaped and erected in the circle and horseshoe monument which still survives. The sarsen circle consisted of thirty uprights, 7 by $3\frac{1}{2}$ feet square and about $13\frac{1}{2}$ feet high, with another 3 to 5 feet buried in the ground. They are placed at intervals of about $3\frac{1}{2}$ feet, and support an equal number of 10-feet lintels, which brings the total height to about 16 feet. The lintels are each dovetailed into one another, and mortised to tenons cut on each of the uprights. The lintels are regularly curved on the inside so as to form a true circle 32

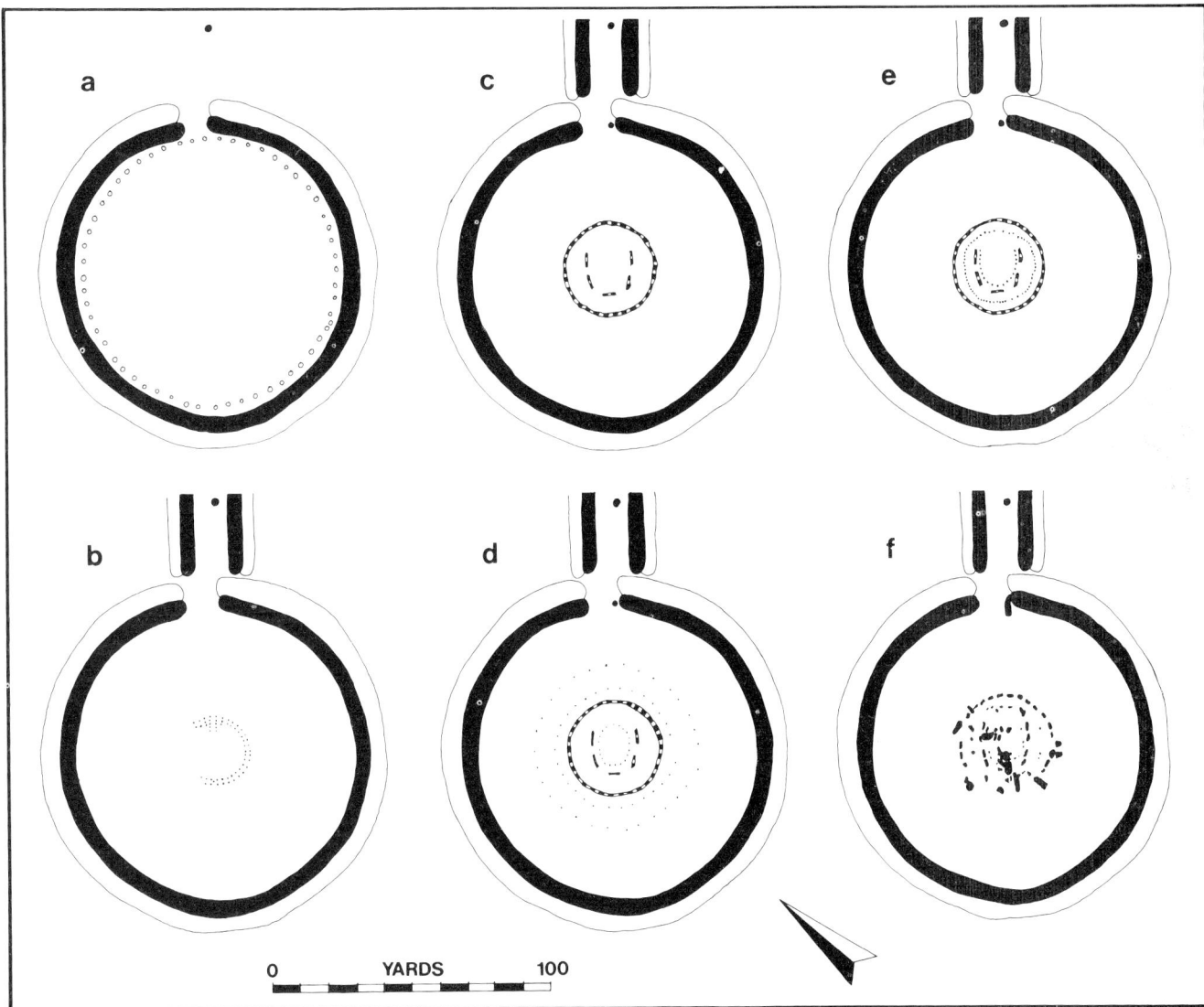

Stonehenge, Wilts: (a–e) stages in its development; (f) present position of stones

Stonehenge, Wilts: aerial view

yards in diameter. Inside this circle stood a horseshoe arrangement of five large free-standing sarsen trilithons, i.e. two uprights supporting a third, and standing 24 feet high. The largest of these uprights weighs some 45 tons. Other sarsens were set in the entrance to form a new gateway, but only one now remains and that fallen (the 'Slaughter Stone').

Then it was decided to reuse the bluestones. Twenty or more were set up in an oval on the inside of the great horseshoe, and holes for two concentric circles of the remainder were dug surrounding the sarsen ring. But then this plan was abandoned and the oval setting demolished. Finally, about 1800 BC, a single circle of sixty bluestones was erected running between the horseshoe and the circle, and a horse-shoe of nineteen inside the great sarsen horseshoe. The largest of these stood about 12 feet high in front of the central sarsen trilithon. It is now fallen beneath a tumble of sarsens, and because of its position was popularly known among early antiquaries as the 'Altar Stone'. (This stone is not actually a dolerite but a sandstone from near Milford Haven, see above, p. 58.)

This erection was achieved with the aid of rollers, levers and ramps, but using tools little more sophisticated than those found in the flint-mines. The dressing of the stones, their jointing and accurate construction were once thought to point to the influence of the urban civilisations of the East Mediterranean: Minoan Crete and Mycenaean Greece. Objects found in barrow

burials of this date certainly point to links between southern England and the East Mediterranean in early times. But recent redating by scientific methods shows that Stonehenge, unique in Europe, was created some five hundred years before the earliest Mycenaean civilisation of Greece began.

From medieval times these enigmatic monuments have aroused speculation and superstition. Many were associated with the Devil, and folklore commonly accounted for stone circles by identifying them as, for instance, groups of dancing girls turned to stone for some misdemeanour (e.g. the Merry Maidens and outlying Pipers, see p. 107). They have been associated mistakenly with the Pharoahs and with the Phoenicians, and in more recent times in an age of computers and space travel the speculation has become increasingly bizarre.

It is evident that such enormous structures requiring so great an investment of labour, and yet neither domestic nor defensive, must have been undertaken under the influence of some very compelling religious or social motive. Their existence implies a high degree of regional organisation and priestly authority. But their meaning remains elusive. Even if we could infer any general ceremony or ritual from the structure of such monuments, we can do no more than guess at the myth they embodied. It is well-nigh impossible to deduce religious beliefs from purely material evidence. But there can be no doubt that the very fact of their circularity was in some way significant.

Professor Alexander Thom has demonstrated that while the great majority of these stone structures form true circles, as at Stanton Drew, the Merry Maidens or Rollright Stones, others are not truly circular but carefully planned ovals like Long Meg and her Daughters, pear-shapes like Castlerigg, or flattened circles as at Callanish. Each design demanded a sophisticated knowledge of geometrical principles. He goes further to conclude that these structures served various calendar and astronomical functions, indicating the point of rising and setting of the sun at the solstices, and may also have been used for the observation of the moon and some of the more prominent stars. For example, at Callanish the northern avenue is exactly aligned on Mt Clisham to the south, which could be a horizon marker for the moon setting at its most southerly mean declination, while the western row of stones points exactly to the two equinoctial sunsets. Most significantly, Professor Thom has established beyond all reasonable doubt that these monuments were constructed on sight-lines framed by major constellations in the position they would have been in the centuries between 2000 and 1700 BC when the majority of stone circles were erected. It seems undeniable that they were designed with great care by people with a sophisticated understanding of mathematical principles. Of course the fact that these structures were laid out in accordance with certain astronomical sightings (just like a modern church), does not mean that they were ever subsequently used as observatories, even some of the time. But preoccupation with the returning seasons seems evident. The two functions of calendar and religious sanctuary are commonly related, even in modern times. It is just possible that the sun and moon may have been worshipped for themselves, or as an outward sign of some interior cosmic mechanism. But in the absence of written records we are still no nearer understanding their basic beliefs. It may be significant that about 500 BC the Greek geographer Hecataeus recorded travellers' tales reporting that the inhabitants of Britain honoured the sun god more than any other, and had built sacred enclosures and a magnificent circular temple, adorned with rich offerings.

The popular connection between monuments such as Stonehenge and the druids is a mistaken one. The druids were a Celtic priesthood who flourished in Britain only for two or three centuries prior to the Roman occupation. When the druids first appeared Stonehenge was more than 1500 years old and may already have fallen into ruins. But if the druids were not responsible for Stonehenge, what was the nature

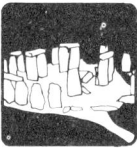

of this religion that so captured the romantic imagination for centuries? We learn of the druids from writers like Caesar or Tacitus only insofar as they came into conflict with Roman imperial expansion. They seem to have formed an honoured priestly caste, exempted from military duty, and the repository of great learning, including astronomical studies. To commit this body of learning to memory took up to twenty years. The authors had learned from hearsay of ceremonies in sacred groves. And they reported lurid accounts of human sacrifice, which the Romans considered particularly barbarous since they had themselves officially abandoned the practice as long ago as 97 BC! But the druids represented an ethnic consciousness hostile to the monolithic interests of Imperial Rome. And the early emperors—who themselves might hope to be deified—took steps to ensure the druids' destruction. In AD 54 Claudius claimed to have abolished the 'barbarous and inhuman' cult in Gaul. But it survived strongly in Britain, which Caesar claimed was the druidical centre, until the military occupation of the island.

It seems likely that the Roman legions systematically destroyed druidical temples, although the records suggest that these priests laid considerable emphasis on natural features like sacred groves (the word 'druid' itself seems probably to be associated with *drus*, the Greek word for oak tree), which would leave no visible remains in any case. There is some slight evidence for the existence of sacred enclosures and temples of this date. A good example was excavated beneath London Airport at Heathrow. Within a large quadrangular earthwork about 150 yards square was found the outline of a dozen circular timber huts; and then set a little apart from these, a massive rectangular timber structure, 6 by 5 yards, with a single door opening out onto a wooden veranda or colonnade forming a precinct—an early forerunner of a well-known Romano-Celtic type of temple (see below).

But if temples of the Heathrow type cannot now be seen, one other class of ceremonial monument

Uffington, Oxfordshire: White Horse, and Ridgeway track hillfort

from this date is visible over wide distances: the hill-figures cut into the chalk of the southern downlands. The most notable of these is the White Horse of Uffington in south Oxfordshire, SU 302866. This is best seen from the Longcott–Fernham road about two miles to the north. On a slope above the Iron Age hillfort and close to the ancient Ridgeway track, turf was removed from over the chalk to form the massive figure of a white horse, sprawling 120 yards long and 45 yards tall. Highly stylised and disjointed, it closely resembles the horse designs on the reverse of certain coins minted by the Atrebates, the tribe that lived in this region in the centuries prior to the Roman invasion. Possibly it represents a totemistic figure significant to these people.

Many other 'white horses' are found cut into the chalk slopes of southern England, all of them more realistically drawn, and all apparently originating at various times since the eighteenth century. One of these below Bratton Castle hillfort near Westbury in Wiltshire, ST 898517, is said to have been recut by

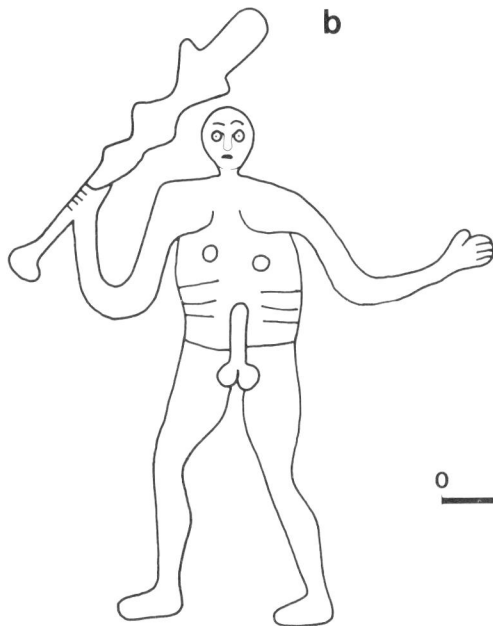

Chalk-cut hill figures: (a) Uffington White Horse, Oxfordshire; (b) Cerne Abbas Giant, Dorset; (c) Long Man of Wilmington, Sussex

a local landowner in 1778 so as to resemble a 'breed animal'. The figure it replaced might have been very ancient indeed.

The figure of a splendidly phallic, club-wielding giant, striding across the hillside above Cerne Abbas in Dorset, ST 667016, may well belong to the period at the end of the second century AD when the Roman Emperor Commodus attempted to revive the cult of Hercules. Ninety yards in height, it was made by trenches 2 feet deep filled with chalk rubble. Hill-figures require regular cleaning if they are to remain visible, and over the years this activity attracted considerable folklore and superstition. Immediately above the Cerne Abbas giant is a small rectangular embanked enclosure about 30 by 35 yards, perhaps originally an Iron Age sacred or burial-enclosure. It was used until relatively recently for May Day celebrations including maypole dancing, a ceremony significantly connected with phallus worship and fertility cults. The Church could have found frequent occasions for discouraging the continuous attention these figures require, and many may have perished on this account. The figures of two club-wielding giants are said formerly to have stood on Plymouth Hoe in Devon.

The Long Man of Wilmington behind Eastbourne in East Sussex, TQ 542035, is best seen from the Weald to the north, where the rather attenuated 77-yard figure is foreshortened and assumes more natural proportions. If the shafts he holds in either hand were originally drawn with spearheads, then very probably he represents Woden and can be associated with the pagan South Saxons of the fifth and sixth centuries. The figure was restored in 1874 by a local clergyman, and it is possible that all sorts of internal details, as well as the spearheads, have been obliterated.

The Roman legions brought with them their gods of the Classical world, although some no doubt could be identified with Celtic deities already worshipped in Britain. Temples in the Mediterranean style were soon erected. At Chichester, for instance, a temple in honour of Neptune and Minerva was dedicated on the authority of the local native king Cogidubnus, for whom the nearly palace at Fishbourne was built (see p. 29) Of the temple itself nothing remains to be seen, but the dedicatory tablet has been found and built into the wall of the Assembly Rooms in North Street. The inscription may be translated: 'To Neptune and Minerva this temple is erected for the well-being of the divine Imperial family at the direction of Tiberius Claudius Cogidubnus, King and Imperial Legate in Britain, by the Guild of Artificers and its associates from personal contributions, the site being given by Clemens son of Pudentius.'

At Bath, the goddess Minerva was identified with the native goddess Sulis, who presided over the hot springs. And a temple was built, apparently on classical lines, attached to the bath-complex there. Several finely carved fragments of sculpture survive and may be seen in the museum. They include reliefs from an elaborate triangular pediment for the façade and altars dedicated to other gods like Mercury, Hercules and Jupiter.

At Colchester the colony of retired legionaries would worship at a temple dedicated to the deified Emperor Claudius, who had been responsible for the conquest of Britain. Of this building only the massive foundation survives below the Norman castle keep. But classical temples of this order were built to a more or less stereotyped design, and with additional evidence from excavation, it is possible to reconstruct in our minds its original appearance. The foundation was built from barnacle-encrusted rubble, presumably from a beach, and perhaps brought to the site as ballast. It supported a raised rectangular platform 32 yards long by 14 wide. This was surrounded by a colonnade, within which stood the shrine itself set back behind a porch fronted with further columns which almost certainly supported a sculptured triangular pediment. The exterior resembled the present-day frontage of the British Museum or St Martin in the Fields. Thirty yards in front of the temple

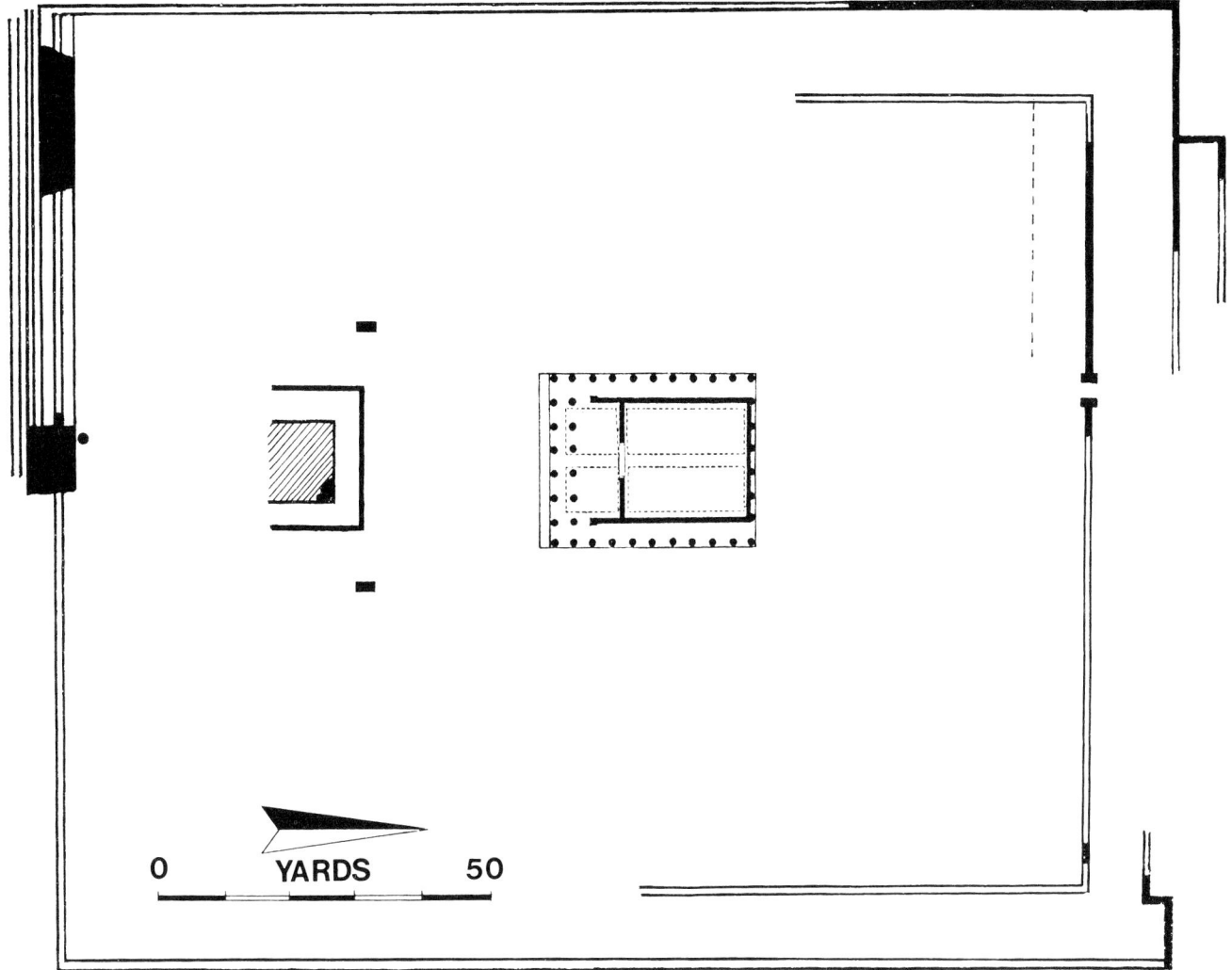

Colchester, Essex: excavation plan of the Roman temple of the Divine Claudius (after Hull)

0   YARDS   50

steps, and surrounded by a drain, stood the base of a large altar which was presumably used for open-air public sacrifices. And flanking the altar stood two pedestals, $1\frac{1}{2}$ yards wide by at least 3 yards long, which probably supported life-size equestrian statues. The entire area was enclosed with a massive wall, finely decorated with imported marble veneers, and the whole precinct was obviously such as befitted the new imperial cult. According to the contemporary historian Tacitus, it was taxes levied for the construction and maintenance of this superb temple which was one of the prime causes of the native Queen Boudicca's rebellion in AD 61. When Colchester was overrun the temple was certainly burned; but it was soon rebuilt and all traces of the fire expunged.

The temple of the divine Claudius was, of course, exceptional. The kind of temple most commonly found in Roman Britain was a standardised form of the native Heathrow type. Built in stone, this consisted of a small inner shrine which would contain a cult statue and altar, surrounded by a portico or veranda used for personal memorials or votive offerings. The whole was sometimes enclosed within a sacred precinct—perhaps a garden—where meditation or teaching could take place.

The foundations of this kind of temple are visible on Jordan Hill near Weymouth in Dorset, SY 698821. In one corner had been dug a 12-feet-deep ritual shaft, into which were placed sixteen separate bird-sacrifices, each accompanied by a coin and separated from the next by a layer of tiles and ashes. Four miles to the north a similar temple was built within the abandoned hillfort at Maiden Castle, SY 668885 (see p. 82). Here the interior shrine was floored in black-and-white mosaic, and the outer veranda in red. Adjoining the temple was a small two-roomed building, which may represent accommodation for the officiating priest. A round native hut a few yards away on the other side of the temple probably housed a servant. In a temple in an urban setting at Caerwent (see p. 29), the inner shrine had an apse at its further end, in which presumably stood a statue of the god—in this case probably Mars Ocelus. Outside the east wall at Caerwent a small octagonal version of the standard shrine plan can be found. And the foundations of a circular temple are visible on the slope above and behind the rich Roman villa at Lullingstone (see p. 27): 6 yards in diameter, its walls $1\frac{1}{4}$ feet thick. A rectangular space in front of the entrance was surrounded by a plastered and painted wooden screen. It was approached by steps up the hillside from the east.

All sorts of small and purely local shrines were built to invoke or placate particular deities. Roman quarrymen at Chester cut a niche-shrine in which stands a statue of their patron goddess Minerva, now much weathered (see p. 49). Amphitheatres and their military equivalent the ludus contained small square rooms close to the entrance where participants could make or pay appropriate vows before the altar of Nemesis, goddess of Fate (see p. 92). Shrines dedicated to water-nymphs were especially popular. A domestic nymphaeum stood adjacent to the fine courtyard villa at Chedworth, enclosing an octagonal pool which supplied the inhabitants with their water (see p. 27). A room in the nearby villa at Great Witcombe (see p. 27) has been interpreted in the same way. A few yards to the west of the Hadrian's Wall fort at Carrawbrough, NY 859712, a swampy spring now marks the site of a shrine dedicated to the nymph Coventina; thousands of coins and small trinkets had been thrown into the pool as votive offerings. Due reverence paid to the local water goddess was not only an attractive and undemanding cult, it could be eminently practical; the spring at Chedworth has never failed, even during the severest droughts of recent years!

However, the best-known example of a complete cult centre was that built over the remains of a failed iron-mine in the long-abandoned hillfort at Lydney overlooking the Severn (see p. 50). Excavation

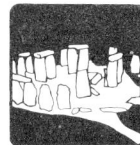

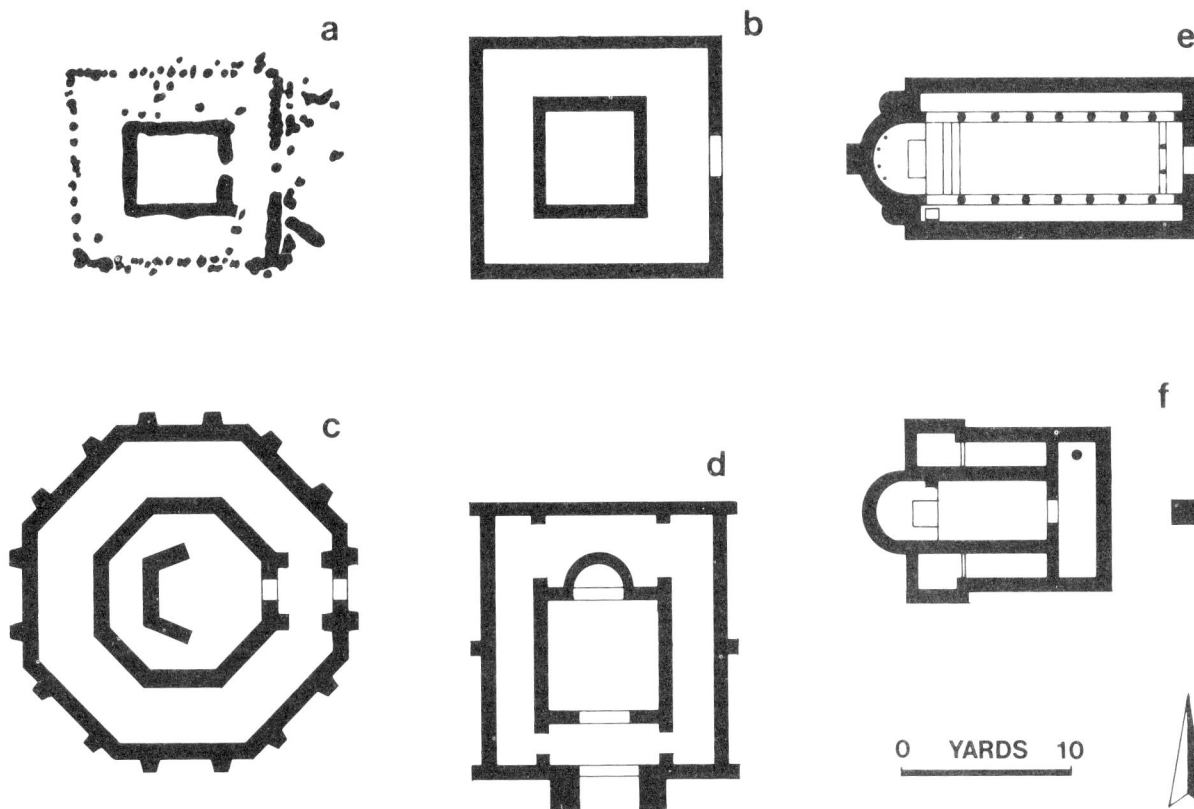

Comparative plans of Romano-British temples: (a) Heathrow, Greater London; (b) Maiden Castle, Dorset; (c) Pagans Hill, Somerset (not now visible); (d) Caerwent, Gwent; (e) City of London Mithraeum; (f) Christian church, Silchester, Hants

showed that this elegant and elaborate centre was built during the pagan revival which took place during the second half of the fourth century. It was dedicated to the native British god Nodens, who was connected with hunting and the sea. The main mosaic in the shrine (not now visible) depicted sea monsters and fish, and was dedicated to the god by one Flavius Senilis, a naval officer in charge of a supply depot,

probably at Cardiff. It seems to have been a curative shrine. Excavation brought to light numerous votive objects including three hundred bracelets and a bronze arm, and almost four hundred bronze and bone pins, traditionally offered by women at the time of childbirth. An oculist's stamp was found, and stone and bronze statuettes of dogs, which were associated with healing in the ancient world. A lead tablet had

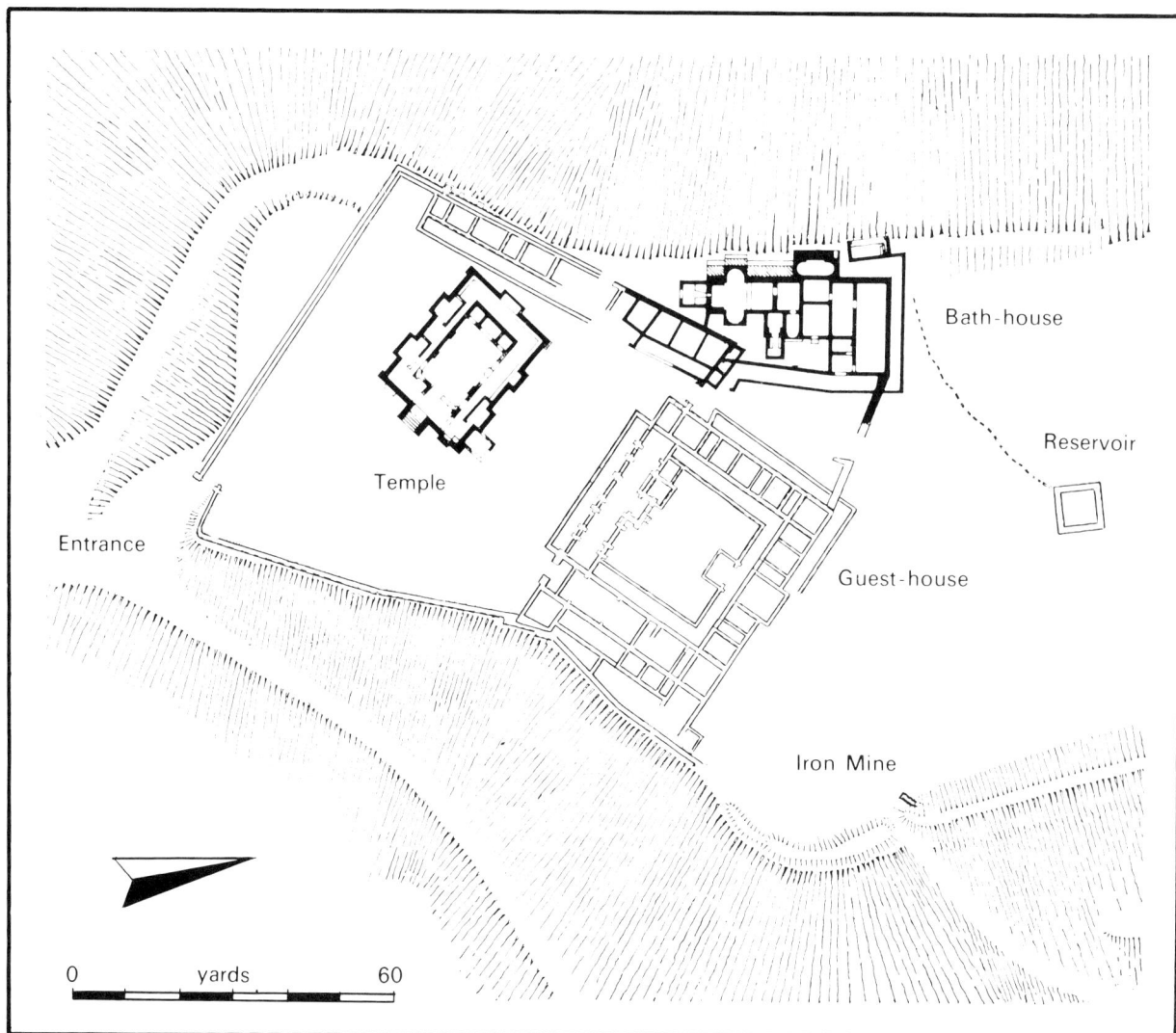

Lydney, Gloucs: plan of Roman cult centre (after Wheeler)

Temple

Entrance

Bath-house

Reservoir

Guest-house

Iron Mine

0   yards   60

Carrawbrough, Northumberland: Mithraeum

been inscribed with a curse. A certain Silvanius has lost a ring at the temple; he promises half its value to Nodens upon its recovery, and prays that in the meantime good health should be denied a man called Senicianus whom he suspects of stealing it.

The sacred precinct, surrounded by a wall, occupied the entire southern half of the interior of the hillfort. The temple itself, measuring about 20 by 27 yards, faced the entrance. A flight of steps led up to the surrounding veranda or portico which contained five bays or alcoves, perhaps best interpreted as side chapels or subsidiary shrines. The inner sanctuary itself ended in three bays, perhaps intended for separate altars. A small rear door either side led out on to the veranda. The cult seems to have attracted a wealthy and sophisticated clientèle. A large guest-house built in the fashion of the best courtyard villas could provide accommodation for a limited number of initiates, perhaps travelling from distant towns like Bath or Caerwent. The excavators found no less than eight thousand coins on the site. An elaborate suite

of baths was supplied from a reservoir tank some yards to the north. This may have served both the social needs of the residents, and the curative purposes of the shrine. A long narrow building running along the enclosure wall behind the temple, and consisting of a dozen rooms leading off a corridor or veranda, may have provided accommodation for diseased patients expecting a cure, or for the ritual sleep known in some cults; or perhaps they represent small lockup shops selling souvenirs or votive offerings to the faithful, in the manner of modern Roman Catholic cult centres.

Of the various Oriental cults introduced by the Romans, the most distinctive was the worship of the Persian god of light, Mithras. Its ritual required that the shrine resemble a cave, and consequently these temples were built underground, or partly so, with no windows. The mithraeum is typically a rectangular building entered through a shallow antechamber at one end, so as to exclude natural light from the interior. A narrow doorway led on to a sunken central aisle,

121

flanked by raised benches on which the initiates could recline. At the far end stood a sculptured relief depicting the basic Mithras myth, showing the god in the act of slaying a bull, plunging a dagger into its throat. Either side usually stood separate statues of torch-bearing attendants, one holding his torch upwards, the other downwards and extinguished.

The most famous mithraeum is that excavated in a blaze of publicity during the 1950s at Walbrook in the City of London. The remains have since been re-erected in Queen Victoria Street, about 60 yards north-west of its original site. About 20 yards long by 8 wide, this was a fine building appropriately furnished for urban sophisticates, who reclined on

Sculptured relief depicting the Mithraic myth from Walbrook, City of London. The inscription reads: Ulpius Silvanus, discharged soldier of the 2nd (Augusta) Legion, pays his vow; discharged at Orange (in France)

couches of black leather adorned with gold leaf. But the secret and ascetic Mithraic cult attracted many devotees among the army, and no less than three mithraea have been found along Hadrian's Wall. The Persian god proved strong competition for the nymph Coventina at Carrawbrough, where a rough but strongly-built mithraeum still contains broken representations of the torch-bearers and several altars, the best of them reproductions, NY 858711. (A splendid full-size reconstruction of this building can be seen in Newcastle University Museum.)

All the mithraea, except that in London, show signs of having been deliberately wrecked—mostly in the fourth century. (In London the Mithraic sculptures seem to have been carefully hidden away, thus accounting for their splendid state of preservation.) Almost certainly this violent opposition was the work of militant followers of another Oriental cult recently introduced to Britain: Christianity. They found the Mithraic ritual—and especially the sacred meal—particularly abhorrent because it apparently mocked their own ceremonies. Properly speaking, most Christian monuments belong to medieval rather than Early Britain. But in the Roman town of Silchester, the excavators revealed a small Christian chapel of the late fourth century (see p. 30). This was an apsidal building 14 yards long by 11 yards wide with a porch and side aisles, oriented east—west. Outside the entrance a masonry foundation, 4 feet square, with a soakaway, probably represents the site of the separate baptistry usual at this date.

At about the same time, one of the rooms in the magnificent villa at Lullingstone (where previously wall paintings of nymphs were found), was converted to use as a Christian chapel and painted with the chi-rho monogram of Christ and figures standing between columns in the classical attitude of prayer. (These paintings have been restored and are displayed at the British Museum.)

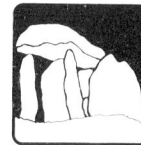

FUNERARY MONUMENTS

Grave mounds of different kinds are by far the most numerous remains of early man in Britain. And if not as impressive to look at as the great hillforts or ceremonial sanctuaries, they are often much more instructive to the excavator. By close examination of the remains of their bodies and from the various equipment thought necessary to furnish the grave, archaeologists have been able to reconstruct a relatively accurate picture of the everyday life led by early men—their tools, utensils, weapons and jewellery, now often displayed in local museums. The manner in which they disposed of the body gives some insight into early religious beliefs—at least insofar as these concerned an afterlife.

The concept of a life beyond the grave, into which the spirit entered by means of a journey or perhaps some sort of rebirth, is an ancient and more or less universal one. During Old Stone Age times a dead man might be buried deep in the inner galleries of the cave whose entrance had afforded him shelter during his lifetime. The notion of a return to the womb of Mother Earth is reinforced by the fact that often the body was trussed into a crouched or 'foetal' position; and in some cases, at Paviland and elsewhere, tne effort to secure rebirth could be furthered by impregnating the entire body and grave with blood-like red ochre. Personal trinkets and symbols of status might be added to the grave, and the dead man pro-vided with food and drink to sustain him on a journey (see above, pp. 16–17).

As with other religious and ceremonial activities, however, it was not until Neolithic times that recognisable funerary structures were built. Then, instead of burying their dead deep inside caves, or leaving the remains to be disposed of by animals, they were lain on the surface of the earth with due ceremony, and covered over with a mound or 'barrow' of earth—or a cairn of stones in rocky regions of the north and west. The early pastoral communities responsible for the first great earthen henge monuments and cause-wayed camps of the Windmill Hill type found on the chalk downlands south of the Thames, favoured long earthen barrows. Most are between 50 and 100 yards long, 15 to 30 yards wide, and anything between 4 and 12 feet high. They have a tendency to be rather higher and broader at one end—which is commonly found to be oriented towards the eastern sunrise. Long barrows are normally found singly, although they often attracted a cluster of later round barrows. Good examples can be seen in such 'cemeteries' in the vicinity of Stonehenge: at Winterbourne Stoke crossroads, SU 101417, at Lake just a little to the south-west, SU 109402, and a small one at Norman-ton Down on the skyline half a mile south of Stone-henge, SU 118413 (see generally p. 134).

As they now appear, grassed over and rounded by

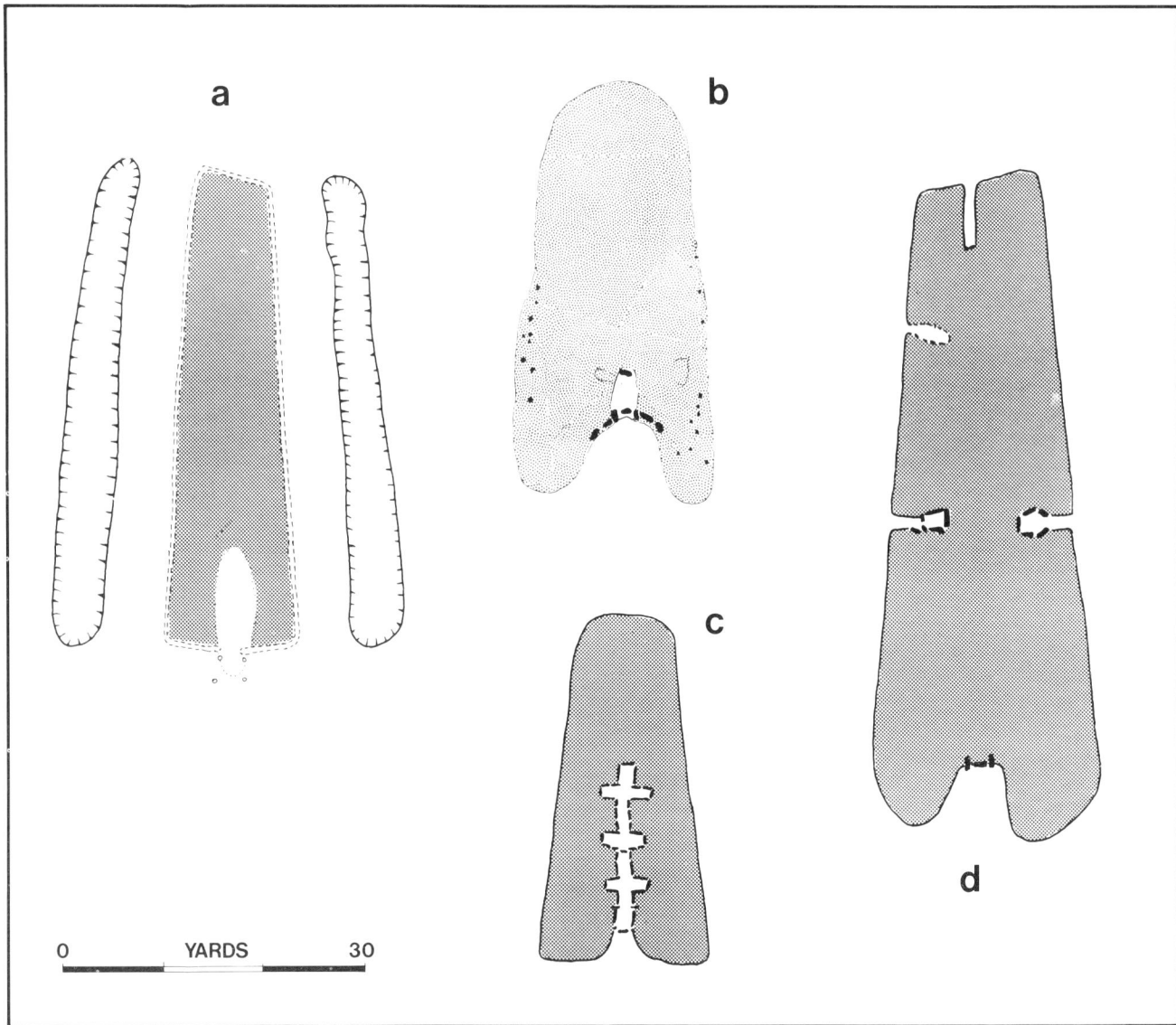

Comparative plans of long barrows and chambered tombs: (a) Clarendon Park, Wilts, SU 192324; (b) Pentre Ifan, Dyfed; (c) Stoney Littleton, Avon; (d) Belas Knap, Gloucs

the weather, their flanking ditches largely silted up, they form long oval or slightly pear-shaped mounds. However, excavation shows that originally these were much more box-like constructions, wedge-shaped in plan, and having vertical sides revetted with timber. A level platform separated this construction from a straight length of steep-sided ditch which flanked it on either side, and from where the material was quarried for the body of the monument. This might seem an over-extravagant tomb for a single man, however powerful. And the evidence shows that they were in fact communal graves, of which the raised mound we see represents only the final completed stage.

In most cases the first phase consisted of a rectangular or wedge-shaped wooden mortuary-house. Some, perhaps most, were tent-shaped, with a porch at one end. Here bodies were assembled over a fairly lengthy period, some at least placed in a crouched position. As later bodies were deposited, the earlier ones were moved to one side, and are found as piles of disarticulated bones. In one instance more than fifty individuals were represented. When it was decided that the mortuary-house could, or should, receive no further bodies, it was burned. The area was then fenced with a timber enclosure, which was then filled with earth and rubble taken from flanking ditches. In some cases no doubt the timber walls were covered with a sloping ramp of earth making a smooth profile into the edge of the ditch. The broader higher end of the monument must still have been conceived as the 'entrance' end, and was often built with a slightly concave façade so as to form a forecourt, Facing eastwards towards the rising sun, it formed an appropriate setting in which various rituals associated with the dead might be performed.

The completion of such a monument must have been an occasion of some importance to the community, and was presumably accompanied by additional social ceremonies. Possibly it was for such an occasion that the kind of earthwork known as a 'cursus' was constructed. These enigmatic structures take the form of parallel lengths of low embankment with an outer ditch running cross-country for some distance and commonly incorporating long barrows in their course. They have curved or squared-off ends which sometimes terminate directly on a long barrow. One such cursus lies half a mile to the north of Stonehenge, roughly 100 yards across, running east–west for a distance of three-quarters of a mile, and terminating at its eastern end with long barrow lying transversely and blocking its route, SU 109429–137433 (see p. 134). Much of its course has been obliterated by cultivation. Better preserved, at least in parts, is the lengthier Dorset Cursus. This is one of the largest prehistoric constructions in the country. It is built to much the same pattern as the Stonehenge example, but extends over six and a quarter miles. Starting from two long barrows on Thickthorn Down north-east of Blandford Forum, ST 970124, it runs roughly parallel with and to the south of the A354; it incorporates two other long barrows, one lying transversely across its line on Gussage Hill, ST 995140, and another within the line of its northern bank passing through Salisbury Plantation on Bottlebush Down, SU 026169; and it terminates near two more close to the great Bokerly Dyke, SU 040192. Its line was cut by Ackling Dyke Roman road as it crosses Wyke Down, SU 012153. The Dorset Cursus seems to have been laid out in two distinct phases. First the three-and-a-half mile south-western section was built, and then later this was extended to the north-east for a further two and a half miles. It is unlikely that we shall ever know for certain what part these strange structures played in the social life of the Neolithic community. It is possible that, like some stone avenues, they were used for astronomical sightings; or they may have formed processional routes; or, in view of their intimate association with long barrows, they may have marked the course of races forming part of the kind of funeral games described by some ancient authors writing about tribes in the Baltic.

Some two hundred earthen long barrows are known (by no means all of them leaving significant traces). The great majority occur in the region of the causewayed camps, that is the chalk downlands from Dorset to Sussex; but two or three are found in the Chilterns, and a small outlying group in the Lincoln and Yorkshire Wolds. Elsewhere in Britain, especially in the north and west where plentiful supplies of stone were available, there developed distinctive types of 'megalithic' tombs (so-called because constructed of very large stones). They are best thought of as mortuary-houses and long barrows combined. Like long barrows they were used for collective burial, and, equipped with a permanent stone entrance to the burial chamber, they remained open for more or less continuous use. Perhaps the tomb was ritually sealed between burials. The doorway might be closed with a temporary blocking of dry-stone walling which could be easily removed whenever necessary. However, this measure of open access has frequently led to the destruction of the contents of the tombs by treasure-hunters and other intruders over the centuries. The mound itself might be composed of earth or rubble. But instead of a timber mortuary-house at the centre, a more or less elaborate chamber was constructed out of large stones. Very often, especially in the south where composed of earth rather than a stone cairn, the covering mound has weathered away completely, leaving the denuded and sometimes ruined chamber standing as an isolated phenomenon, known locally as a 'dolmen' or 'cromlech': usually three or more uprights supporting a massive capstone. Occasionally they attract the same kind of folklore as some of the stone circles. In some cases it is possible to trace the outline of a denuded mound from the position of large kerb-stones originally used to retain the outer edge of the monument.

The remains of about 350 megalithic tombs are known in England and Wales, and perhaps twice as many in Scotland. Many conform to the overall plan and proportions of the earthen long barrows, although

nowhere are they as long. They are occasionally rectangular, but most frequently wedge-shaped in plan, with sometimes emphatically crescentic, even horn-shaped entrance façades. The simplest form of mausoleum consisted merely of a roughly rectangular chamber set immediately behind the entrance. This is the type found, for example, at Tinkinswood west of Cardiff, ST 092733, where the enormous capstone weighs some 40 tons. The Tinkinswood tomb originally contained the remains of at least fifty individuals. A mile away the denuded and ruined remains of another can be seen at St Lythans, ST 101723. The largely denuded but still superb chamber of Pentre Ifan in Pembrokeshire, SN 099370, is of the same order.

Pentre Ifan, Dyfed: denuded chamber

An outlying group clustered in the Medway valley in Kent seem also to be of this type. All are denuded and more or less ruined. The best known is Kit's Coty House, lying beside the A229 between Maidstone and Chatham, TQ 745608. But better preserved are The Chestnuts tomb at Addington, TQ 652592, and the Coldrum tomb a mile to the north near Trottiscliffe, TQ 654607.

Other much more elaborately-designed chambered tombs are found. 'Wayland's Smithy' lies on the Ridgeway just a mile and half west of the Uffington White horse in Oxfordshire, SU 281854: a wedge-shaped mound of chalk rubble, 62 yards long, with several sarsen kerb-stones still in place. Behind a blocking-stone in the monumental 9-feet façade lies a narrow gallery with one pair of side chambers and an end chamber, resulting in a cruciform plan. Presumably these individual chambers were intended to receive separate interments; excavation shows that at least eight individuals had been buried here.

More commonly two pairs of opposing chambers are found. This is the case in one of the largest such tombs known, at West Kennet close to the stone avenue leading to Avebury, SU 104677. This is an enormous wedge-shaped mound of rubble, 115 yards long and 8 feet high, quarried from two enormous flanking ditches, 10 feet deep and 7 yards across. One large and several smaller blocking-stones filled the concave façade and concealed the entrance. Several uprights in the gallery show areas of polishing where the builders sharpened their stone axes. About thirty individuals were buried here. Other tombs with chambers of this kind can be seen in the Cotswolds at Notgrove, SP 095212 and at Hetty Pegler's Tump, south-west of Stroud, SO 790000, and near to the Cat's Hole cave-dwelling at Parc le Breos six miles west of Swansea, SS 538898. But the most elaborate example is to be found in the magnificently preserved tomb at Stoney Littleton in Avon, ST 735572, in which no less than three opposing pairs of chambers flank a vaulted gallery leading some 17 yards from a funnel-shaped forecourt into the body of the mound.

A curious variant is well represented by the tomb known as Belas Knap, some five miles north-west of Notgrove in the Cotswolds, SP 021254. Within the funnel-shaped forecourt there stands what at first sight appears a conventionally blocked door. But this is quite false, since no chamber lies beyond. Perhaps it was intended to mislead tomb-robbers, or more likely evil spirits of the kind that might be supposed to intrude upon the dead. In fact the remains were placed in small chambers located in the flanks and rear of the monument. Evidence for some thirty or forty burials in all were found by the excavators. This monument is rather unusual in that it is oriented directly north—south.

In north-east Scotland, Orkney and Caithness, a regional type is found in which transeptal chambers are not made separately, but formed by slabs of stone projecting from the wall creating a series of stall-like compartments along the gallery. Of several examples on the island of Rousay, a particularly fine one stands on the seashore close to the Midhowe broch, HY 372306. An oval cairn 36 yards long by 14 wide covers a long narrow gallery with a dozen pairs of opposing stalls, those on the east containing low stone benches on which groups of bones were found—presumably representing separate family vaults.

In most of England and Wales and in parts of Scotland, the long chambered tomb was favoured, a megalithic version of the long barrow. But around the whole of the Atlantic sea-board a tradition of round chambered cairns is found. These characteristically contain a narrow passage leading to a square or irregular-shaped chamber at or near the centre of the mound.

Undoubtedly the finest of all such monuments is Maeshowe, which stands close to the Ring of Stenness, nine miles west of Kirkwall in Orkney, HY 318127. An impressive cairn, 24 feet high and 37 yards in diameter, is separated by a level 17-yard plat-

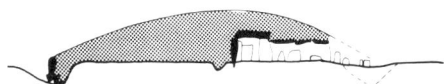
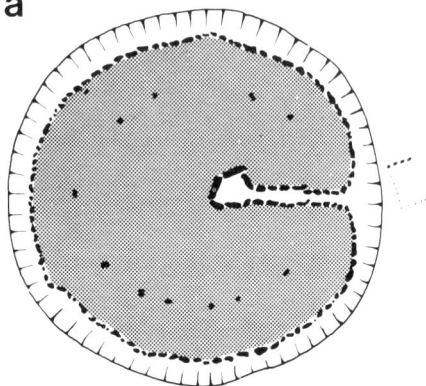
a

c
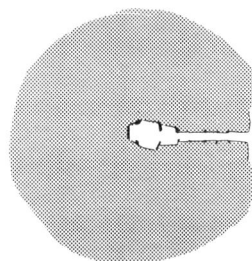

d
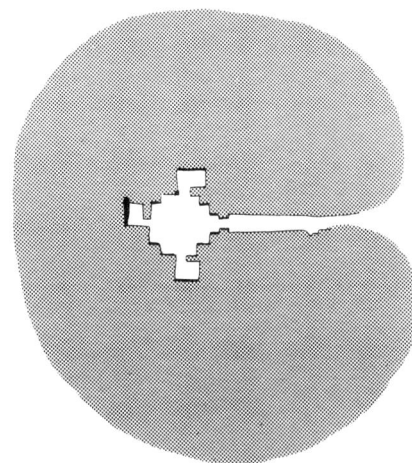

b
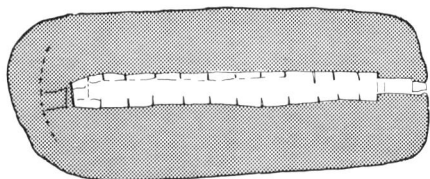

0	YARDS	30

Comparative plans of chambered round barrows: (a) Bryn Celli Ddu, Anglesey; (b) Midhowe, Orkney; (c) Camster, Caithness;
(d) Maeshowe, Orkney

form from a massive surrounding ditch about 13 yards across. The internal structure is finely built from large monolithic slabs and smooth regularly-coursed dry-stone walling. A straight passage, low and narrow, 12 yards long, 3 feet wide and $4\frac{1}{2}$ feet high, leads to the central chamber. Five yards square, each corner

Maeshowe, Orkney: interior of chambered tomb showing entrance to subsidiary chamber with fallen blocking-stone

buttressed by a substantial monolith, the vaulted roof still rises $12\frac{1}{2}$ feet, and originally rose at least a further 4 feet. On three faces small window-like openings, $2\frac{1}{2}$ feet square and 3 feet above the floor, give access into three small subsidiary chambers, 7 by 5 feet square and $3\frac{1}{2}$ feet high. Three large stones found on the floor of the main chamber were presumably used to block off these cells. Maeshowe is a superbly planned and executed monument which compares favourably with some Mycenaean structures. It has been ransacked many times over the centuries, most notably by Viking treasure-hunters in the twelfth century who left a remarkable series of graffiti on the walls of the chamber and passageway.

Some other round cairns in Orkney and Caithness contain galleries 'stalled' by projecting slabs in the manner of the Midhowe tomb (see above, p. 127). At Camster in Caithness good examples of both round and long stalled tombs lie close together just 100 yards off the road, ND 260443. The round cairn is 20 yards in diameter, with a passage $2\frac{1}{2}$ feet wide leading 6 yards to an ante-chamber and then into the main chamber, 10 feet high and divided into several stalls. Two hundred yards to the north lies a long stalled chamber tomb with a funnel-shaped forecourt, but entered in fact from the flank as with Belas Knap.

Two particularly fine 'passage-tombs' are found in Anglesey. Bryn Celli Ddu (i.e. 'The Hill of the Dark Grove'), lies just a mile or two from the Menai Bridge, SH 507702. It was originally some 30 yards across, but has been restored to only half its width to allow an inner circle of retaining stones to be seen. A passageway 3 feet across and about 8 yards long leads to a small irregularly shaped chamber roughly $2\frac{1}{2}$ yards square. At the further end stood an upright stone pillar decorated with a meander design, beside which had been dug a ritual pit containing a human ear. Within a small stall in front of the entrance an ox had been sacrificed. Farther west in Anglesey on the edge of the sea-cliff stands Barclodiad y Gawres (i.e. 'The Giantess's Apronful'), SH 329708. The

mound was 30 yards in diameter, but had no retaining stones and is now barely 3 feet high. The surviving length of passage, some 7 or 8 yards long, leads into a polygonal chamber about 4 yards across with three subsidiary chambers forming a roughly cruciform plan. The wall slabs at the rear of each side chamber and several others at the end of the passageway are decorated with carved chevrons, spirals and concentric circles. Occasionally megalithic tombs bear the mysterious cup-and-ring symbols already noticed on some standing stones. They are found, for instance, on a fallen stone from the partly denuded Arthur's Stone chambered tomb in west Herefordshire, SO 318431.

In the extreme south-west, in west Cornwall and the Isles of Scilly, are found numbers of small round cairns containing rectangular chambers entered directly from a portal in the side without any passageway. Good examples can be seen near the Carn Euny village, SW 402282 (see p. 44): a chamber $7\frac{1}{2}$ by 4 feet covered by a barrow 6 yards across and $6\frac{1}{2}$ feet high, or another called The Giant's House, three-quarters of a mile south-west of Zennor, SW 448376.

The marked distribution of passage-graves along the Atlantic seaboard suggests that perhaps this tradition was introduced via the western sea-ways. Collective burial was practised in more or less contemporary cave-tombs in the Mediterranean, and it is possible that these northern megalithic tombs represent an artificial man-made version used by immigrant folk for a similar ritual but in a land where natural caves are rare. Burial practices are notoriously conservative among all peoples.

With the coming of the Bronze Age, however, the Neolithic custom of collective burial in tribal or communal mausolea seems to have been abandoned in favour of individual interment. Most, whether inhumed or cremated, were simply buried in the ground with no visible marker—or at least none sufficiently substantial to have survived. But many others were covered with various kinds of circular mounds of earth or stones. Bronze Age round barrows are by far the most familiar of all prehistoric monuments, and may perhaps be numbered in tens of thousands. They occur in all parts of the country, either singly or in groups.

By far the commonest form are simple 'bowl' barrows, so called because they resemble an inverted bowl. These vary greatly in size, the smallest only some 5 yards across and 3 feet high, the largest 40 or 50 yards in diameter and 20 feet or more in height. The profile has invariably eroded. Commonly the material is taken from a surrounding ditch, which may sometimes have an outer bank. The ditch is often completely silted up, appearing, if at all, only as a ring of darker grass. Sometimes there was no ditch, in which case the material for the mound must presumably have been scraped up over a relatively large area. The present appearance of these barrows is deceptively simple. Careful excavation has shown that sometimes they incorporated circular enclosures fenced with wooden stakes or alternatively small round or rectangular hut-like structures. Ethnological parallels suggest that this might represent the symbolic 'house of the dead' where the body lay before burial. The depression sometimes found in the top of round barrows (where this does not mark the depredations of treasure-hunters in recent times), may have been caused by the collapse of such internal features. In stone cairns these wooden features are replaced by concentric D-shaped or crescentic settings of larger stones. Some barrows show signs of having been surmounted by a standing stone or timber post, which may have been structural, allowing a higher cone of material to be built up around it, or which may have borne a symbolic marker of some kind.

Sometimes the original ground surface beneath the barrow shows signs of burning, and occasionally ritual pits and ditches are found filled with ashes, hinting at various kinds of funeral feasts and other ceremonies. Before being covered with the mound, in-

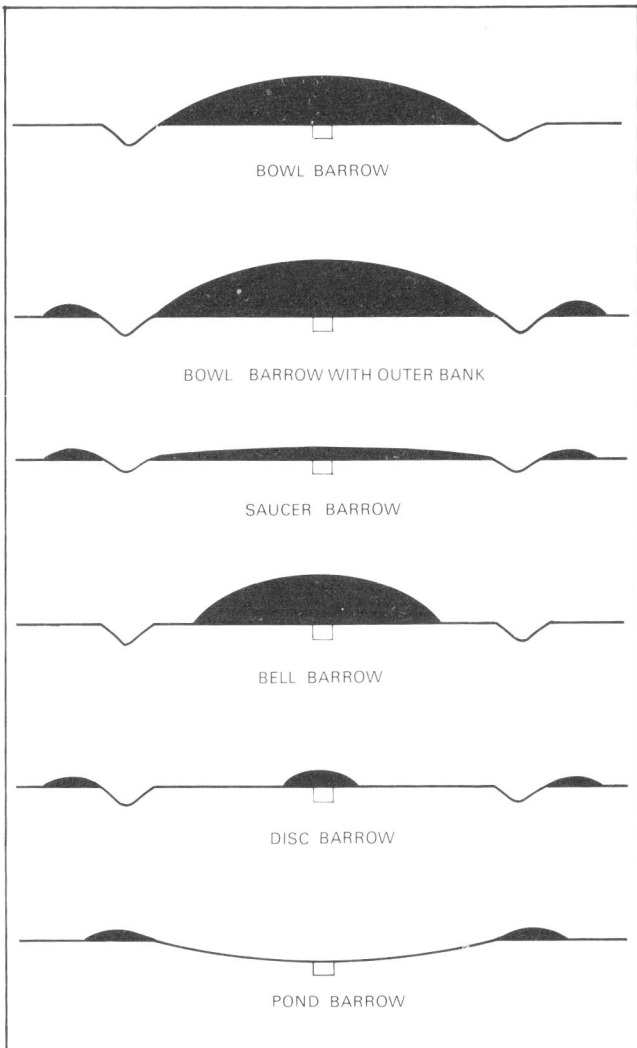

Types of Bronze Age round barrow profiles

BOWL BARROW

BOWL BARROW WITH OUTER BANK

SAUCER BARROW

BELL BARROW

DISC BARROW

POND BARROW

Cist grave uncovered in cairn, Ri Cruin, Kilmartin, Argyll

humed bodies might be placed either on the surface, or on a low platform, or in a grave-pit dug into the ground. They are found either fully extended, or lying on their side crouched in the 'foetal' posture. Sometimes in stony regions the grave-pit was lined with slabs to form a box-like 'cist', which becomes visible when the covering mound has been eroded away. On Dartmoor a good example can be found at Lakehead Hill near Postbridge, SX 644774. Numerous examples occur in Scotland; that illustrated can be seen just south of Kilmartin in Argyll, NR 826971. A rock-cut grave beneath the cairn built within the henge at Cairnpapple Hill (see p. 106) has been reconstructed and can be entered. In the south and east where stone was not so easily available the grave might be lined

Barrow cemetery at Winterbourne Stoke cross-roads, Wilts

with timber planks; or sometimes a wooden coffin was hollowed out of a tree trunk. The deceased was commonly supplied with a beaker of drink or food and occasionally a bronze knife to accompany him on his journey to the afterlife.

During the course of the Bronze Age cremation became increasingly fashionable as a means of disposing of the dead. Sometimes the burned remains were simply piled on the ground or in a pit; but in time a distinctive kind of pottery urn, 12–15 inches high, was developed to contain the ashes. This was covered with a small stone slab and placed either on the surface, or in a small pit dug for the purpose. While the original burial is found at the centre of the barrow, sometimes subsequent 'secondary' burials were deposited in pits dug into the flanks of the mound. This may have been merely a matter of convenience; but possibly some barrows were always intended as family graves.

In Wessex especially, but occasionally elsewhere, there developed various distinctive types of earthen round barrow. Particularly low bowl barrows, only a couple of feet high although sometimes more than 20 yards across, and always surrounded by a ditch and outer bank, are known appropriately as 'saucer barrows'. Other small bowl barrows separated from the surrounding ditch by a flat level platform or berm between 3 and 7 yards wide, are known from the resulting profile as 'bell barrows'. In some the central

mound is very small indeed, so that the area enclosed by bank and ditch is more disc-like. Occasionally two or three small mounds are found in these 'disc barrows'. These seem to be characteristically the graves of women. Particularly unusual, and something of a contradiction in terms, is the so-called 'pond barrow', which consists not of a mound but a shallow circular depression up to 40 yards in diameter and surrounded by a ditch and embankment. Possibly these should be considered primarily as fenced enclosures for the exposure of bodies prior to burial.

One unique barrow-like monument deserves mention: Silbury Hill, a prominent landmark standing a mile south of Avebury and a mile west of The Sanctuary, SU 100685, (see p.105). One hundred and thirty feet high and 180 yards in diameter, covering more than five acres, this is the largest man-made mound in Europe. It is surrounded by a ditch now largely silted up but originally 20 feet deep. It contains about 360 thousand cubic yards of chalk rubble, and clearly involved a considerable expenditure of manpower. But its original purpose remains a mystery. Excavations at various times have revealed no evidence for a burial. But radio-active carbon dating shows that its construction was contemporary with Avebury, The Sanctuary and the first phase at Stonehenge. It may conceivably have served some related ceremonial or religious function.

Round barrows are not infrequent occurrences in

valleys and other low-lying places, and the ditches of many now ploughed flat are often revealed by aerial photography. But they are most commonly found in upland or downland regions. Sometimes they were sited just below the crest of a hill so as to appear on the skyline when viewed from a neighbouring valley, which may indicate where the community lived that was responsible for their erection. Although isolated single barrows are not uncommon, they frequently occur in groups, sometimes sufficient clustering together to be considered a barrow 'cemetery'. Sometimes the barrows are all of a kind; at other times several types are found together. Very often such a cemetery gathered around, or aligned itself with, an already extant monument like a Neolithic long barrow, presumably because of its long-established sanctity. They very commonly accumulate in the vicinity of large stone circles like Stonehenge, much as later burial-grounds are found sharing the sacred precincts of a medieval church or cathedral.

Good examples of nucleated barrow cemeteries occur in all parts of the country. For example, almost thirty clustered around the Thornborough henges in North Yorkshire (see p. 105), although like the henge circles themselves, these have been extensively levelled by ploughing. On Stanton Moor north-west of Matlock in Derbyshire, SK 247634, no less than seventy small cairns can be found scattered over a broad area south of the Nine Ladies stone circle. And in the Lincolnshire Wolds two miles south of Louth, the 'Bully Hills' are seven impressive bowl barrows strung out along the skyline, TF 330827. Close to the Icknield Way on Therfield Heath in Hertfordshire, lies the most extensive group in the Chilterns: eight bowl barrows between 3 and 8 feet high situated to the north of a Neolithic long barrow, TL 342402. The 'Devil's Jumps' four miles south-west of Midhurst on the South Downs in west Sussex, SU 824173, form a fine alignment of six bell barrows between 6 and 16 feet high and between 28 and 38 yards in diameter.

A mile or two south of Uffington on the Berkshire–Oxfordshire border a fine cemetery of thirty or forty barrows lies either side of the Lambourn–Kingston Lisle road, close to a ruined chambered long barrow, SU 328828. Those to the north of the road include two east–west alignments.

In north Dorset more than two dozen barrows of various types are found where the Ackling Dyke Roman road crosses Oakley Down, SU 007154. The embankment of the road cuts across the line of two disc barrows. In the south of the county the 'Poor Lot' cemetery six miles west of Dorchester, SY 588907, consists of forty or so barrows of all kinds lying to the north-east of two Neolithic long barrows. Two miles south of Honiton in east Devon, sixty or so round barrows of various kinds are scattered over a length of three miles beside the B3174 between Gittisham Hill and Broad Down, SY 163970–172933. Farther west in Cornwall an east–west alignment of eight bowl barrows is found at Braddock three miles north of Lostwithiel, SX 142634, while at Pelynt, two miles north of Polperro, two dozen bowl barrows of varying sizes can be found, SX 200545. One of these contained a long Mycenaean bronze dagger, witness to the extensive trade routes at this early date.

However, by far the greatest concentrations of barrows are found on the Wiltshire Downs in the neighbourhood of Avebury and Stonehenge. Half a mile north of Stonehenge a fine row of six bell barrows and one bowl are aligned parallel with and to the south of the Cursus. Half a mile to the south of Stonehenge the Normanton cemetery, one of the finest in the country, consists of a dozen or so barrows of most types, some in alignment. Several contained the burials of richly equipped warriors who carried bronze daggers and wore sheet-gold ornaments and necklaces of amber, shale, gold and blue Egyptian faience. These grave-goods are preserved in Devizes Museum.

The most accessible group containing barrows of all types lies one and a half miles west of Stonehenge in the north-east angle of the Winterbourne Stoke

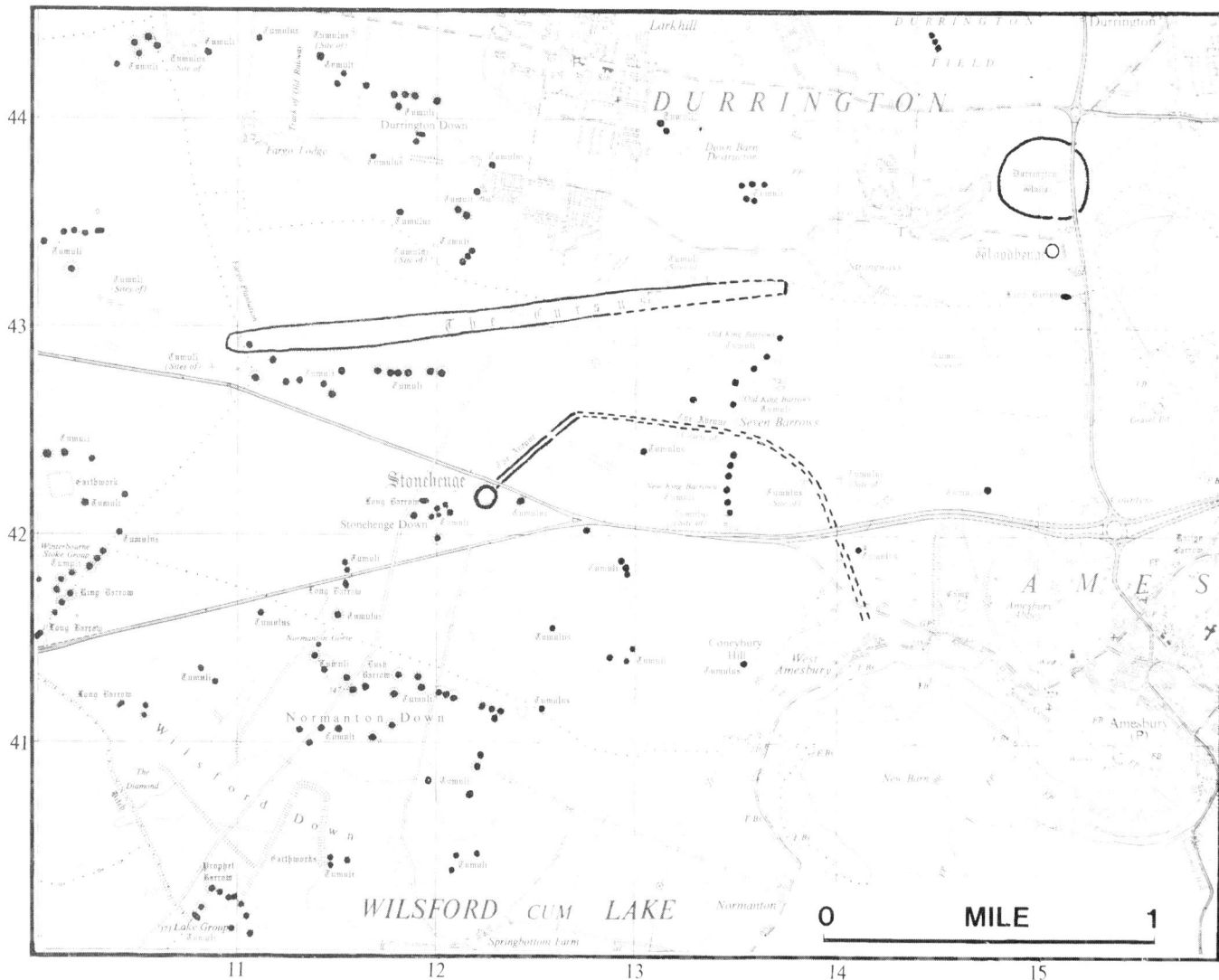

Distribution of barrow cemeteries in the vicinity of Stonehenge, Wilts (based on Ordnance Survey 2½-inch map)

junction of the A303 and A360, SU 101417. Closest to the junction (now a roundabout) lies a Neolithic long barrow, about 80 yards long and 10 feet high. Beyond this lie some two dozen round barrows, some in alignment including: seventeen bowl barrows of varying sizes, two bell, two disc (the northernmost with three small mounds), and two pond barrows (see p. 132). Some contained burials equally as rich as those at Normanton.

Subsequently during the Iron Age, barrow burial continued to be practised, although few sites are known. Close to Kilham in the wolds of East Yorkshire lie remains of one extensive barrow cemetery known as Danes Graves, TA 018633. Over two hundred out of an original five hundred or so small round barrows can be seen, between 1 and $3\frac{1}{2}$ feet high and from 3 to 10 yards across, many surrounded with slight indications of ditches. They contained the crouched burials of both men and women. The pins, brooches, armlets and beads found show that they had been buried in their clothes. Many were supplied with pots of drink and food (joints of pork). One particularly interesting barrow contained the remains of two men buried with a two-wheeled war-chariot and horse's harness and trappings, although not the horse itself which was presumably too much prized to be disposed of in this way.

We know that the pre-Roman aristocrats of this region favoured chariot warfare. Several other chariot burials have been excavated in the Wolds. One is said, perhaps over-romantically, to have accompanied the skeleton of a muscular woman—a veritable Boudicca figure! But only in one instance at Arras, three miles west of Market Weighton, SE 925417, were the horses (two small ponies), sacrificed. And as yet no material evidence has been found for the scythes on the wheels reported by Pomponius Mela, writing at the time of the Roman invasion.

One particularly rich Iron Age burial was found in a large barrow at Lexden in the outskirts of Colchester, TL 975247, some $6\frac{1}{2}$ feet high and 30 yards across, surrounded by a wide deep ditch. The body had been cremated and placed on a bier surrounded by a splendid array of funeral goods, many of which had been deliberately mutilated before burial—perhaps to dissuade possible tomb-robbers, perhaps a ritual destruction intended to allow their spirit to accompany that of the dead man. These furnishings (now displayed in Colchester Museum), included silver-studded chain mail, gold-embroidered clothing, decorative ears of wheat made in silver, jars full of wine, and a series of classically inspired bronze statuettes including a griffin, bull, boar and cupid. Colchester was the capital of the native tribe of Trinovantes before the Romans established their colony there, and almost certainly the Lexden barrow was the tomb of one of their kings or high-ranking aristocrats.

Barrow-burial continued sporadically during the Roman occupation. Perhaps it was still favoured by the more conservative native families. Roman barrows are for the most part larger and more conical than those of prehistoric times. Characteristically they cover cremations placed in glass jars, often within leaden caskets, and surrounded by a variety of grave goods. Most are to be found in the south-east of the province. Roman law forbade burial within city precincts and, following Continental practice, Roman burial grounds are commonly found close to or lining the side of a Roman road leading away from a town. Sometimes they can be found lining the sides of roads well away from any known town. Three lie beside Watling Street (now the A2), where it crosses Barham Downs on its way from Dover to Canterbury, TR 202518—later surrounded by numerous smaller barrows of Saxon date. In Hertfordshire the 'Six Hills', each now about 10 feet high and 20 yards across, form a row lying beside a roundabout on what is now the A1(M) at Stevenage, TL 237237.

Most impressive of all, however, is the row of four, out of an original eight, at Bartlow on the Cambridge–Essex border, TL 586448. Three lie one side and one the other of a now disused railway line. The largest

Bartlow Hills, Esssex, Roman barrows

is still 45 feet high and 50 yards across at the base. An earthwork which can be picked up a few yards to the north-west between the barrows and Bartlow parish church, may represent a cemetery-enclosure of some kind. An isolated barrow on Mersea Island on the coast of Essex, TM 023143, 22 feet high and 40 yards across, covered a small brick-built vault, 18 inches square—containing a glass cremation urn within a lead casket (now in Colchester Museum). The site of this vault can still be reached by way of a tunnel built into the side of the mound.

Examples of classical-style Roman mausolea are known, although from early times these have been robbed for building stone, and only foundations now remain. At Harpenden in Hertfordshire (in the grounds of the Rothamstead Experimental Station,

TL 119136), an area about 33 yards square was enclosed with a masonry wall surrounded in turn by a ditch, and entered by a single door in the middle of one side. At the centre of this space lay a substantial circular mausoleum, 4 yards in diameter. It had a squared-off façade, and was almost certainly domed. A plinth in the centre probably represents the foundation of an altar tomb; and an alcove was provided at the rear to receive a statue of the deceased, fragments of which were found by the excavator. Two cremation burials were found elsewhere within the enclosure, and perhaps others were intended.

Other mausolea are to be found at Keston in the London Borough of Bromley, TQ 415634. An impressive drum-like foundation, 10 yards in diameter, may have supported walls up to 20 feet high. It is sup-

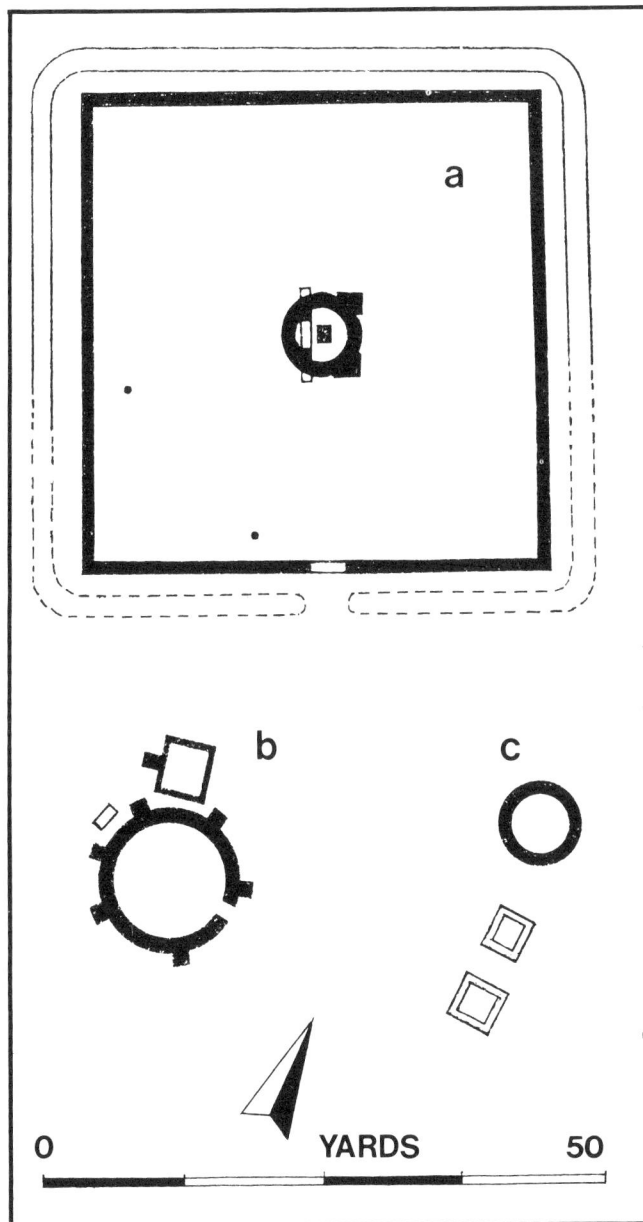

ported by six buttresses, and entered by a small door. The flint rubble walls were plastered on the exterior and painted red. Adjacent lies a smaller rectangular tomb with a foundation for steps, or perhaps a pedestal, on one side. Buried six or seven feet deep inside was a stone coffin (smashed by a German bomb in World War II, but now returned to the site). A third small vault lay between two of the buttresses of the circular tomb, lined with tile and visible beneath a modern trapdoor. In it was found a cremation in a lead casket.

A similar group of circular and rectangular tombs lay beside Roman Dere Street where it runs 700 yards to the south of the fort at High Rochester in the Cheviots, NY 835985, although all that remains visible are the lower courses of one drum-like tomb, one stone of which is carved with the head of an animal. At the remarkable Lullingstone villa in Kent (see p. 27), the family provided itself with a square temple-like mausoleum built close to the temple on the hillside above the house. A deep grave cut into the chalk contained the remains of a young man and woman, buried with a set of gaming pieces. But this mausoleum was apparently abandoned after the coming of Christianity to the household.

For the most part, Roman burials, whether by cremation or inhumation, in lead or stone coffins, were laid out 'flat' in the modern manner with no visible structure surviving above ground. Especially in the military region of the north, however, graves were occasionally marked by sculptured and inscribed tombstones. But none remains in place and these can be examined only in museums.

Comparative plans of Roman mausolea: (a) Harpenden, Herts; (b) Keston, Greater London; (c) High Rochester, Northumberland

137

APPENDIX: GAZETTEER

Only those sites mentioned in the body of the text are referred to here; many others may be found by a study of the $1\frac{1}{4}$-inch Ordnance Survey maps.

London and the Home Counties

Many monuments are to be found within a half-day's excursion from the capital. Along the North Downs through *Surrey and Kent* we can walk long stretches of the 'Pilgrims' Way' prehistoric thoroughfare; it passes close to the site of the Mesolithic hut at Abinger (permission to visit from Abinger Manor), the hillforts and rock-shelters at Oldbury and High Rocks and the fine Lullingstone Roman villa, before crossing the Medway near to the Kentish group of megalithic tombs; one branch of the Pilgrims' Way eventually leads to the hillfort at Bigbury, while the other ends on the Kentish cliffs near to the Folkestone Roman villa. Around the coast there are Saxon Shore forts at Pevensey, Lympne, Richborough and Reculver, and a Roman lighthouse at Dover. Roman town-houses can be seen at Dover and Canterbury. In the Weald can be found innumerable signs of Roman and earlier iron-workings and the slag-surfaced section of Roman road at Holtye. On the South Downs in *Sussex* there are Neolithic flint-mines and causewayed camps, Iron Age hillforts like Cissbury, the Roman villa at Bignor and the chalk-cut hill-figure of the Long Man of Wilmington. And down on the estuary lies the unique Roman palace of Fishbourne.

In the *Chilterns* to the north of London, where the Icknield Way crosses Pitstone Hill there can be found flint-mines, Celtic fields and Iron Age boundary ditches; another boundary ditch is visible at Beech Bottom near the Roman town of St Albans. And there are Roman tombs at Harpenden (permission to visit from Rothamstead Experimental Station). In *Essex* there are Roman barrows at Bartlow Hills and on Mersea Island, the remains of the temple of Claudius at Colchester and salt-workings along the margins of the estuaries. In *London* itself, stretches of the Roman wall and the temple of Mithras can be visited, while on the south-eastern outskirts there are dene-holes at Bexley, the Chiselhurst chalk-caves and Roman tombs at Keston (permission to visit from Keston Bird Farm).

Central-Southern England

The chalk downlands south of the Thames are a classic hunting-ground for ancient burial-mounds, earthworks and field-systems of all types. Its centre on Salisbury Plain is the location of many of the most famous monuments of prehistoric Britain: henges and circles like Stonehenge, Woodhenge, The Sanctuary, Avebury and Durrington Walls, and associated monuments like Silbury Hill, the Cursus and Kennet Avenue.

Nearby are the Windmill Hill causewayed camp and the West Kennet megalithic tomb. And there are hillforts like Liddington Castle and Figsbury Rings. Towards the Thames, the *Berkshire* Ridgeway passes close to Wayland's Smithy megalithic tomb, Uffington Castle hillfort and the chalk-cut white horse, and the Grim's Ditch boundary dykes. In *Hampshire* there are hillforts like Quarley Hill—and an interesting unfinished example at Ladle Hill—a Roman town at Silchester, a Saxon Shore fort at Portchester, and villas at Rockbourne and on the Isle of Wight at Brading and Newport. And there are the experimental prehistoric farming plots at Butser Hill.

Farther west in *Dorset* there are important hillforts like Maiden Castle, together with its later Roman temple—and another nearby on Jordan Hill; the Dorset Cursus, incorporating long barrows in its length, crosses the embankment of Ackling Dyke Roman road, and finishes at the great Bokerly Dyke defensive earthwork. Outside Dorchester can be found the remains of a Roman amphitheatre and the town aqueduct, and a little to the north the hill-figure of the Cerne Abbas giant. In *Somerset* there are remarkable Roman remains at Bath, the Stanton Drew stone circle, Stoney Littleton megalithic tomb, and the Pen Pits quarries. In the Mendips are found the Priddy Circles henge monuments, and the series of cave-dwellings in Cheddar Gorge. In the Somerset Levels can be found Ponters Ball defensive dyke, and in the Brendon Hills an unfinished hillfort at Elworthy Burrows.

The South-West

The granite moorlands of Dartmoor and Bodmin Moor abound with early settlement-sites of the Rough Tor and Grimspound type, and in *Cornwall* there are the remarkable nucleated villages of Chysauster and Carn Euny, and the enigmatic underground fogous. Good examples of standing stone circles are found in The Hurlers, Fernacre and the Merry Maidens. Early clapper-bridges are common. There are small Iron Age hillforts like Chun Castle and larger hill-towns like Carn Brea, while round the rocky coast many cliff-castles are to be found. On the north *Devon* coast there are Roman signal stations. In south Devon there is an impressive cave-dwelling at Torquay, and fine stretches of Roman town wall to be seen at Exeter.

The Midlands

The rich arable land of the *East Midlands* has been continuously worked over the centuries, obliterating many superficial traces of early occupation. But it is still possible to find the remains of the henge at Arminghall, and to descend a flint-mine at Grimes' Graves. The Devil's Ditch defensive dyke controlling Icknield Way where it crosses Newmarket Heath is among the most impressive earthworks in the country, while the lengthy Roman canal system of Car and Foss Dykes is unique. There is a fine Saxon Shore fort, now slightly inland, at Burgh Castle in Suffolk, and a variety of Roman town remains, with walls and interior buildings, at Caistor St Edmund, Great Casterton and Lincoln.

In and around the *Cotswolds* fine Roman villas are to be seen at Chedworth, Great Witcombe and North Leigh, and a Roman amphitheatre at Cirencester. There are important megalithic tombs at Notgrove, Hetty Pegler's Tump and Belas Knap. And the sole Midland example of a stone circle can be found in the Rollright Stones. There are boundary-dykes like those on Minchinhampton Common, and hillforts like Bredon Hill. Across the Severn at Lydney is the important sequence of hillfort, Roman iron mine and later cult-centre (permission to visit from Lydney Estate Office), and the remains of iron-workings in the Forest of Dean, with an excavated section of Roman road at Blackpool Bridge.

Farther north lie the Corndon Hill axe-factory, hillforts like Old Oswestry, and a wide range of Roman towns like Wroxeter, Wall and Leicester, the legionary fortress at Chester with its amphitheatre and the important reconstructions of the Lunt fort at Coventry.

North of England

The *Pennine Chain* from the Peak District to the Cheviots contains a wide range of monuments of all kinds. There are cave-dwellings in Cresswell Crags and in Victoria Cave, henges and stone circles like Arbor Low, areas of cup-and-ring markings like those at Roughtinglinn, hillforts like Yeavering Bell, and an important quarry at Wharncliffe. But this region is especially rich in Roman monuments: the remarkable length of Roman road on Blackstone Edge, marching-camps at Rey Cross and Chew Green, and the superb series of forts associated with the Hadrian's Wall frontier work, with related earthworks, temples and tombs.

To the west in the *Lake District* there are axe-factories at Pike of Stickle and Great Langdale, stone circles like Castlerigg and Long Meg and her Daughters, a Roman fort in a spectacular position at Hard Knott, and a Roman milestone still in position at Temple Sowerby. On the other side of the Pennines in *North and East Yorkshire*, there are the henge monuments and associated barrows at Thornborough, huge monoliths at Boroughbridge, Rudston and elsewhere, and strange duplex dykes at Scamridge and Huggate Wolds. There is a section of Roman road open across Wheeldale Moor, passing the practice-camps at Cawthorn; and there are signal stations around the coastline. There are the perimeter walls of a legionary fortress at York and of a civilian town at Aldborough together with its quarry.

Wales

In *South Wales* there is a series of early cave-dwellings in the Gower peninsula and elsewhere, megalithic tombs west of Cardiff at Tinkinswood and St Lythan, and a string of important Roman sites: the town at Caerwent, the fort and ludus at Caerleon, the reconstructed fort at Cardiff and amphitheatre at Carmarthen. Roman sites further inland include the marching- and practice-camps at Y Pigwyn and Llandrindod Wells, and the unique gold-mining works at Dolaucothi. In *North Wales* there are cave-dwellings in the Vale of Clwyd, a Roman fort at Caernarvon and fine megalithic tombs on Anglesey—notably Barclodiad y Gawres and Bryn Celli Ddu. In the Lleyn peninsula can be found the Mynydd Rhiw quarry pits, and the prehistoric hill-towns of Garn Boduan and Tre'r Ceiri.

Scotland

In *South-Western Scotland* there are burial cairns, extensive areas of cup-and-ring markings in Wigtown, an impressive stretch of open Roman road at Craik Cross, and unique Roman siege-works around the hillfort at Burnswark. Within reach of *Edinburgh* there are middens at Inveravon on the Forth, an important henge and cairn at Cairnpapple Hill, and the largest of Scottish hillforts at Eildon Hill. Significant Roman sites in *Central Scotland* include the Antonine Wall and its associated forts, the site of the Inchtuthill legionary fortress and the Gask Ridge line of signal stations. On the *Western Coast* there are cave-dwellings at Oban, extensive middens on Colonsay, cairns, duns and brochs in Argyll and Skye. In *North-Eastern Scotland* there are found souterrains and the distinctive type of 'recumbent' stone circles, and various kinds of chambered tombs. In the far north and in *Orkney and Shetland* are preserved nucleated villages of the Skara Brae type, impressive henges and stone circles, exceptionally fine megalithic tombs, and distinctive pillared souterrains.